T0352369

Queen FAQ

Queen FAQ

All That's Left to Know About Britain's Most Eccentric Band

Daniel Ross

Backbeat
Books

Guilford, Connecticut

Backbeat Books
An imprint of The Rowman & Littlefield Publishing Group, Inc.
4501 Forbes Blvd., Ste. 200
Lanham, MD 20706
www.rowman.com

Distributed by NATIONAL BOOK NETWORK

The FAQ series was conceived by Robert Rodriquez and developed with Stuart Shea.

Book design by Snow Creative Services

British Library Cataloguing in Publication Information available

Library of Congress Cataloging-in-Publication Data available

ISBN 978-1-61713-728-0 (paperback)
ISBN 978-1-4930-5141-0 (e-book)

∞™ The paper used in this publication meets the minimum requirements of American National Standard for Information Sciences—Permanence of Paper for Printed Library Materials, ANSI/NISO Z39.48-1992

Contents

Acknowledgments

There is only one author name listed on the cover of this book but, as is so often the case with works relying on research and reference and recounting, there are many individuals to whom that one name is indebted. To those who spoke to me directly for the book, providing new insight on well-discussed topics and adding color to the story, and to those who provided crucial information, pictures, and advice, my sincere thanks: Brian May, Tim Staffell, Morgan Fisher, Howard Blake, Bruce Murray, Doug Bogie, Tony Stewart, Mark Grehan, Martin Skala of Queenconcerts.com, Peter Gifford, Alice Lorenzini (lunaelive.com), Davide Traversi and the Official Italian Fan Club, Andreas Voigts, Janis Davidson, Carol Demont, Owen Hopkin, Rupert White of Queen in Cornwall: you've all made this book much richer than I could have alone.

Everyone at Rowman & Littlefield and Backbeat, for your editorial support and hard work, particularly Paula, Carol, Barbara, Bruce, and John: thank you. Same goes to Robert Lecker, who was game enough to suggest I write this book in the first place—I valued your belief and enthusiasm from the very beginning.

My wonderful in-laws Stuart and Liz were kind enough to let me dog-sit in their mercifully silent and unbelievably comfortable house for long stretches while I was in the final stages of the first draft. My parents, who bought Queen CDs and guitar chord books when their youngest son pestered them, and my older brothers, who donated home-recorded mixtapes of Queen's Greatest Hits (with The Muppet Show album on the other side), are the reason I am able to write about music today.

Finally, my love and everlasting puppyish gratitude goes to Emily, Wilson, and Roy, the family who had to put up with my writing this book for many months, accompany my crate-digging for original Flash Gordon LPs, work at our bookshop in my absence, and then smile and nod at my continual "sounding out" of deeply ephemeral theories around Queen trivia. I hope it wasn't too annoying for you.

Introduction

The Rehearsal Room

In the days leading up to perhaps the most important event in the band's history—their July 1985 appearance at Live Aid—Queen took to a London rehearsal room to work. The footage of their preparations in a nondescript practice space shows a hermetic ensemble, a stadium rock performance introverted, in miniature. There are bum notes. Fingers slip on guitar necks. Roger Taylor laughs from behind the drum kit as Brian May's guitar wobbles off-key in the build to the chorus of "Radio Ga Ga." But, crucially, all the ingredients for a defining moment in pop music history are present and appreciable. What's most telling about this rehearsal is the manner in which Queen, a band of four utterly distinct personalities, appears to be completely collegiate and collaborative, even professional, a full fifteen years into a career that had seen them conquer the music industry and be ignored by it, take all its money, and suffer its fickleness. The point is that, obvious as it may sound, *music* was always at the center of Queen. Performance, showmanship, virtuosity, compositional rigor: as long as these tenets stood strong in the band, everything just worked.

In that footage, Freddie Mercury smiles as his band plays the introduction to "Radio Ga Ga." He preens around the rehearsal room, obviously proud of the band's mammoth sound in this tiny rehearsal space and aware of the cameras, but he is as much a technician as his colleagues are. As they move on to the opening of "Bohemian Rhapsody," we can see John Deacon standing behind Mercury's piano, his moves utterly instinctual as his muscle memory twitches through the bass line. It is obviously effortless. It might not be too fanciful to think that during this rehearsal, just days before Queen would be the undoubted runaway winners of Live Aid (and by many accounts it *was* a form of competition), the band knew they were an unimpeachable musical force. Through incessant touring and recording across the previous decade, they had reached a technical zenith that few artists from pop history could rival. In short, they were, in the words of Francis Rossi from Status Quo, who opened the show at Live Aid, "shit-hot."

Doesn't all this fly completely in the face of what we imagine when we think of Queen? Shouldn't they be peeling charcuterie from the skin of a naked dwarf? Where's that cigarette Freddie would endlessly be stubbing out and replacing during TV interviews? And why hasn't someone shoved a camera into his permanently amused visage? Their legendary lavishness and Mercury's lifestyle in particular made the headlines more than any of Queen's albums ever did, but at its heart the band was a model of musical proficiency and skill. This is the central dichotomy in their story.

To distill these opposing elements into one book has been attempted numerous times in the past, but the sheer volume of available material, both musical and journalistic, could fill entire libraries. The narrative of Freddie Mercury's demise, heartbreaking in both sweep and severity, has been told in infinitely more detail than these pages allow, as has the story of Queen's various triumphs and missteps as they've glided through the music industry since the early 1970s. Inevitably, things will be missed. So with this book, the aim is to gild that narrative with specific, new details, providing some fresh insight to those well-told stories. Certain areas that other volumes might skip past benefit from deeper research here in the hope of casting the known story of the band in a different light.

And what of the band's career post-Mercury? After his death and bassist John Deacon's retreat into anonymity, Queen's fan base remains buoyant—rampant even. The band's pulling power still sees Roger Taylor and Brian May effortlessly fill arenas worldwide (with help from hired hands, naturally), and their work on musicals, movies, and various solo projects continues to maintain a grip on the wider public consciousness: we'll be diving deep into those areas too. *We Will Rock You*, the international hit musical that jimmied the Queen songbook into an invented dystopian narrative, is surely one of the most visible projects of its kind in history, while Roger Taylor and Brian May can still effortlessly fill arenas worldwide with their collaborations with singers like Paul Rodgers (formerly of Free) and Adam Lambert (the *American Idol* winner and star of musicals). Even as recently as 2018, the feverish reception for the troubled movie version of the band's career, *Bohemian Rhapsody*, dominated news in the entertainment world.

As the band becomes more and more comfortable with its "brand" status, the distance from here to the student's union hall at Kings College London seems impossibly, improbably large, and that's something the book attempts to convey through its chapters. Naturally, as the series title suggests, the focus for this book is also on answering questions. Thanks to the generous participation of some key figures in the life of the band, I've been able to ask those questions to the people who were actually there and dutifully note their answers. I am grateful for their honesty, and I hope in all cases that I asked something they hadn't heard before.

For my part, Queen is a band I discovered through family, when I was too young to really know what a band was. My eldest brother made his own customized cassette edition of Queen's first greatest-hits volume, the cover of which was a photograph of Freddie Mercury in 1986 taken from the video for "Princes of the Universe" (presumably scissored from the pages of *Look-in*) with neon highlighter decoration all around. The track listing was painstakingly copied out by hand from the official version he must have borrowed from a school friend. Completely divorced from their public personae, to me, hearing "Save Me" in the early 1990s, they were just fun songs full of sci-fi guitar noises, marshalled into place by the mustached guy's bizarre voice. I didn't even know that Freddie Mercury had died while I was growing up, nor can I remember a moment when I found out. I listened to Queen throughout my childhood with a sense of oblivious innocence.

Even when I finally began to realize that they were a real band made up of real people, I thought they were American (largely thanks to a live recording in which Mercury, in the middle of an a cappella call-and-response routine, shouts, "You bastards can sing higher than I can!" with a distinctly Yankee twang). As I fell into music journalism as a quasi career, I began to think differently about Queen and, more important, to write about them. To now be given free rein to add to that library of existing material on the band's story and music is a formidable joy, and with my intentions now laid out, I hope I can fulfill them.

One thing I will make clear at the outset is that Queen is one of the most exhaustively documented bands to ever pierce the public consciousness. Their rampant fan base doesn't just collect the records and watch the concerts: its constituent members have logged every moment of the band's history in its various incarnations with an intimidating degree of accuracy. There are, naturally, occasions on which accounts of the same events can differ: perhaps some dates don't quite work, some guest lists seem incomplete, or some credits on single sleeves appear to omit certain personnel. Where those anomalies or discrepancies have occurred, I've tried to find the most plausible answer and make the reader aware that, even then, it's hard to be completely sure. What I'm saying is, if you're looking for a long list of statistics relating to precise dates in the band's history, there are amateur and professional catalogers out there who have done it all for you, and you can read it for free. All I can give you is my impression of what many others have pored over for the past fifty years, supplemented by my own discoveries along the way.

On that note, it's worth explaining here just whom we're talking about. There's a strong chance, of course, that having picked up this book you'll already be familiar with its subjects. But on the off chance that you're not, I think it's enough to briefly explain Queen like this: four apparently English men, one of them not English, met and saw in each other a chance to make music in a fashion more spectacular than any of their peers could imagine. It took them a long time, and they made mistakes, but at the peak of their powers, they were world-beaters, one of the most famous and popular to have ever existed. They whirled in and out of control and sobriety, continued to make music that borrowed from and built on their influences, and sold an inconceivable number of concert tickets to shows that took on an epochal quality. And then, at Live

Aid, where their rehearsals had been so careful and meticulous, they played for about twenty minutes and became cultural immortals. There followed a mingled morass of tragedy and controversy and ever-complexifying music and then an entire second life as their fans continued to rediscover them through musicals, movies, and merchandise, turning what was once a band of four apparently English men into a multinational brand.

It is one of the strangest stories in rock history but also one of the best. At its heart were Farrokh Bulsara, John Deacon, Brian May, and Roger Taylor.

Queen in 1975, from left to right: John Deacon, Brian May, Roger Taylor and Freddie Mercury.
Andre Csillag/Shutterstock

1

What Did Queen Do before They Were Queen?

Farrokh Bulsara

In the Zoroastrian religion, it is a widely held belief that humans are responsible for their own actions. It is a complete rejection of the idea of predestination. In other words, no matter how astrally fortunate or unfortunate your life or circumstances might seem, fate has nothing to do with it. On that basis, Farrokh Bulsara, born September 5, 1946, into the Zoroastrian faith in Stone Town, Zanzibar, must have had a dash more tenacity than the average Gujarati Parsi. By all accounts a rambunctious and charming child with a performative streak, he was loved by his family. He took piano lessons and had, as one would expect of a child in a reasonably well-to-do family who had been sent away to an English boarding school in India, access to certain pervasive elements of Western culture, most notably rock 'n' roll.

It was at St. Peter's Boarding School in Panchgani, near Bombay (now Mumbai), that Farrokh's performative nature came to the fore. Much later, he would tell *Melody Maker* in an interview, "I was a precocious child. My parents thought boarding school would do me good so they sent me to one when I was seven.... I look back on it and I think it was marvellous. You learn to look after yourself and it taught me to have responsibility." In 1958 at age twelve, he formed the Hectics with four classmates (the other classmates being Bruce Murray, Derrick Branche, Farang Irani, and Victory Rana). A covers band, they energetically tackled songs by British and American heartthrobs like Cliff Richard and Little Richard at school assemblies and events but were strictly forbidden from seeking opportunities outside of the school itself. Songs on their limited set list included Lieber and Stoller's "Yakety Yak," Elvis Presley's "Girl of My Best Friend," and Jim Reeves's version of "Ramona."

Fellow Hectic and classmate Bruce Murray noted Farrokh (at this time known as "Bucky" thanks to his overbite) as a natural musician and performer but one with a certain shyness. "He was the quiet one, shy to the extent of not being there, but always came alive when we were on stage. [Was he] destined to be the frontman? Not in a million years." Early on in his life as a performer, we can already begin to see the duality that defined much of his life, one that cuts his life into two warring parts: the flamboyant performer dedicated to exciting those around him and the terminal introvert. But for Murray and the Hectics, it was that prodigious musicality that mattered: "Freddie was the only proper musician in the band. He could listen to a song and then go and play it on the piano instantly."

Farrokh was also a generous musician from the beginning. His bandmates in the Hectics would cheerfully admit that he was the real impetus in the band forming and maintaining itself throughout their school years, until 1962. Murray also notes an occasion when the roles were reversed, when the young Bulsara stepped aside for him: "I did meet Freddie once in Bombay. He came over and we played a few songs for my aunt. I sang, Fred played. I was the singer in the band, he was just my piano player!"

In 1964, the Zanzibar Revolution, which saw the sultan overthrown and the country turned into a republic (a status that lasted just a year), was cause enough for the Bulsara family to leave. And leave they did, ending up in Feltham, Middlesex, a distinctly indistinct town to the far west of London. One thing Feltham did offer the now seventeen-year-old Farrokh Bulsara was a direct train to Kensington, where a few years later he would end up selling second-hand clothes in Kensington market, and access to nearby Heathrow Airport, where he took a job as a baggage handler. Before that, though, he studied art at both Isleworth Polytechnic and Ealing Art College, where his prowess with the visual arts and fashion design came into its own.

Musically, Bulsara still held a torch for his rock 'n' roll heroes like Little Richard, the very same artists who had so influenced the Hectics. But now, with London emerging as the hip capital of the Western world, other influences began to seep in. The Who, Cream, the Beatles—they all left their indelible marks on Bulsara. He joined a blues outfit called Ibex and moved to Liverpool for some months, staying in a room above the Dovedale Towers pub on Penny Lane.

It is around this time that Bulsara's history begins to mingle with that of other members of Queen. With him in Ibex was Richard Thompson on drums, who happened to play in Brian May's first band in 1984. It can safely be assumed that May and Roger Taylor, who began playing with Smile in late 1968, would by now be aware of Bulsara as a performing entity, but it would still be some years before they would work together.

In what seems on paper like quite an unbelievable story, an Ibex gig in September 1969 (actually from before Thompson's time in the band, though he and Bulsara had been friends since 1966) took place at the Sink in Liverpool. Smile also happened to be playing the same city that night and, according to accounts from Ibex's roadie Geoff Higgins, popped in to see Ibex's early set. Higgins happened to be recording the set (it's now available online), but the tape runs out

The Dovedale Towers on Penny Lane, Liverpool, where a young Farrokh Bulsara stayed while he was a member of Ibex. *Old Ropewalks Ltd.*

before a momentous development in the evening: according to Higgins, quoted in *Record Collector*, both May and Taylor were eager to join in with their friend of a friend Freddie and proceeded to play a few Smile numbers with which Bulsara would no doubt be competently familiar. Whether there's a record of this performance or not, the thought of it is tantalizing to Queen enthusiasts: the first time three core members of the band would share a stage.

When Ibex, who just weeks later changed their name to Wreckage, didn't work out, Bulsara returned south and joined yet another outfit, Sour Milk Sea. He was now fully ensconced in the same musical scene as Smile and, therefore, his fellow future members of Queen, but Sour Milk Sea was not destined for longevity—internal fractiousness led to their demise in early 1970, leaving Bulsara a free agent without a gig.

John Richard Deacon

Thanks to the discreet way in which he vanished from the limelight once the dust around Freddie Mercury's death had settled, John Deacon has a modern reputation of being something of a recluse. But looking back at his childhood reveals that he was just as musically sociable and ambitious as the rest of the band. Born on August 19, 1951, in Leicester, it would be slightly cruel yet completely possible to characterize Deacon's early life as "humdrum." His father, Arthur, worked for Norwich Union, a job that would have afforded the family (John had a younger sister) a certain amount of stability, that most precious of postwar objectives for the British middle classes. After early years spent close to the center of Leicester, the family moved farther out to the affluent suburb of Oadby, where Mark Hodkinson argues in his book *Queen: The Early Years* that the young John Deacon became "a ghost of a boy."

It seems that Deacon was, like Brian May, studious and methodical in his manner but devoid of the social nous that came so easily to Roger Taylor. Deacon's father died when he was just ten, in 1962, and his mother, Molly, according to accounts in Hodkinson's book, sought to keep her son on the path to academic success rather than willingly urge him toward rock 'n' roll excess. All this is not to say he was an introvert: he joined his first band, the Opposition, around the age of fourteen, originally playing guitar. They played Yardbirds covers and hits from the Motown stable, very much the same musical wheelhouse in which Roger Taylor's the Reaction found themselves.

Known to his friends as "Deaks," John eventually switched to playing bass after the original incumbent, Clive Castledine, proved unable to keep up with his bandmates' musical progression. The group's singer, Peter Bartholomew, characterized Deacon's playing as "so relaxed . . . always so confident," which holds true when you watch footage of his time in Queen. Still, Deacon's manner was markedly quieter than his peers, and his time with the Opposition was spent being swept along rather than taking a musical lead, though the group's frequent appearances in the pubs and clubs of Leicestershire would have been the ideal grounding for what was to come. The Opposition eventually became the New Opposition and then the Art before Deacon left in late 1969 with around four years of solid experience.

While the band were still together, all members, including Deacon, trekked to London's Royal Albert Hall to take in Deep Purple's now legendary Concerto for Group and Orchestra under the baton of Malcolm Arnold and featuring the Royal Philharmonic Orchestra on September 24, 1969. It's not too fanciful to view this as something of a musical awakening for Deacon. The influence it had on the young man's formative creative brain must have been seismic. All of Deep Purple's members were superlative musical technicians, and to see them as equals with an orchestra would surely have been inspiring to Deacon, already an accomplished and gifted musician himself. The concert itself was only three or four short years ahead of Queen's earliest recordings, and, stylistically, the exploratory fuzz and ambition of Jon Lord's composition seems in hindsight to be something of a landmark in Deacon's musical development.

But there were some years still to go before he found the outfit that would change his life. As an enthusiastic home engineer from childhood and now, about to turn eighteen, as the proud owner of eight "O" levels and three "A" levels (all at grade A), Deacon was accepted into Chelsea College in West London to study electronics. Music wasn't completely forgotten from his life (although he did initially leave his bass in Oadby), but it wasn't until October 1970 that he came to see the trio of Bulsara, Taylor, and May performing as an embryonic version of Queen. When he first saw the newly formed Queen (the band was cycling through potential bassists with alarming speed, and Deacon all but completely sidestepped the whole Smile period), he was decidedly unimpressed, later claiming, "They didn't make a lasting impression on me."

CHELSEA COLLEGE, Manresa Road, S.W.3

HARDIN YORK

IDLE RACE :: DEACON

Booked through Marquee Martin

SATURDAY, NOVEMBER 21st, 8-11.30 p.m.

Admission 7/-, Door 8/-

Phone 352 6421, ext. 109 for details

An advert for a London support slot from Deacon in 1970.

Martin Skala, QueenConcerts.com

Unlike the more extroverted members of the band he was to join, Deacon's enthusiasms and mannerisms remained quiet as he began his new life in London, but he was still musically active, specifically in a short-lived project simply named Deacon. It doesn't take forensic evaluation of the group's dynamics to see why the trio warmed to Deacy, as he was known by then. A demeanor that wouldn't draw the spotlight away from the middle of the stage and a certain musical tastefulness and methodical approach (not to mention the chops to repair any exploded amplifiers) meant he was always going to fit in.

Brian Harold May

A studious child, Brian May was also the only one born to Harold and Ruth May, arriving on July 19, 1947, and afterward resident in Feltham. Coincidentally, the May family home in this otherwise notably unnotable town wasn't far from the Bulsara family home, where Farrokh was to spend a large portion of his teenage years. Although there were certainly traits of it in young Brian's upbringing, the stereotype of the overindulged, undersocialized only child didn't seem to quite fit him. Despite a low family income, Brian's was a childhood split between two highly aspirational and high-minded passions—astronomy and music. Both manifested themselves in a close relationship with his father, who worked as an electronics engineer and also at the Ministry of Aviation.

Brian would read endless books on astronomy throughout his childhood. In partnership with Harold, he would build telescopes, scouring electronics shops for interesting parts to experiment with and better serve his interest in the night sky. But Brian's passion for music (and perhaps the seeds of his combining the two) first arrived when he was shown a few ukulele chords by Harold when he was just six years old. A year later, he was given a Spanish acoustic guitar for Christmas. Lonnie Donegan records followed. Listening to Radio Luxembourg underneath the covers, May's musical mind expanded. He loved Gustav Holst's *Planets* suite and the orchestral sweeps of Mantovani. It was, though modest, an idyllic and enriching childhood that laid a foundation for one of rock music's most noted technicians.

Finding academic studies to be well within his grasp, Brian's extracurricular enthusiasms began to take over as he entered his teenage years. From 1958, he was a student at Hampton School (motto: "Wisdom surpasses wealth"; former pupils include Yardbirds founders and members Paul Samwell-Smith and Jim McCarty as well as Vic Briggs of the Animals), where he excelled in the sciences and mathematics throughout. But it was in his late teens that Brian's more serious musical ambitions began to take hold. From around 1963, just as they had done with homemade telescopes, Brian and Harold set about creating an electric guitar—the Red Special. The exact specifications of this most legendary of rock instruments is explored later in this book, but for now it's enough to call it a labor of love, a truly significant example of amateur perfectionism and craftsmanship that has gone on to achieve more than almost any musical instrument before or since. With the Red Special now safely in his possession, Brian May was ready to let music take over his life.

At Hampton, Brian met Tim Staffell, with whom he would go on to form Smile, the band generally agreed on to be the immediate precursor to Queen. This meeting and subsequent musical collaboration is perhaps one of the most important in the whole story of the band and its myriad offshoots. When they first worked together musically, Brian had already been recording home demos with a friend, Dave Dilloway, but their first solid project was a band named 1984 (rejected names included the Mind Boggles), formed in 1964.

Primarily covering American rhythm-and-blues staples like "My Girl" and "Knock on Wood," 1984's musical output seems on first inspection to be a long way from May's wheelhouse. But Staffell's voice and occasional harmonica antics drove the group in a bluesier direction, and they added Jimi Hendrix's "Purple Haze" to their canon. Recordings from a 1967 session at Thames Television studio can be found online and allow us to hear Brian and his Red Special in full flow. In particular, the group's version of "Purple Haze" shows the guitarist to be a confident ape of Hendrix's style and the distinct sound of the Red Special as still immature, but what impresses the most, as with many of Queen's early recordings with other ensembles, is the sheer professional verve of the musicianship. May's playing is technically superb, even flamboyant.

Firmly entrenched in his studies at Imperial College in Kensington, May and 1984 continued to gig around West London and, quite incredibly, actually managed to support Jimi Hendrix when he played at the college in May 1967. It is now bizarre to think of these two guitar legends playing on the same bill, a musical generation apart from one another.

As with so many nascent bands split across locations and academic institutions, 1984 eventually fizzled out. But with Staffell and May now firm friends and collaborators with reasonable gigging experience, it was time for Smile to emerge. In 1968, Brian placed an ad on a college notice board asking for any potential drummers to get in touch, and Roger Taylor answered.

Roger Meddows Taylor

When Queen was in their first flush of fame, *Sounds* magazine interviewed Taylor and summed up his pre-Queen life story thusly: "Roger has 'O' and 'A' levels, a biology degree and is a former dropout from dental college." Of all the members of Queen, it could be argued that Taylor's early life was the most balanced and comfortable. If you were asked to describe the upbringing of a quintessential British rock star of the 1970s and all the attendant privileges (a countryside setting, a boarding school, a natural shock of malleable blond hair, and a gravel-lined throat), chances are you'd tick off the defining factors of the early life of Roger Meddows Taylor. Born on July 26, 1949, in a maternity unit that had recently been opened by Queen Elizabeth II and raised variously in the postcardish towns of King's Lynn in Norfolk and Truro in Cornwall (a place that wears its connection to the Queen story with fierce pride), the young Roger Taylor's early life was defined by music.

After an initial stint as ukulele player in an outfit named the Bubblingover Boys when he was just seven years old, Taylor's musical prowess was evident from an early stage. While he was a day boy (a male boarding school student who lives at home) at Truro School (motto: "To be, rather than to seem to be"), he was involved in several short-lived musical projects, going by various names: Beat Unlimited, the Cousin Jacks, and the Falcons are all either remembered or half-remembered monikers for makeshift ensembles playing covers in the local area. In 1964, when he was fifteen, Taylor joined the Reaction (later "Johnny Quale & the Reaction" once they'd engaged a vocalist), a band known best for playing rock standards from the likes of Ray Charles and Elvis Presley. It's interesting to note that in the few years prior to Taylor's musical formation, Bulsara was experiencing something stylistically very similar in the Hectics, several thousand miles away.

Recordings of the Reaction do exist, surprisingly, and one in particular from 1966 shows Taylor's early musical tics in a stark manner, tics that would later come to embody his contribution to Queen. A cover of Wilson Pickett's "In the Midnight Hour," recorded at Wadebridge Cinema (a current Google review reads, "Very smelly, sticky and generally run down place"), features Taylor on drums and lead vocals and displays in its infancy the growl that would later grace his tracks on early Queen albums. The voice is strong and ebullient in character and sounds older than its owner. The drumming, more notably, is frantic, heavy, and somehow still nimble. The recording begins with an elaborate free-form drumroll before the song itself kicks in, and all throughout, the snare has an unpracticed "ring" to it, no doubt by dint of the recording conditions but also indicative of a restless energy. The tempo, too, is considerably faster than the Pickett original that Taylor and his friends would no doubt have been studying meticulously.

As is so often the way with bands formed in adolescence, the lineup of the Reaction changed drastically as the 1960s wore on, and by 1967, it was reduced to just three members: Mike Dudley, Ricky Penrose, and Taylor. Musically, however, the band had progressed from rock 'n' roll and soul covers to material altogether more psychedelic and heavy, tackling songs by Jimi Hendrix (who counted among his musicians drummer Mitch Mitchell, an acknowledged influence on Taylor). Of the period, bassist Ricky Penrose recalled in an article by Andy Davis and John S. Stuart in *Record Collector*, "Yeah, we had dreadful flowery trousers. The worst thing about them was the look you got when you stopped for petrol." The band remained in constant demand and played shows across Cornwall to audiences numbering around 300.

Studies complete, "O" and "A" levels obtained, Taylor left Cornwall in 1967 for London to study dentistry at the London Hospital Medical College, where the next chapter of his musical life was set to begin as a member of Smile. Before that, Taylor did return to Truro to play with the Reaction for one last summer in 1968, but it was to be their last stint together. Back in London in late 1968, when bassist Tim Staffell and guitarist Brian May were auditioning for a

"Ginger Baker–type drummer," Taylor's natural gifts in this area made him the perfect candidate, and Smile was solidified.

One thread that runs through Taylor's early musical life, as it does with all other members of Queen, is sheer consistency and inventiveness. As well as working tirelessly as a musician, gaining that all-important comfort onstage, it was never enough for Taylor to ape his influences: it was his conscious desire to improve on them with his own innovations and stylistic signatures.

2

Which Artists Influenced Queen?

Because all four of them played extensively in other ensembles before forming Queen, it's no surprise that much of the band's formative musical influences came from a deep fondness for early rock music. For example, a steady diet of Led Zeppelin, David Bowie, and, perhaps inevitably, the Beatles is traceable in most of Queen's early recordings and those of Smile. However, Queen being one of the more magpie-ish acts of their generation, that base layer of influence was supplemented by a more esoteric range of enthusiasms, stretching from music hall to opera and gospel and forming a willfully diverse and eccentric box of tricks into which they would regularly delve. Here are a few of the most intriguing musical influences that made the band's sound what it was.

Annunzio Paolo Mantovani

One of the founding fathers of "light music," Mantovani's enormous mid-century popularity was such that the members of Queen would likely have been familiar with the gentle sounds of his oeuvre. More than that, Brian May even based the guitar solo from "Killer Queen" on the composer and bandleader's signature sound, describing it as "a conscious attempt to create a certain type of bell-like effect I heard in Mantovani's music." As well as the bells, in May's more layered guitar solos (the lengthy solo from 1974's "Brighton Rock" is a good example), the "cascading" effect that Mantovani relied on to create washes of sound is in full evidence.

Mantovani's career trajectory seems an unbelievable one now: an orchestral arranger and bandleader with impeccable musical heritage and training (his father was concertmaster at La Scala in Milan during the great conductor Arturo Toscanini's stewardship, and Annunzio himself studied at London's Trinity College of Music) who then managed to find widespread intergenerational appeal

Mantovani receives a gold disc in Amstelveen. The composer and arranger was an important early influence on Brian May especially.
Bert Verhoeff, National Archives of the Netherlands / Anefo

and huge commercial success—all thanks to his relentless gigging at the dance halls of prewar Birmingham.

An interesting way of separating Queen from the Beatles in a purely aesthetic sense would be to consider Paul McCartney's response when George Martin suggested a string arrangement be employed to augment his "Yesterday." McCartney reportedly told Martin that under no circumstances did he want his song to sound "like Mantovani." May's more reverential attitude to the composer suggests a sympathy for populism that would go on to permeate the band's entire career.

Jimi Hendrix

Repeatedly and throughout the band's career, all four core members make explicit reference to the influence of Jimi Hendrix on Queen's music. As a guitarist, Brian May was naturally the most likely to be directly influenced by the virtuoso psychedelic firebrand (especially as he managed to book Hendrix for a show at Imperial College in 1967 as part of his role on the Entertainments Committee), but Hendrix's natural charisma as a performer would undoubtedly have ignited the young Freddie Mercury's imagination. Regardless of the obvious virtuosity Hendrix displayed, his effortless showmanship was revolutionary to the student crowds of the late 1960s, the guitarist seemingly able to control the mass reaction of thousands with the merest roll of a finger on a fretboard. His sense of visual presentation, a sort of impeccably unprepared and feathery flamboyance, is part of the same lineage that includes Freddie Mercury's peacock suit in the "It's a Hard Life" music video and Björk's infamous Marjan Pekoski "swan" dress at the 2001 Academy Awards ceremony.

Beyond Hendrix himself, Roger Taylor often cited Hendrix's drummer Mitch Mitchell as a key influence on his own playing style.

Aretha Franklin

The gospel influence on a song like "Somebody to Love" is clearly audible, but in particular Freddie Mercury's performative style owes an acknowledged debt to the late Queen of Soul Aretha Franklin. As he told *Night Flight* in 1984, "It's all spontaneous phrasing, which is what I love. I sometimes try to do that.... I'm mad that George Michael did a duet, I could've done it better." Mercury's affection for female singers was clear throughout his career. One thing that seemingly unites the majority of these influences is rawness, both emotional and musical, but also the ability to control and manipulate that rawness. Certainly this is the case with Franklin, whose legendary vocal improvisations were aped and adapted by Mercury. Just listen to "I Want to Break Free" or "Another One Bites the Dust," specifically the way in which Mercury ends even the simplest vocal lines with a Franklin-esque flourish.

Michael Jackson

The King of Pop's influence on Freddie Mercury as a performer was potent and powerful as Queen moved into their most world-beating phase during the 1980s. Not only did the pair work together on songs that have only recently seen the light of day, but Jackson's veteran status as a stadium-filling entertainment act formed not only a kind of prototype for the Queen live experience but also another fleet-footed example of how to command a crowd with only the tiniest of gestures. Mercury in particular would undoubtedly have seen Jackson as a powerful rival on the world stage.

Chic

This influence didn't begin to show itself until later in the band's career, most obviously on 1982's *Hot Space* album, but the music of guitarist and songwriter

Nile Rodgers's funk collective nonetheless inspired John Deacon to push his creativity into ever-more-commercial territory. Deacon had in fact spent time with Chic prior to writing "Another One Bites the Dust," to the chagrin of May and Taylor. Aside from Deacon's songwriting, listening to *Hot Space* reveals the true extent of Rodgers's influence on Brian May's guitar sound, albeit short-lived: by the time the album was done and dusted, it was extremely rare to hear May's lithely overdriven guitar figuring on the recording at all, the instrument's sound now drastically thinned and decidedly more trebly. The incidental guitar licks in songs like "Staying Power" from *Hot Space* and "Another One Bites the Dust," for example, could easily have found a home on a perkier Parliament record.

Liza Minnelli

It would've been a proud moment for Freddie Mercury to witness Liza Minnelli herself performing Queen's "We Are the Champions" at Wembley Stadium in his honor (see chapter 30), but while he was alive, her influence as a prime example of how a singer should deliver a song was unsurpassed. Drama was such a feature of her life both on- and off-screen that Mercury was transfixed. According to a legendary account from Andy Warhol, Minnelli once arrived at a party and demanded that the host furnish her with every possible intoxicant on the premises, the kind of performative request it wouldn't be hard to imagine Mercury himself making.

As an artist, Minnelli funneled that drama and destructiveness into her performance, her mezzo voice so often at its limits so as to wring every possible emotion from her material. Again, this is something in which Mercury specialized, a superhuman level of commitment to each performance regardless of what damage it might do to his instrument.

Mott the Hoople

Perhaps inevitably given that Mott the Hoople (or simply "Mott" as Queen knew them) was an early touring partner, early musical pointers were taken from headliner and filtered down into support act. Despite this, Mercury noted in interviews later that the billing on such tours was, in his view, very much the wrong way around. Mott's most noted song, "All the Young Dudes," was written for them by none other than future Queen collaborator David Bowie in 1972 and by 1974 was a common penultimate feature of their touring set list. Although there are commonalities beyond it, this one song is a neat barometer of Mott the Hoople's influence on Queen. Anthemic in the extreme, it also plays with gender fluidity and androgyny in its lyrics, itself arguably a clear Bowie fingerprint.

Led Zeppelin

Early Queen album reviews often pointed to the influence of Led Zeppelin on the band's sound. Roger Taylor told *Sounds* magazine in 1974 that "I still think John Bonham is one of the most underrated rock drummers, so I suppose we've absorbed some of that somewhere," and countless riffs from the first few Queen albums could've been adapted from material originated by Jimmy Page. This was simply an aesthetic influence, however: Led Zeppelin's decidedly more elemental subject matter was far too lofty for Queen to be doing, and the band quite quickly shed their enthusiasm for mythology in their songwriting as the hits began to rack up.

Classical Music

It takes only the first few seconds of Queen's "It's a Hard Life" for a listener to detect Ruggero Leoncavallo's influence on Freddie Mercury in both delivery and composition. Those bellowed first lines, "I don't want your freedom / There's no

Ruggero Leoncavallo, who provided direct inspiration for the introduction to Queen's "It's A Hard Life."
Wikimedia Commons / Public Domain

reason for living with a broken heart" not only are operatic in gesture but also quote almost exactly a melodic motif from Leoncavallo's own "Vesti la giubba," an aria from the opera *Pagliacci*. The mirroring line in the aria is "Laugh, clown, at your broken love," which seems rather apt considering the lyrical content of "It's a Hard Life."

Beyond this stark example, though, runs a deeper connection to opera and ballet, one quite specific to Freddie Mercury. The most notable example of this is, perhaps obviously, "Bohemian Rhapsody," thanks to its legendary cod-operatic midsection, which is discussed later in this book. But this was only the beginning of Mercury's experiments in the genre, an incurable musical dabbling that saw him reference the ballet productions of Vaslav Nijinsky in the video for 1984's "I Want to Break Free" and record a collaborative album with soprano Montserrat Caballé in 1987 (which spawned the popular single "Barcelona"). Ballet in particular left its stylistic mark on Mercury. It was not at all unusual for him to sport ballet shoes during live shows in the 1970s, and his preference for leotards was not just an attempt to play with androgyny—this was a conscious effort to re-create the aesthetics of Sergei Diaghilev's productions of Stravinsky's ballets (including *The Rite of Spring*, initially choreographed by Nijinsky).

Elements of classical music also stalked the band's musical arrangements as they became more ambitious. Timpani, gongs, and bell trees would adorn Roger Taylor's drum set, Brian May faithfully covered Richard Wagner's "Bridal March" from *Lohengrin* for the sound track of *Flash Gordon* ("I love to turn my guitar into an orchestra"), and Mercury's own falsetto voice would rattle with a tight vibrato in its upper reaches. Much of this would be derided by some detractors as mere pastiche, but the study and knowing references to various composers suggest a far deeper connection.

Umm Kalthum

Sitting alongside Little Richard and Tommy Steele in the young Farrokh Bulsara's listening diet was the singer sometimes known as Egypt's fourth pyramid, Umm Kalthum. Over a remarkable career that lasted into the 1970s, the singer's status in her homeland and across the Arab nations was comparable to Elvis Presley in terms of the sheer adoration she received (ably demonstrated by record sales in excess of 80 million units). Her enunciatory and trilling style of singing was most notably aped by Mercury on Queen's "Mustapha," but more generally her delivery of songs as self-contained confessional pieces directly influenced Mercury's performance style, both singers working as an actor does in locating dramatic meaning in each individual artistic gesture.

3

Doing All Right

From Smile to Queen

It was Roger Taylor who eventually answered Brian May's advertisement on a college bulletin board asking for a "Ginger Baker–type drummer" to join him and Tim Staffell in an as-yet-nameless new group. This was in 1968, when all three were studying in London (Staffell was at Ealing Art College and friendly with Freddie Bulsara, who would eventually replace him), and all three had now sufficiently experienced a variety of musical groups and influences to begin something more serious.

Not only was Taylor able to keep time and tune his drums (a novelty and a sign of a muso's musician in the rock world), but he was also able to secure gigs outside London, specifically at venues in his native Cornwall, giving the trio some initial road experience. Most gigs were at Imperial College, where May was studying, and included support slots with the Troggs and Pink Floyd. Musically, the band began to play with more elaborate cover versions and their own material, a lot of it technically adventurous and most easily labeled as heavy blues, though the psychedelic influence of bands like Yes and Procol Harum began to permeate as their instrumental sections grew in length and daring. They were filled out in live shows by keyboardist Chris Smith but were equally comfortable as a three-piece unit.

Although May described Smile as merely "semi-professional," they did make substantial headway beyond this and managed to bag a slot near the bottom of the bill at London's legendary Royal Albert Hall, specifically at a charity concert for the National Council of the Unmarried Mother and Her Child in February 1969. They were on immediately after a then recently formed outfit named Free, who would go on to sell 20 million albums and achieve rock immortality with their song "All Right Now." Incidentally, their vocalist was one Paul Rodgers, someone with whom Queen would eventually collaborate many decades after their paths first crossed. There was a feeling that Smile, with their Stones-predating "lips" logo and their increasingly flouncy presentation, could go somewhere.

The Smile logo, as designed by Tim Staffell.
©Tim Staffell

Indeed, 1969 saw a Smile demo tape find its way into the hands of a Mercury Records artists and repertoire man, John Anthony, and the resulting promise of a single to be recorded for the U.S. market led the band to Trident Studios in Soho in June of that year. They committed three original numbers to tape: "Step on Me," "Earth," and "Doin' Alright," the latter being the only Smile song that ended up also being a Queen song, with a writing credit shared between Brian May and Tim Staffell. "Earth" was the lead song on the single, and "Step on Me" was the B-side (also one of the only compositional hangovers from Staffell and May's time playing in 1984), but it didn't chart. Another venture into the studio (this time at De Lane Lea Studios in Wembley, North London—along with Trident, an important and formative place for Queen) produced three more songs: "Blag," "Polar Bear," and "April Lady," the last of which appears to have been donated to the band by one Stanley Lucas at Mercury Records. That song ended up having a second life as a song by Southern Comfort (previously Matthews Southern Comfort, featuring Iain Matthews of Fairport Convention). These recordings were ostensibly for an album, even though they'd been contracted for only a single, but that album never fully materialized.

What Did Smile Sound Like?

The scant available recordings of Smile show them to be a taut ensemble, with more than a few foreshadowing elements of Brian May's later songwriting as part of Queen. "Polar Bear," for example, could've jostled with material on either of Queen's first two albums (although the bizarre lyrics about the titular stuffed mammal perhaps catch May in an inconsequential mood). Staffell's elastic vocals on Smile's recording of the song are, surprisingly, more histrionic than a later recording of the song made with Bulsara at the microphone.

"Doin' Alright" was the only song to make it fully intact onto a Queen album (as "Doing All Right"), but it's not the most obvious sonic link between both ensembles. It has a milder, more loose character than many cuts from the band's early albums but does allow May's guitar playing to come to the fore in its second, more boisterous half. It's worth noting that the opening section has the distinct character of a Led Zeppelin acoustic doodle (specifically, "That's the Way" from *Led Zeppelin III*), which is in keeping with much of the early criticism Queen received as mere Zeppelin rip-offs. Lyrically, too, it is indistinct, indicating a lack of life experience on the part of the young writers, but also a sign that the lore and fantasy that dominated the first Queen albums was yet to show itself.

Of all the available Smile recordings, the one with the strongest fingerprint on future Queen compositions is "Blag," the middle section of which is basically a transplant of a guitar solo that Brian May would later incorporate into "Brighton Rock" on Queen's third album, *Sheer Heart Attack*, in 1974. On either side of that section, "Blag" is essentially a wordless jam composed solely by May and, as such, could be mistaken for an outtake from an early Queen session.

It would be wrong to conclude that Smile were simply an embryonic version of Queen. Staffell's propensity for blues histrionics was contained by May and Taylor's more rock 'n' roll leanings, but it was enough to make them a different proposition, and it could be argued that the duo's ability to operate in a band pulled in different musical directions was honed during this time. Today, especially since the inclusion of "Doing All Right" in the *Bohemian Rhapsody* movie sound track, Smile's position has been elevated to one of almost mythic importance in the Queen story, with Staffell's step aside akin to Pete Best being fired from the Beatles. In truth, all the members of Smile admitted their frustrations with their limited success. More important, the group's musical development was, in comparison to what would happen to Queen in the next five or so years, far slower.

How Did Smile Become Queen?

Smile had grown stagnant. Tim Staffell, frustrated with their lack of progress and eager for a new challenge, left the group for a burgeoning folk rock act named Humpy Bong. We already know that Freddie Bulsara was a fan of Smile and had reportedly already performed live with May and Taylor, but their musical connection was now to become permanent. It would be wrong to say that Bulsara joined Smile—more accurate is to say that he simply joined May and Taylor, who were in something of a funk with their situation. Bulsara had been part of the same social circle and, with Ibex and Sour Milk Sea, part of their musical circle as well. He would come backstage and offer enthusiastic suggestions for how Smile might improve their sound or their performative presentation.

Eventually, with his dropped hints finding their mark and with May and Taylor reluctant to start from scratch with a completely new musical outfit, Bulsara became the singer of what used to be Smile. Crucially, however, Bulsara did not play the bass guitar as Tim Staffell had done. This group could not function as a trio if it was going to achieve a conventional rock balance of sound, and the exhaustive search for the perfect bassist began.

Before they settled on John Deacon, the trio auditioned and gigged with a surprisingly large number of candidates (though not the Spinal Tap–esque litany that some have claimed). This was an ensemble in transition, still technically named Smile. When they booked another gig in Truro for June 1970, organized by Roger Taylor's mother, Win, it was with fellow Cornwall native Mike Grose on bass and under the band's existing name (two advertisements in local newspapers stated as much). But by the time the band arrived at Truro's City Hall, they were going by something much more eyebrow raising: Queen.

Bulsara delighted in the regal connotations of the new name, boasting about the great fortunes and notoriety the band was now destined to experience. But it was more than that: the inevitable suggestion of involvement in Kensington's foppish and camp arts scene was an intentional one designed to make people blush. In 1974, Taylor told *Sounds* magazine, "It was just a reflection of the social world we were in at the time.... I didn't like the name originally and neither did Brian, but we got used to it." Bulsara, ever the charming houseguest, stayed in the attic room of a Taylor family friend and practiced his yoga poses by balancing against the walls, then weeded the garden.

Although the band's name was now fixed, their identity wasn't. Playing a mixture of Smile songs, Elvis covers, and newly composed Queen numbers (among them "Stone Cold Crazy" and even *Queen II* material like "Father to Son"), they cycled through bassists including Grose, Barry Mitchell, and Doug Bogie before John Deacon's unassuming style and handiness with a soldering iron won them over.

Enter the Deacon: Queen Completed

Sources disagree over exactly when and where Deacon's first gig with Queen took place, but it can be narrowed down to July 1971, when the band were becoming a popular draw in their own London colleges (Brian May had a role on the events team at Imperial College) and farther out into leafy Surrey to the southwest of the city. With the band now comfortably formed, utilizing the local connections (and celebrity) he'd accrued in his youth as a member of the Reaction, Roger Taylor managed to bolt together an itinerary of gigs across Cornwall.

Deacon, the newest member of the band, saw it as an important bonding experience, telling *Music Star* magazine in 1974, "We got to know each other really well and it settled us as a group. Roger did manage to find us half a dozen or so gigs as well, so we broke even."

The last of the band's shows in Cornwall was at the haughtily titled Tregye Festival of Contemporary Music, an all-day event that saw Queen lingering at

Promotion for the Tregye Festival of Contemporary Music.
Queen is featured toward the bottom.
Martin Skala, QueenConcerts.com

the bottom of the bill, well below names like Hawkwind and Arthur Brown's Kingdom Come (one poster also advertised "Food—Freaks—Licensed Bar"). Joining them on the bill was a band called Graphite, whose guitarist David Hook described seeing Queen backstage to Queenconcerts.com: "In the dressing room

Queen ... had a real presence, a real aura. They weren't casual like the rest of us hippies. They seemed more arty. And they had hangers-on."

Queen had been professional in their approach as soon as they'd officially formed, a more calculated and serious band than their peers. Their musical chemistry, too, bordered on the miraculous: all members had differing experiences of performing but enough in common for a telepathy to develop among them. Bulsara's microphone stand was by now an essential prop, being snapped a third from the bottom and thus allowing him to ape and parody May's guitar stance, flip it around his head, or clutch it tightly while he sang to it. The broken microphone stand stayed with Mercury throughout his career with Queen, becoming nearly as iconic as his moustache or his yellow military jacket, but unlike these later examples, it was unplanned, even serendipitous. The microphone stand, the all-in-one leotards, and the adapted costumes became as integral to the show as the songs themselves, turning it into a regal circus driven by Bulsara's onstage personality. It was time to capture the magic.

In December, Queen made their first official recordings at De Lane Lea Studios, where the likes of Jimi Hendrix and Pink Floyd had previously committed their work to tape (and Smile, of course). The tracks laid down were "Keep Yourself Alive," "The Night Comes Down," "Great King Rat," "Jesus," and "Liar," a mixture of Bulsara and May compositions, all of which went on to feature on the band's debut album. This was physical proof that Queen was now a band—and a serious one. Ending 1971 with a New Year's Eve show at Twickenham Rugby Club, just a few miles down the road from Bulsara's family home in Feltham, was not the most glamorous way to ring in the coming year, but with a demo tape now firmly in their possession, 1972 was set to be decidedly more fruitful.

4

Murky Beginnings

Queen's First Record

It's bizarre to think with the benefit of hindsight that Queen, with their litany of commercially bulletproof singles, would have encountered any difficulty in securing a record deal. But in 1972, having only just settled into a regular lineup and being mostly confined to playing student nights around London, they were a tricky commercial sell thanks to their complicated aesthetic mix of dorky academic and jumpsuited preener, and that's without even mentioning their still-settling musical offering.

Enter brothers Norman and Barry Sheffield, who, having discovered the band's demo tape (recorded at De Lane Lea Studios in December 1971—now widely available on the 2011 remaster of *Queen*), were willing to let the band record in their own Trident Studios and, given that the band had none in place, provide general management. A crucial caveat of this deal was that Queen would be allowed full access to the Sheffield brothers' state-of-the-art recording facilities, but recording sessions would be restricted to "off-peak" hours.

In a fashion that would come to typify much of the band's early activity, *Queen* (also informally known as *Queen I* to differentiate it from *Queen II*, which followed in 1974) was a hodgepodge of a debut. Fractious late-night recording sessions were slotted around those of more important Trident clients throughout the second half of 1972 (Carly Simon's "You're So Vain" was recorded there while Queen could well have been lingering in the corridor).

It was during this period, hanging around Trident waiting for the more notable artists to vacate the premises for the day, that Bulsara was asked by engineer Robin Cable to provide vocals for two non-Queen recordings: covers of Phil Spector's "I Can Hear Music" and Goffin and King's "Goin' Back." The songs eventually surfaced on a 1973 single under the name of Larry Lurex (see chapter 5).

Bulsara's solo dalliances aside, the band cemented a unified work ethic in this crucible, rubbing up against their newly assigned producer, Roy Thomas Baker. Having recorded a handful of the tracks written for the album in demo form at De Lane Lea, the band was reluctant to veer too drastically from what

The entrance to Trident Studios in St. Anne's Court, Soho, London. *Author's collection*

they'd already established. Baker, on the other hand, was a creative firebrand of equal heat and convinced the band to rerecord with Trident's superior equipment. The band disliked Baker's results, but after significant cajoling, he eventually won out (with the exception of "The Night Comes Down": the De Lane Lea version ended up on the album).

Along with Baker, *Queen* also saw the first contributions of Mike Stone, a studio hand at Trident with whom the band clicked professionally and went on to work with them on subsequent records, trusted as a shared visionary of their ideal sound.

The character of this now solid band of distinct personalities was perhaps summed up by an early suggested (and swiftly rejected) title for *Queen*. Mercury's answer to everything at that time, be it a studio mishap or a personal inconvenience, was a shaken-headed "Dearie Me." It's not clear who exactly quashed the notion that this should be the name of the album, but it's amusing to imagine the career that followed having begun with such a misstep. Despite recording an album that aimed at sonic and conceptual triumph, Queen still consisted essentially of losers.

Three Songwriters Emerge

Much of the album's material was written by individual members while the final lineup was still solidifying, with the notable exception of "Stone Cold Crazy," which was a leftover from Bulsara's time with Wreckage in the previous decade. The song was so elaborately reworked and reorganized when it was taken to May, Taylor, and Deacon that it was eventually credited to the entire band. However, across the rest of the album, individual songwriting characteristics that would go on to define the band's entire catalog were already becoming clear.

Bulsara penned five of the album's ten songs, a huge contribution for an interloping vocalist. Of those five songs, four contain significant folkloric and religious imagery, suggesting an early fixation. Of particular note is "My Fairy King," which provided Bulsara with the stage name that would define him until his death: "Mother Mercury, look what they've done to me," he sings, and so christened his onstage persona. Also significant among Mercury's tracks here is "Liar," the album's longest and most complex song, as it foreshadows a penchant for the long form that would last through all of his career.

Brian May provided four numbers if you count "Doing All Right" (Tim Staffell received substantial royalties for his cowriting credit). But it was the album's opener, "Keep Yourself Alive," that showed May's songwriting gift most fully. A fixture of live shows until the 1980s, it's a fair summary of all the musical elements that defined the band's early sound. Alongside the traces of Led Zeppelin and Black Sabbath, there's a bouncing affection for the blues as well as the first appearance of Mercury, Taylor, and May's multipart vocal harmonies in the chorus. May's guitar solo would also be most listeners' first encounter with the distinctive zip of his Red Special (unless they'd happened to come across Smile or 1984), and the lyrics are perfectly in line with the joyous decadence that the band would collectively enjoy in years to come: "I've loved a million women in a belladonic haze / and I ate a million dinners brought to me on silver trays."

Consistent with several later Queen records, Roger Taylor (billed on *Queen* as Roger Meddows-Taylor) contributed one absurdly rambunctious number, a charming enough stomper that was no doubt custom-built for live shows but the album's sorest thumb. "Modern Times Rock 'n' Roll" is a fine showcase for Taylor's high tenor, a stylistic cousin to Rod Stewart's careworn rasp, but his sophistication as a songwriter was, based on this cut, yet to develop.

John Deacon, credited on the album as Deacon John, contributed no songs, but in a 1977 radio interview, he provided some context around the album's composition: "They're songs that we just used to play. And we just went in and recorded them." At its core, though the album hangs roughly together in a thematic sense, it's a narrow snapshot of a Queen live show, a sketch of the more accomplished band that would come to fruition in the year that followed.

Doing All Right?

Queen was finally released in July 1973 after Trident had spent several months attempting to find a willing label to release it. Ultimately, Norman Sheffield was able to convince EMI to release the album in conjunction with Trident, but it became nothing more than a commercial footnote, limping to number eighty-three in the United States and not making a dent on the U.K. album charts at the first time of asking.

Critically, the album fared a little better. Certain areas of the music press saw the folk references and blues-metal riffs and drew a direct line between Queen and Led Zeppelin (the *Winnipeg Free Press* complained in an otherwise gentle review that "the material is so derivative it hurts"), but on the whole, the album was received with a quiet warmth.

The cover of Queen's self-titled debut.   *Author's collection*

What's more notable about the album, though, is what it foretells in the context of the band's story. Through the second half of 1973 and into 1974, Queen toured the album and wrote another. By the time most people heard *Queen*, the band had already completed most of the work on its follow-up and were a demonstrably different ensemble both musically and aesthetically. Tellingly, the cover of *Queen* is a fuzzed-to-hell photograph of very little at all, taken by photographer and friend of the band Douglas Puddifoot. A stage light pours diagonally downward onto a triumphant—but not yet fully flamboyant—Freddie Mercury, arms aloft and holding the half microphone stand that would become a trademark. In a possibly unconscious nod to Jimi Hendrix, a purple haze clouds the whole picture. It's representative of the album and elements of Queen's sound at this formative point in their career, but equally, it's the perfect symbol of their promise. For the few people who bought the album on its release, this would be the first visual clue to the audiovisual brio that would follow, the chaotic, genre-exploding music that would leave an indelible scribble on the next two decades of popular rock music.

The Queen emblem, designed by Freddie Mercury, as it appears on the reverse of their debut album sleeve.   *Author's collection*

Is *Queen* What the Band Really Sounded Like?

With the dust settling on the album's release in the late summer of 1973 and regardless of Mike Stone and Roy Thomas Baker's efforts to make *Queen* sound as "live" as possible, the band wasted no time in jettisoning much of the material when it came to their concerts. A bootleg recording of a performance at Golders Green Hippodrome on September 13 of the same year shows a set list that looks forward to their next album, *Queen II*, stuffed as it is with then unreleased compositions like "Father to Son" and "Ogre Battle." Only three songs from *Queen* make the cut—"Son and Daughter," "Liar," and "Keep Yourself Alive"—while set lists from the following months show a similar lean to newer material.

Interestingly, the band was still steeped in cover versions at this point in their career. A hangover from previous ensembles and incarnations of the band, the practice of including covers in set lists ran deeply in the band's musical DNA, but what's most revealing is the choice of material. That same bootlegged recording from Golders Green Hippodrome is typical of other shows around the same time, and on it, we can see a medley of rock 'n' roll classics that played into Mercury's tastes: "Jailhouse Rock" flows into momentary versions of "Shake, Rattle and Roll," "Stupid Cupid," and "Be-Bop-a-Lula" before circling back around to "Jailhouse Rock" once again (all in under four minutes).

More revealing still—and a truly overt expression of the delight Mercury took in his own androgyny—is the cover of "Big Spender" from the musical *Sweet Charity* that follows (the song became a singles chart success thanks to Shirley Bassey's 1967 recording). Queen's version would sit comfortably toward the end of live sets from this early period and through the mid-1970s as well as occasional outings into the 1980s. Worth noting also is Mercury's tweak to the song's lyrics addressed to a male: presumably in an effort to mask the most overt verbal references to his own sexuality, Mercury removes any signifiers of gender, singing, "I could see you were a *one* of distinction" and "I don't pop my cork for every *one* I see" rather than the "man" of the original, a rather coy and guarded move that perhaps reflects attitudes of the time rather than Mercury's.

Typical sets of this time would close with Little Richard's "Bama Lama Bama Loo," another return to the rock 'n' roll roots of the Hectics that Mercury would have been only too happy to trot out. On the Golders Green recording, his glee is palpable as he muffs one of the final refrains and trades "Yeah!"s with Roger Taylor. It has a lightness, almost a silliness, that the album they were touring didn't show but would become an important weapon in their arsenal as they began to attack the music industry and all notions of their beloved rock 'n' roll.

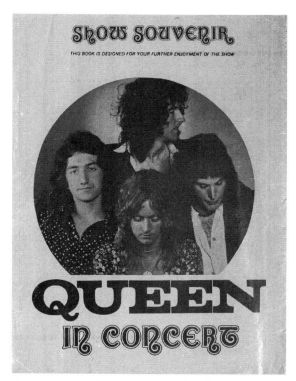

An early program that accompanied live shows in 1973 and 1974, "designed for your further enjoyment of the show."
Martin Skala, QueenConcerts.com

A Musical Identity Crisis

The Hippodrome performance shows that *Queen* was in no way a definitive capture of the band's sound in 1973. That so much of the material for *Queen II* had already been written by the release of their debut suggests that Queen had moved on. The heavy psychedelic blues of Smile had been ground out of them and replaced by a real performative zing that is evident in their live recordings, but they were still a difficult commercial sell. Nevertheless, the venues they played began to grow in capacity, but the music that filled them was a strange mix of fantastical, ponderous epics with lyrics that sang simultaneously of mythical stories and the hedonistic delights of worlds real and imagined, with the occasional vaudeville romp thrown in for good measure.

Quite simply, Queen was operating too many musical levers at once, seemingly unable to choose just one. *Queen* is the manifestation of just one of those levers being pulled, and it would take a serious stylistic, technological, and even industrial development to even begin to satisfy their full range.

5

Mercury Rising

Larry Lurex

During recording sessions for *Queen*, Trident Studios engineer Robin Cable was in an experimental mood. He'd worked on rock classics like Elton John's *Tumbleweed Connection* back in 1970 and would go on to be a regular fixture on records by Chris De Burgh, Carly Simon, and Nilsson, but it just so happened that when Queen was at Trident, Cable wanted to emulate the sounds of the past, specifically, Phil Spector's "Wall of Sound" recording technique, wherein instrumental parts would be doubled or augmented to create a much fuller sound, an almost literal "wall" of musical force.

For his experiment, Cable wanted to cover two pop staples from the previous decade and put them out on EMI. The songs were Phil Spector's own "I Can Hear Music" (which had been a successful number for the Beach Boys and, to a lesser extent, the Ronettes) and Carole King and Gerry Goffin's "Goin' Back" (also a notable Dusty Springfield recording). On the face of it, Freddie Mercury was perhaps not a natural choice for a vocalist for this doubleheader. Although his childhood was steeped in pop history, Mercury's penchant was for the rawer end of the spectrum, such as the likes of Little Richard and Elvis. But seeing his natural talent for interpreting the work of others, Cable cajoled Mercury into recording vocals for the songs, and according to some accounts, Mercury in turn roped in Brian May and Roger Taylor to record instrumental parts, resulting in a curious seven-inch released under the name of Larry Lurex (itself a wink to British glam-rock star Gary Glitter, who was peaking in popularity around this time).

What Does Freddie Mercury's First-Ever Single Sound Like?

Curious it may be, but this single was also the first commercially released example of Mercury's recorded singing voice, showing it to be already preternaturally competent. "I Can Hear Music" is indebted, naturally, to the Beach Boys' already

The cover for Larry Lurex's only seven-inch single, "I Can Hear Music." *Photo by Mark Grehan*

well-established version, and Lurex's vocals ape the tics and flourishes of Carl Wilson. This is not yet a Mercury vocal, impressive as it is. Limited accounts of the recording process mean that any speculation as to Freddie's mind-set during those sessions must remain exactly that, but listening dispassionately, it's easy to imagine that this was all a bit of fun for Mercury, May, and Taylor. While Taylor isn't immediately traceable on the recording (perhaps he's the tambourine?), May's guitar solo toward the end is immediately recognizable, swooping and harmonized in a manner completely his own. The arrangement is an elaboration, closer even perhaps to a pastiche, of Spector's orchestral excess. Surprisingly rich in texture and assault, it absolutely succeeds in marrying Spector's production ethos with Lurex's emerging vocal prowess.

On the other side of the record, Goffin and King's "Goin' Back," Mercury sounds just like a mezzo-soprano, the same vocal type as the singer who initially made the song famous in 1968: Dusty Springfield. He sings it in the same key and at the same pitch albeit a little more breezily and without Springfield's trademark rhythmic playfulness. Again, the production is somewhat reduced in comparison to its definitive version, but it's Mercury's performance that is most interesting. Emotionally, it is surprisingly blank: not unfeeling but certainly not dramatic in the way listeners would come to associate with him. Listening to "Goin' Back" alongside Queen songs like "Nevermore" and "Funny How Love Is" shows just how the influence of his female vocal idols carried through into the band's early work.

Surprisingly, given the low profile of the release, it managed to chart in the United States, specifically at number 115 in the *Billboard* "Bubbling Under the Hot 100" chart. Although not a spectacular performance by any means, this doubleheader remains an important document in the gestation of Queen's early recorded sound. It's evidence that, as an ensemble (minus John Deacon in this case, we have to assume), they were more than comfortable to flit between genres and that they harbored a not-so-latent fondness for "straight" pop records.

What Happened to the Singles Themselves?

Prices for original copies of the seven-inch in its various iterations, usually without spelling mistakes (an early pressing displays the title as "I Can Her Music"), can vary. In some cases, supposedly unplayed examples of the record are listed on eBay for around $200, so its value is not insignificant to the Queen completist. Given that it made it only to number 115 in the United States, it's safe to assume that there weren't too many copies of the seven-inch itself in circulation. One persistent online rumor also states that Mercury himself had a number of singles pressed a few years later to give to family and friends.

The misprinted version of the Larry Lurex single. *AV_Queen/45cat.com*

Among the copies circulating the collectible seven-inch market, however, it's unlikely you'll find the very first acetate of the single, which lists the artists (handwritten in the spidery scrawl of someone working quickly) as Larry Lurex and the Voles from Venus, extending the gentle lampoon of Gary Glitter to take in David Bowie's Spiders from Mars as well.

While the physical item might be costly and of interest mostly to collectors, the music it contains is a surprisingly revealing glimpse into what Queen could have sounded like had they taken a different stylistic route or simply become session musicians.

6

"... And Nobody Played Synthesizer"

Queen the Engineers

This was the quiet but defiant mantra that graced each of Queen's first four record sleeves, usually after the ever-lengthening notes listing each and every instrument played by individual members.

Barry Sheffield and all the Trident People.) Queen's equipment supervised by JOHN HARRIS. Queen's photographer Douglas Puddifoot; cover design Douglas, Freddie and Brian ... and nobody played synthesizer.

The famous caption that appeared on early Queen albums (this example is from their debut).

Author's collection

℗ 1974 Trident Audio Productions Ltd.
Virtuoso castanets by Roy Thomas Baker ... *and nobody played synthesizer ... again.*

The same declaration, adapted slightly for *Queen II*.

Author's collection

Did Queen Hate Synthesizers?

The band's early reticence in including synthesized sounds (we can call them "created" electronic sounds rather than electronic or amplified sounds that have a genesis in striking a drum or plucking a string) can be interpreted in various ways. Were they pompously rising above the fashion for synthesizers as man-ufacturers like Dr. Robert Moog's instruments began to filter out into the rock mainstream? The Beatles, Stevie Wonder, Rick Wakeman of Yes, and Keith Emer-son of Emerson, Lake & Palmer were all early adopters of Moog synthesizers in particular from the turn of the 1970s on, so it would've been perfectly natural for Queen to do the same. But they didn't. Were they just too good for synthesizers or maybe unwilling to see the potential benefits?

Another theory might be that Queen consisted of instrumental purists. In this philosophy, any sound, even if it had been modified with studio technology, should come from an accepted tool of the instrumental mainstream (guitar, piano, drums, banjo, auxiliary percussion, and so on), not from something entirely synthetic. Pointing this out in the liner notes of their early albums by printing ". . . and nobody played synthesizer" is a two-finger salute to listeners who couldn't accept that the mind-boggling sounds they were hearing were made by mere traditional rock instruments. You can imagine the thought pro-cess: "*surely* there must be some kind of wizardry going on there—no normal instrument can make those sounds."

The most likely answer is, inevitably, a mixture of these ideas. The band prided themselves on their superior musicianship, and it would be perfectly within their character to exercise a certain haughtiness in finding synthesizers unnecessary and even delight in tricking listeners into thinking that their more incendiary sounds came from the depths of a Moog Modular 55.

It should be noted that once the band did accept synthesizers (they first appeared in their sound around the time of *The Game* in 1980), they approached them with a zeal and inventiveness that was at least consistent with their con-temporaries. But Queen was a band of engineers, and nowhere is this more evident than in two significant inventions that defined their early sound: Brian May's homemade guitar, the Red Special, and John Deacon's modified guitar amplifier that it connected to, known as the Deacy Amp.

The Red Special

It's hard to overstate the impact that this one musical instrument had on the history and progression of rock music in the twentieth century, but it is equally surprising to learn of its humble origins. Brian May's guitar was the result of a collaborative project with his father, Harold, begun simply because there was no money in the family for Brian to buy an expensive Fender or Gibson elec-tric guitar. May has stated that there wasn't even enough money for a cheaper imitation model, such as a Hofner, so the only option was for the two of them to build a guitar together, matching exactly with his specific tonal needs. They began work on the guitar in 1963, when Brian was just sixteen years old, and sourced the materials required from whatever happened to be close at hand. As a result of this thriftiness, a list of the main components of the guitar resembles the items you might find in a garden shed. They are as follows:

- Main body—made from softwood and weighted with parts of an oak table-top, finished with a mahogany veneer
- Neck—twenty-four frets, fashioned from an oak mantelpiece and riddled with wormholes (plugged by May with matchsticks)
- Neck markers—custom configuration (e.g., buttons)

Brian May's homemade Red Special guitar.   *Andrea Leone/Shutterstock*

A double-necked version of Brian May's Red Special, as seen in 2012 at Queen + Adam Lambert's first London show.   *Davide Traversi / We Will Rock You Official Italian Queen Fan Club*

- Fret wire—from Clifford Essex, Cambridge Circus
- Tremolo arm—made from a discarded steel part from a bicycle saddle and finished with a knitting needle belonging to Brian May's mother

On a technical level, it is this unusual combination of resonant elements that gives the guitar its unique sound. Combined with prepurchased electrical pickups (the only significant monetary spend made on the guitar during its construction), it's perhaps no wonder the guitar itself is instantly recognizable as the Red Special. In a move indicative of May's perfectionism and musical idiosyncrasy, those pickups were specially configured to allow for many more sound combinations than a traditional electric guitar.

On the few Queen songs where May opted for another instrument, the difference in sound is clear: a good example of this is the guitar solo for "Crazy Little Thing Called Love," on which May uses a Fender Esquire to achieve a brighter and more traditional rock 'n' roll tone.

Such is the uniqueness and impact of the Red Special that there have been inevitable attempts to re-create it for a wider commercial release so that amateurs and Queen fans could make themselves sound like Brian May. Manufacturers like the Guild Guitar Company and Burns Guitars have released replicas to the mass market, while more specialist luthiers have worked directly with May to create more bespoke reproduction models for backup use by May himself. In 2003, X-ray photographs of the guitar were made at St. Bartholomew's Hospital in London so that a more accurate replica could be made.

Today, there's an official Brian May Guitars online retail site, which is a true marker of the distance traveled by this one instrument cobbled together at home by two enthusiasts. All its imperfections have now become standardized for a commercial marketplace, allowing the unique sound of the Red Special to be owned and adapted by anyone who wants it.

The Deacy Amp

John Deacon, like Brian May, was an enterprising scavenger and manipulator of electrical goods. The instinct to find and adapt materials so that they served a new sonic purpose was very strong in both, but in keen electronics student Deacon, the instinct extended less to instruments and more to amplification. Rifling through a dumpster in 1971, the recently joined Queen bassist liberated a tatty circuit board with indeterminate origins (later thought to be from a cheap transistor radio, a model mass-produced in South Africa) and wedged it into an old bookshelf speaker with the intention of using it as a practice amplifier for his own use.

This homemade amplifier really sang only at the top of its voice, so the volume control was removed, leaving it in a permanent state of maximum noise that just so happened to chime with the construction of Brian May's Red Special, a guitar that was already sensitive to the kind of feedback noise and audible clutter that May was able to marshall so well. Combined with a treble booster pedal (also constructed by May), the two components were malleable enough that a large range of instrumental noises could be created. An early example of this is May's "Procession," which opens the *Queen II* album. Not only does May utilize the full pitch range of the guitar, but he also exploits the temperament of the Deacy Amp to make the sustained notes sound almost orchestral in tone. Similarly, from 1975's *A Night at the Opera*, Brian May's song "Good Company" makes extensive use of the Deacy Amp to re-create the individual sounds of Dixieland revivalists like the Temperance Seven, most obviously the oompah of lower brass and the melodic whirling of clarinets.

Like the Red Special, the Deacy Amp too has been forensically examined and re-created for commercial and enthusiast purposes. According to Greg Fryer of Fryer Guitars (who has been deeply involved in re-creating both the guitar and the amplifier), the basic circuitry consisted of "a 1950s audio style Germanium transistor push-pull circuit, utilising in its front end an AC125 and AC126 respectively, with the push-pull Output stage comprising two AC128

Germanium transistors." Many attempts to tweak and improve the likeness of commercial replicas have been made in much the same way as with the Red Special, implying that their true individuality cannot be completely copied.

Primitive yet Inimitable?

Until their budgetary restrictions were eased and the idea of synthesizers became more palatable, it was these two engineering feats that gave Queen a signature sound aside from Mercury and Taylor's vocals. Something of that spirit of combining disparate elements and working with them until they sounded correct survived in the band throughout its lifetime, but nowhere was it more apparent on a sonic level than in their earliest albums. Those recordings are in many ways a marvel of studio engineering rather than electrical engineering, but behind all the posturing associated with claiming that synthesizers were somehow beneath them, Queen at least had the technological nous to back them up. May and Deacon's engineering skills are indicative of a true craft, and, arguably, the sign of that true craftsmanship is just how much work goes into its re-creation without ever fully achieving it.

7

Becoming Iconic

Queen II

There are many reasons why *Queen II* holds a special place in the hearts of many Queen devotees. It is the first glimpse we have of the band as innovators in technology as well as composers and their most unified artistic statement by that point in their careers. This extended to all areas of the band: stage aesthetics, album photography, and the company they kept. Influences that had been percolating within the band suddenly seemed to burst out of Mercury and May in particular, each of whom penned a side of the LP (except for the obligatory Roger Taylor contribution on side 1). *Queen II* is still many stylistic steps from the Queen that the casual fan would come to appreciate, but deep within this pivotal album's murky extravagances are detectable clues of what was to come. It would also produce their first commercial hit single and introduce them to a national audience sitting in front of their television sets as the caped, catsuited, and coiffed quartet made their first appearance on *Top of the Pops*.

First, though, they had to actually record the thing.

Back to Trident

The promotional tour for *Queen* had seen the band essentially promoting material from the album that would follow it rather than lingering on the album that they were actually supposed to be flogging. The wrangles and frustrations of recording that imperfect first album had left their mark, and the band resolved to make things easier on themselves this time around: no more late-night recording sessions to keep things cheap.

Keen to honor their influences, none other than David Bowie was initially approached to produce the album, but his commitment to recording his covers album *Pinups* in the north of France at the same time meant he had to refuse. Now they would record at sociable hours with Roy Thomas Baker and Mike Stone back behind the desk, trusted foils and cheerleaders dedicated to helping them realize their sonic goals. Also fine-tuning things in a coproduction role was Robin Geoffrey Cable, who had previously been behind Freddie Mercury's recorded stint as Larry Lurex.

Incredibly, *Queen II* took only a month to record, right off the back of a grueling national tour and before another in the new year. Their existing deal with Trident meant that the album could be made to the best of everyone's technical ability without having any specific label backing or a deadline for release, and it was in this atmosphere of frenzied creativity that May and Mercury marked their compositional territory with an entire side of the album each, May with the first "Side White" and Mercury with the flip "Side Black."

Side White

Like the albums that both preceded and succeeded it, *Queen II* begins with a showcase for Brian May's Red Special. After the thudding bass drum introduction, May's multitracked composition takes on the character of a Bach chorale, an overture for the song that follows it. "Father to Son" is one of Queen's longest songs and May's most personal. Given the time he spent in his youth working on various careworn science projects with his father, Harold, it's impossible not to read this as a direct and fond message to him. Musically, "Father to Son" begins to crystallize the idea of Queen as purveyors of the rock epic, featuring a midsection that borrows Beach Boys harmonies and the shuffling acceleration of the Who's Keith Moon. Simply put, long songs suited the band in the early to mid-1970s (though the commercial zenith of this, "Bohemian Rhapsody," was still to come).

"White Queen (As It Began)" and "Some Day One Day" round out May's main compositional contributions to *Queen II*, and all are unified by his more emotional approach. "White Queen" in particular could be read as the ultimate geeky love letter to a girl in May's biology class on whom he had a crush, the humdrumness of the source material elevated by arcane, Tolkien-esque lyrics ("How did thee fare, what have thee seen? The mother of the willow green!") and those omnipresent multitracked lines of guitar. On an instrumental level, May proved to be as resourceful as ever and approximated the sound of a sitar by wedging some fret wire under the strings of his battered Hallfredh acoustic, perhaps a nod to their reverence for Led Zeppelin.

Roger Meddows Taylor's (he was still billed as such on the album sleeve) sole composition on *Queen II* makes a perfect bedfellow for "Modern Times Rock 'n' Roll" from *Queen*, albeit a more aggressively swaggering one. "Loser in the End" is a grinding workout that could have been written only by a drummer (and not just because the drum part utilizes not one but two cowbells), undoubtedly indebted to glam-rock staples like T-Rex, but the lyrical content is worthy of mention thanks to its maternal fixations. The song has the sound of a steamy strut but the lyric of a cautionary telling-off. He sings of the mother in the song, "Misuse her and you'll lose her as a friend / She's Ma, on whom you can always depend." Was Taylor inspired to fall into thematic line by May's paternal proclamations in "Father to Son," or was he just a bit stumped for something to write about? Either way, it's unusual lyrical fare for a song that is so brazenly glam and full of rock posture and the album's least musically ambitious moment.

Side Black

In a way, the entire second side of *Queen II* (listed as "Side Black") is Freddie Mercury's most significant early composition. It is almost completely through-composed, with only two between-song silences in a suite of six thematically linked works that show more musical range than the material on May's Side White and hint tantalizingly once again at the band's aptitude for the epic.

That being said, the first impression we get of this second side is of the technological prowess now available among the band and their team of producers and engineers at Trident. "Ogre Battle" begins with a "mirrored" section, a fifteen-second series of riffs played backward and then seamlessly forward before the song's main verses begin. The riff itself goes a step harder than their acknowledged debts to Led Zeppelin and sounds decidedly more aligned with early heavy metal templates established by Uriah Heep and Black Sabbath, though May's playing is understandably more nimble than Tony Iommi's iconically leaden techniques (the result of an industrial accident in the sheet metal factory where he worked as a teenager—he lost the tips of his middle and ring fingers on his left hand).

Like May, Mercury is lyrically more cautious when dealing with human emotion and, for the most part, prefers to revel in the fantastical. "Ogre Battle" is a prime example, with its vaguely comprehensible tale of the titular grudge match between bands of "ogre men" who emerge from their "two-way mirror mountain," and "The Fairy Feller's Master-Stroke" goes even deeper. The song is completely inspired by the painting of the same name by the English artist Richard Dadd, most famous for his depictions of detailed myth and fantasy scenes and for creating them while incarcerated in various asylums after murdering his father in 1844. In 1973 as it does now, the painting hung in the Tate Britain in central London, and Mercury would drag his bandmates (possibly it wasn't so much of a wrench to convince May, a fellow fan of all things folklore inspired, to join him) to marvel at its intricacies, its separate narratives, and its characters that all nonetheless coalesced in a strange visual chaos. The resulting song is similarly chaotic and intricate, featuring harpsichord and dueling guitar lines battling with Mercury's extreme falsetto. Lines like "Tatterdemalion and the junketer / There's a thief and a dragonfly trumpeter" make direct reference to the painting itself, but it's crucial to note that all of this is mere wordplay and description, another example of Mercury's reticence to glom onto emotional truth in favor of something more whimsical.

Furthermore, two utterances in the song of the phrase "what a quaere fellow" might understandably be construed as a comment on Mercury's own sexuality (the nature of which was still couched in the prevailing attitudes toward homosexuality of 1970s Britain), but the more likely explanation is the simple delight in using an arcane word. Why, for example, would Mercury coyly adapt the lyrics of "Big Spender" to make it a sexuality-free discussion only to negate it by pronouncing his own "quaereness" in a song mainly about folklore? It would be some years still until Mercury could write more openly about this then shaded area of his life.

"Nevermore" showcases in a quieter fashion the current state of Mercury's emotional songwriting. It is a ballad, straightforward and brief at under ninety seconds in length, but in it Mercury displays a distinctly classical trick of gently undulating the song's tempo (known as "rubato" playing) to delay harmonic gratification or perhaps to increase drama or tension. Classical influences on the band have been noted in other chapters, but this is one of the earlier and simpler examples.

Queen's second-longest song across all of their albums clocks in at just over six and a half minutes long and is another example of their early reluctance for chart-friendly immediacy. "March of the Black Queen" is the counterpart to May's "White Queen" but rivals "Bohemian Rhapsody" in complexity and in-studio invention. Notable features include tubular bells, frequent tempo changes, Rachmaninov-indebted piano lines, and some of Roger Taylor's most hair-raising backing vocals, overdubbed until they sound quite alien, another instrument altogether fighting in a deliriously cluttered mix.

After "Funny How Love Is," perhaps the only other song that explicitly deals with actual human emotion alongside "Nevermore" (albeit in a breezier, Beach Boys–like strum-along style), the final three minutes of *Queen II* opened them up to the nation for the first time in their career.

Queen's First Hit

On February 21, 1974, Queen appeared on the BBC's *Top of the Pops* program for the first time in their career, miming along to "Seven Seas of Rhye." Due to a cancellation from David Bowie and the band's inclusion on a *Sounds* magazine list of bands to watch in 1974 (they were at number three behind Nazareth and Blue), their booking came before *Queen II*'s official release date of March 8. Also on the lineup that particular week were performances (mimed, prerecorded, or otherwise) from the likes of Barry White and the Isley Brothers, pegging Queen as one of the lesser-known acts to feature. Nevertheless, their dingily lit sing-along contained the hallmarks of their live show on display for the whole nation to enjoy. All in black with flashes of white frill (thanks to Zandra Rhodes's designs), it is an arresting enough performance that identifies Mercury as the front man and focal point and May as a preening yet serious-faced deputy with Deacon and Taylor afforded comparatively scant screen time (a shame given the magnificent open-chested leotard that Taylor had opted to wear).

The program's audience size and reputation was such that a seven-inch single release of "Seven Seas of Rhye" was rushed to press (with "See What a Fool I've Been" from the band's debut LP tacked on as a B-side) and available in shops by February 23, all of which resulted in Queen's first top-ten single in the United Kingdom—peaking at number ten.

Looking at the lyric sheet for the song might not immediately mark it out as a single with significant commercial appeal, but the sound of it marks a turning point in the band's discography. A popular gripe among management at Trident—and indeed in the studio with Roy Thomas Baker—was that the band's songs simply took too long to build up to their most memorable passages. The hooks were there, but they were hiding behind elaborate piano introductions and waltzing guitar solos. With "Seven Seas of Rhye," the band's sound is distilled and compacted into a salable chunk that features all major elements in the opening twenty seconds: athletic piano and the looping squall of the Red Special and the grunt of Deacon and Taylor's rhythm section, all before Mercury's vocal arrives. There isn't a chorus to speak of other than the iteration of the song's title, but its brevity and bracing tempo were enough to lodge it in the minds of the public after just one airing.

Additionally, as well as providing the band with a hit, "Seven Seas of Rhye" also binds its parent album to the albums that precede and follow it. The single takes its initial motifs from the instrumental track of the same name that closes the second side of *Queen*, and then the outro of the *Queen II* version of the song sees the instruments faded down as a brassy version of "Oh I Do Like to Be Beside the Seaside" steadily increases in volume until it dominates. This soundscape (complete with whistled reiteration of "Oh I Do Like to Be...") is then resurrected in the opening seconds of "Brighton Rock," the first track from the album that follows: *Sheer Heart Attack*—proof (not that it was needed) that Queen was still operating very much as an "albums band" rather than a singles factory.

The Dietrich Diamond

Perhaps the most lasting aesthetic aspect of this period of the band's history is the cover of *Queen II*, the first time Queen was pictured together in the famous "diamond" formation that would reappear in their music video for "Bohemian Rhapsody" in 1975. The band approached photographer Mick Rock to shoot some potential album covers after seeing his shots of David Bowie (as his official photographer) and the cover of the Stooges' *Raw Power* album from earlier in 1973. Rock later stated in an interview that Mercury "looks as if he's on his way to bloody heaven," such was the ethereal quality of the shot.

The cover of *Queen II*, showing Mick Rock's photograph of the band in the Marlene Dietrich-inspired image.   *Author's collection*

It was in fact inspired by a black-and-white picture of Marlene Dietrich in the movie *Shanghai Express* that shows the actor lit from above and clutching her face, which remains plaintive as a cigarette burns close to her fingers. Mercury, the most outwardly excited during the photo session, was happy with this idea after Rock showed him the Dietrich picture, and the rest of the band was photographed in the same way while Rock stood on a ladder.

A "white" version of the photograph was also shot for the inside of the album's gatefold vinyl, but the styling is considerably more gauche (even by Mercury standards), a more comical counterpart to the soon-to-be-iconic original.

Now I'm Here, Now I'm There

As the end of 1973 approached, with *Queen II* recorded and awaiting release, Queen embarked on their only tour as a support act for Mott the Hoople's twenty-two-date jaunt around the United Kingdom. Taking in various universities, guildhalls, town halls, and civic centers, it culminated in two nights at the Hammersmith Odeon. Mott the Hoople's most notable single, 1972's "All the Young Dudes" (written and donated to them by David Bowie), crowned a model headliner's set, jammed with anthems and ceremony, a unity and focus that Queen hadn't yet cracked for themselves. Brian May later described watching Mott on those dates: "We were in the presence of something great, something highly evolved, close to the centre of the spirit of rock 'n' roll, something to breathe in and learn from."

But it would still take some months for those learnings to show themselves. When, after the album release, Queen went on their own headline tour of the United Kingdom beginning in March, their power as a live act was hugely magnified. Multiple encores were demanded at venues the length and breadth of the nation, most notably in Stirling, Scotland: when the band refused to return to the stage for a fourth time having delivered three encores, a small riot ensued in which two members of the band's road crew were hospitalized. A combination of this and reports of the band being questioned extensively by police resulted in the following night's concert in Birmingham being postponed.

Ticket stub for the band's Rainbow Theatre show.   *Martin Skala, QueenConcerts.com*

The appetite for this band of unutterably strange musical influences had suddenly become ravenous in their home country (though reports of a particularly grim festival slot at Sunbury in Australia in January 1974 had them down as mere "Pommie poofs"). A climactic show at the Rainbow Theatre in Finsbury Park, North London, was recorded on March 31 of the same year and became a key live document for fans, capturing a set typical of the time and one shot through with that enigmatic "headliner" quality they'd learned to harness from their now considerable concert experiences.

After they'd torn across the United Kingdom in fine style and exhausted a set list not dissimilar from the *Queen* album tour, Queen reunited with Mott the Hoople to take on America for the first time. It was to be an epic jaunt throughout the country and the band's first major international engagement but one that saw the frustration of playing second fiddle come to the fore. Mercury told *Melody Maker* in December 1974 with not a little of his customary woe-is-me exaggeration, "Now we are a headline band we know people have come to see us. Being support is one of the most traumatic experiences of my life."

The tensions were clear despite both bands being on good terms. Queen had tasted success with their live show and sneaking into the singles chart and wanted to headline and get back into the studio to plot their next chart assault, but the list of tour dates stretched out from mid-April to June 1974. But they diligently performed their no-encore support slots throughout the south and

Queen onstage at the Rainbow Theatre, March 31, 1974.   *Ian Dickson/Shutterstock*

east of North America, twenty-one shows in total, until disaster struck: Brian May was discovered to have contracted hepatitis while the band was in Boston at the end of April, and by the time they made it to New York ten days later, he was struggling, eventually collapsing after a show at the city's Uris Theatre (now the Gershwin Theatre). It was a disastrous end to the tour. The band canceled the remainder of their appearances and came home, and May went straight to the hospital.

8

Sheer Heart Attack

How Did Queen Enter the Mainstream?

No Built-In Remedy

After EMI had managed to shift a few more copies of *Queen II* off the back of the chart success of "Seven Seas of Rhye," Trident placed the band on a small salary to cover their expenses. But with no live dates on the horizon and no album to sell, the pressure to make their third record a success was mounting, and the circumstances were far from improving. With Brian May convalescing in the hospital after his bout of hepatitis, it was time for Queen to consider their next move.

The album that followed *Queen II* was recorded only twelve months after and ended up being released in the same calendar year, but the distance between these two records is one of the most marked in their catalog. The Richard Dadd references were gone. The labyrinthine lyrical stories were still there, but they were no longer concerned with mythological characters: these were songs written in the real world, about real people. *Sheer Heart Attack* is a broader, more accessible work on the face of it but was born out of chaotic circumstances, across four studios and with May absent for large parts of the process. To add to their stresses, once May had been discharged from the hospital and the business of songwriting as an ensemble could formally begin in mid-1974, he then developed a stomach ulcer and had to go back to the hospital *again*.

One thing the band did have on their side, however, was the beginnings of some popular momentum. There was a tangible fan base in Britain, and juicy sales territories like the United States and Japan were beginning to show signs of "getting" Queen. May's absence granted the band two things on top of this: first, time for May himself to write alone and, second, time and necessity for Roger Taylor and John Deacon to up their contributions, setting in motion a group dynamic that would yield decades of hits to come. This was to be, in a time of upheaval for the band, the album that introduced Queen to the world, a glamorous, raucous, and (if you discount John Deacon's mildly perplexed expression on the album cover) lusty ensemble, oiled and ready for commercial domination.

Program for the band's Japan tour, featuring artwork from the *Sheer Heart Attack* cover.   *Martin Skala, QueenConcerts.com*

Necessity Breeds Invention

Recording sessions for the album began in July 1974 at Trident, but there was still barely any material written. This fostered a certain sense of breeziness to the songs: these were far less wrought and pored over than those of *Queen II*, a series of potential singles and more accessible epics for the live set, interspersed with the odd doodle-ish genre experiment.

Just as *Queen II* ended with the sounds of "Oh I Do Like to Be Beside the Seaside," so *Sheer Heart Attack* opens with the sound of fairgrounds, convivial hubbub, and crashing waves: the setting for "Brighton Rock." May originally fleshed the song out around the time of the *Queen II* sessions, but it was deemed thematically incompatible (which prompts unanswered questions around the inclusion of "Loser in the End") and thus ended up as the bracing and virtuosic introduction to the album that followed it. May's guitar work on this song is discussed in a later chapter, but it's worth noting here that it has accrued a feted status in the Queen catalog and among guitarists in general.

The story in May's lyrics is a relatively inconsequential one, of sweethearts Jenny and Jimmy and a trip to Brighton, the same fodder of mod bands and indeed mod revivalists of the era (the Who's *Quadrophenia* is an interesting comparison point), but musically, it displays a continuation of the lessons learned on "Seven Seas of Rhye," namely, that directness sells a record. "Brighton Rock" is epic but disciplined, contrasting passages of simplistic riffs and extreme ensemble virtuosity delivered in bite-size chunks, all revolving around May's central guitar solo.

Chart Dynamite?

In the spirit of the album's composition, Freddie Mercury claimed in an interview with *Melody Maker* that he wrote "Killer Queen" in a single day, beginning with the lyrics on a Saturday night and then powering through the music the following Sunday: "I'm not being conceited or anything, but it just fell into place." Despite the speed of its composition in comparison to previous material, the song is no less layered and precisely written. It's no exaggeration to state that "Killer Queen" is one of the most technically remarkable songs to chart in the 1970s (and this is still a year before "Bohemian Rhapsody"). Mercury also likened it to something that Noël Coward might have sung, a lighter song and a departure from the band's more familiar rock dynamics.

With its gently stomping piano and finger clicks, it is indeed the arrival of a distinct new style for Queen but one that suited them. And while Mercury suggested that Noël Coward could be a suitable singer for it, it wouldn't be surprising to hear the likes of Dame Shirley Bassey (who also, it should be noted, is famous for her rendition of "Big Spender," a Mercury favorite) assailing the melody and indeed the song's subject matter, which tells of the gaudy peculiarities and demands of a sex worker.

During recording sessions for the song at Trident, a recuperating Brian May lamented his inability to contribute more to the song, but the band was diligent in leaving him space for a guitar solo that went on to become one of his most memorable and "singable."

Commercially, the song performed better than any they'd released so far. It reached number two on the U.K. singles chart after it was released in October 1974 (just behind David Essex's "Gonna Make You a Star") and went into the top ten in several European countries. Significantly, it also hit number twelve in the United States, a sign that their commercial power was beginning to grow in a significant territory. For many mainstream consumers, "Killer Queen" was the first glimpse they'd had of the band and, interestingly, defined them not as a rock band but as a pop act.

In November, Queen appeared on *Top of the Pops* again, this time in a more polished-looking mime performance that showed Mercury dressed in an opulent fur coat befitting the song's narrator. The rest of the band's attire is marginally more reserved than their previous appearance on the show, and the effect as such is more refined: they are dandies and preeners, not rockers. Any vestige of being indebted to Led Zeppelin had now been nixed.

"Gimme a Good Guitar!"

Roger Taylor's sole composition on *Sheer Heart Attack* acts as a mere segue into a medley of Mercury compositions. "Tenement Funster" is doggedly within Taylor's musical range of louche and lumbering blues rock numbers, presenting a rare moment on the album when pop ambition seems to have been tempered. Taylor's cry of "Gimme a good guitar" is answered by Brian May, who, it could be argued, rather dominates proceedings here before a seamless transition into Mercury's numbers "Flick of the Wrist" and "Lily of the Valley," heralded by the arrival of the piano—the instrument by now utterly indivorcible from and synonymous with his role in the band as chief composer and bandleader. It's interesting to note this reduced songwriting role occupied by Taylor in the band's early albums, especially when considering the magnitude of Queen hits for which he was eventually responsible, but on this album at least, May's guitar still somewhat tramples his contribution.

The clinical environs of a hospital bed were perhaps the inspirational setting that Brian May required to needle out a song that had been bugging him, one that would become a staple of the band's live sets until deep into the 1980s. In "Now I'm Here," he relates his experiences of life on the road during the tour they'd had to leave due to his illness (hence the line "Down in the city, just Hoople and me") with a surprisingly romantic and tender series of couplets. Musically, again, the song bears witness to May's dominant influence on *Sheer Heart Attack*, almost as if because of his absence he was all the more determined to make his guitar heard. The song became the band's second single from the album in January 1975, just missing the top ten and charting at number eleven.

Who-esque suspended guitar chords on "Now I'm Here" show May's then current fondness for the group, and Taylor's rolling drums match the sound world, but it's the main guitar riff that, again, shows *Sheer Heart Attack* to be in many ways one of the most guitar-oriented albums in the band's discography.

On the second side of the album, though it isn't solely a May composition, "Stone Cold Crazy" further emphasized the guitar-toting nature of the band's sound at the time. The song was effectively a bastardized hangover from Mercury's days in Wreckage and Queen's spirited attitude to reworking existing material. The songwriting credit is shared among all four members, which perhaps indicates the jumbled hand-me-down nature of its composition. It is one of the hardest, fastest, and shortest songs in the entire Queen catalog and has many times been held up as a prototypical example of speed and thrash metal. Taylor's drumming isn't inconceivably distant from the blast-beat style that would emerge in more extreme metal subgenres from the 1980s on, while May's guitar once again proves the dominant melodic force for the whole song, bookending Mercury's gabbled verses with multitracked riffs (the idea of Queen as a metal band is explored in the next chapter).

Conversely, "Stone Cold Crazy" is followed by a seventy-second May composition, "Dear Friends," one of the simplest and quietest songs the band ever recorded. May's sentimentality as a lyricist again shows throughout the wrought verse ("So dear friends your love has gone, only tears to dwell upon"), and Mercury's vocal is restrained, anti-histrionic. Of this performance choice, Mercury told the Radio 1 deejay Kenny Everett some years later that as a performer, "People do associate me with the simpering little ballads, but Brian has written some lovely ones in his time."

John Deacon's Songwriting "Misfire"

The title of the first solo composition for the band by bassist and longtime "quiet one" John Deacon has to have been a knowing attempt at self-deprecation. "Misfire" is a ditty, nothing more substantial than a couple of calypso-indebted ideas bolted together with Deacon taking on most of the instrumental responsibilities himself. It's almost cheery, defiantly warm, and uncomplicated, with the only signs of its having been "workshopped" by the band emerging when May's wiggling guitars arrive at the very end and lead a series of escalating key changes.

Unlike Roger Taylor's slow and stubborn development as a songwriter across the span of many Queen albums, Deacon's emergence as a composer in the band is one based solely on play and experimentation, on doodles and single musical motifs rather than overarching themes or grand songwriting goals. The repeating guitar lick and galloping bass line for "Misfire" sits alongside the opening electric piano notes on "You're My Best Friend" or the looped bass line from "Another One Bites the Dust" as evidence of Deacon's more cellular style of writing (this notion is explored in more detail in chapter 41).

"Misfire," though, was omitted from the band's set list on the tour that followed and has been somewhat forgotten, the only notable life beyond the original recording coming from a bluegrass-inflected cover version from Neko Case in 1997.

Penchant for Pastiche?

Sheer Heart Attack closes with three more distinct Queen characteristics. First, Mercury's ukulele-led George Formby pastiche "Bring Back That Leroy Brown" (which is something of a blood relative of Brian May's similarly vaudevillian "Good Company" from *A Night at the Opera*) and then May's somber, lightly experimental "She Makes Me (Stormtrooper in Stilettos)," which closes with ambient sirens and breathing sounds, what May called "New York nightmare sounds."

Following these is another example of what could be considered Freddie Mercury's ongoing attempt to compose the ultimate rock epic: "In the Lap of the Gods . . . Revisited." The wordless refrain of the song so blatantly invites sing-alongs unencumbered by international translation that it's impossible not to conclude that the band now firmly had its sights set on commercial impact and the theatrical power of their live shows at home and abroad (appropriately, the song would close many live sets on the *Sheer Heart Attack* tour).

This final trio of songs distills the creative restlessness the band had encountered during the rushed and frenzied in-studio writing sessions for the album. Inadvertently, Brian May's recurring hospitalizations had allowed room for other songwriting avenues to open up, for space-filling ditties to emerge, and for the band as a whole to define itself once again. Where the overt technical and musical excess of *Queen II* and the subsequent tour had taught the band the value of direct, commercial songwriting, *Sheer Heart Attack* saw them forced to act on these learnings with disciplined intensity. The material for mainstream crossover had been assembled: now they just needed the audience.

Champions Returning

By September 1974, *Queen II* had sold 75,000 copies, making it worthy of a silver disc presentation from a look-alike of Queen Elizabeth II herself, appropriately enough at London's Café Royal. *Top of the Pops* and the band's Mott the Hoople tours had cemented them as a live act capable of matching the raucous hyperbole with which they described themselves. In short, the appetite for Queen was increasing quickly.

The *Sheer Heart Attack* tour began at Manchester's Palace Theatre on October 30, 1974, just as the album itself was rocketing into the charts at number two, and continued around the United Kingdom for the following three weeks, culminating in two more nights at the Rainbow Theatre in Finsbury Park before heading off to Europe, North America, and, for the first time, Japan. The U.K. leg of the tour saw them revisiting venues that by now were primed and ready for the hysteria that was following the band. With finances now looking a little more settled, possibly even rather comfortable, the band spent more money on the shows themselves. Mobile lighting rigs allowed for extensive and malleable atmospheres to be created and amended as the sets progressed, while the Zandra Rhodes winged costumery was mingled with monochromatic outfits.

The level of the band's stagecraft became much more developed. One notable effect for this tour would see a spotlit Freddie Mercury delivering the first line of "Now I'm Here" at one side of the stage, only then for him to apparently reappear on the other side of the stage for the line that follows ("Now I'm there"). The effect was achieved by dressing a roadie in exactly the same clothes as Mercury and positioning him at a conveniently remote location and using the spotlights to imply a teleportation that, while simple, was still hugely effective.

As the end of 1974 approached, Queen began the European leg of the tour, which would take them through the mainland of the continent and into Scandinavia before a typically calamitous event would momentarily halt their progress: a road accident involving the bus that carried their much-mythologized lighting equipment meant that concerts in Copenhagen and Oslo were canceled. Queen also played with Lynyrd Skynyrd during this jaunt, unlikely as it may seem. Although Roger Taylor's opinion of the band has never been a secret, as he told *Mojo* magazine, "They were awful. They were Southern rednecks and they could not believe it when they saw us four caked in make-up and dressed like women."

The North American tour began in February 1975 after the album had managed to climb to number twelve on the *Billboard* charts. Again, concert cancellations rubbed the shine off the success of the tour, this time due to certain venues' inability to safely host the projected volume and rambunctiousness of attendees and, in Vancouver, due to Mercury's coming down with a sore throat.

Set lists for these shows became understandably more epic and varied in length and material, but the band's first-ever tour of Japan allowed them still more freedom. Queen was treated like celebrities (almost deities) in Japan, and the *Sheer Heart Attack* tour was the beginning of a relationship that included mobbings at airports, hysterical concert receptions, magazine features (all four members separately graced the cover of *Ongaku Senka* in 1975), and awkward prerecorded video messages to be broadcast on national television. The natural by-product of this warm welcome was an extended average set time, which allowed for songs written pre-*Queen* to get an airing, songs like "Hangman," performed on the final night of the tour at Budokan Hall in Tokyo as an extended and quite simplistic blues stomp with a surprisingly vicious outro that further plays into the notion of Queen as speed metal pioneers.

Flyer for Queen's show with Lynyrd Skynyrd in Frankfurt.

Martin Skala, QueenConcerts.com

God Save the Queen

Now that Queen effectively consisted of veterans of the live circuit (at least in their home country), a strange thing began to happen. Between songs or while they were waiting for yet another encore, enthusiastic fans would start to sing the national anthem of the United Kingdom, otherwise known as "God Save the Queen." It is, in its sparsest form, a very Queen piece of music: stately, pompous, and self-inflating. It seemed only logical that Brian May should mastermind a multilayered version of it for the band to play live from the *Sheer Heart Attack* tour on, his orchestral leanings coming to the fore in a spectacularly gauche expression of the band's essence. It would be some years before Mercury began parading around the stage in red regal robes and hoisting a crown into the air, but the die was cast: Queen was on its way to becoming rock royalty—in their own minds at least.

9

How Metal Was Queen?

Trying to define exactly where the burgeoning heavy metal scene was at the turn of the 1970s is a task for another, longer chapter than this one, but, by way of setting the scene, it's perhaps enough to characterize the genre at this point as one populated by outsiders. Black Sabbath's second album *Paranoid* topped the U.K. album charts in 1970, Led Zeppelin was gradually easing themselves into the hearts of the American rock mainstream, and the howl of Deep Purple's Ian Gillan was one of the most powerful musical instruments in the world. These three, especially Sabbath, became synonymous with the "heavy metal thunder" that Steppenwolf sang about in 1968's "Born to Be Wild," a darkly thrilling and spartan new musical aesthetic that would permeate culture and disperse its influence across the decades that followed.

Metal in its various forms was and still is a genre that, broadly speaking, champions virtuosity. It was only natural, then, that Queen would adopt some of its stylistic tropes in their music, most notably in their first few albums but also at certain points right up until their final recordings. Brian May and Roger Taylor's blues influences were on full display when they played in Smile, and the harder, more psychedelic edges of their sound were no doubt due to artists like Deep Purple and Jimi Hendrix, traditionally viewed as incubators of what would become the heavy metal sound.

But Queen being Queen, the influence of heavy metal was not simply a tool in their arsenal: it was something to be squeezed and prodded and regurgitated via their complex series of compositional processes. The results, where we can find them littered throughout the back catalog, are revealing.

"Son and Daughter"

In terms of sheer riff magnitude, "Son and Daughter" from *Queen* shows the incubation of those early metal influences like Black Sabbath very clearly. The riff itself is more lead-filled Tony Iommi than spry Ritchie Blackmore or intricate Jimmy Page, one that you sense falls easily under the fingers for May and

Deacon especially. Mercury's vocal, as with the majority of these examples, does not seem touched by the growls or yips synonymous with the genre. It's also one of the very few Queen songs to feature any kind of profanity, specifically when Mercury sings, "The world expects a man to buckle down and shovel shit," and as such can be filed alongside his exhortation on "Death on Two Legs" for you to "Kiss my ass goodbye."

"Father to Son"

This is the first of two candidates on *Queen II* that most obviously show Queen's metal influences. May's "Father to Son" is an epic in the sense of its length and lumber, but the aesthetic evidence of heavy metal is clearest at the song's midpoint, right after Mercury sings, "You'll write it all again before you die," when a truly sludgy and glacially paced Brian May riff arrives. Consisting of barely four notes, it's another calculated interpretation of the work of Black Sabbath's Tony Iommi albeit a shortened and economized version.

"Ogre Battle"

Unusually, this song was written by Freddie Mercury on the guitar rather than his favored compositional tool of the piano. Mercury's guitar skills were markedly inferior to the deftness he showed on the keys. As such, the repetitive, hammered nature of the riffs on this highlight from the second side of *Queen II* is understandable. It's possible to hear a prefiguring of the likes of Motorhead in those relentless, jabbing downstrokes, especially when combined with Roger Taylor's pummeling of the tom-toms, but again, the metal influences are confined to the instrumental sections of the song as Mercury's whimsical lead vocals turn the song back toward the light.

"Stone Cold Crazy"

One way of quantifying the metal credentials of Queen's "Stone Cold Crazy" from *Sheer Heart Attack* would be to mention that none other than perhaps the most successful metal band in history, Metallica, recorded and performed a cover of it on numerous occasions. Musically, the song combines blues and metal with a rare proficiency, a shuffling riff that borrows equally from both genres. It is apposite that Metallica was the band to recognize the song's root-level metal attributes, as their cover version (which originally appeared on an Elektra Records compilation in 1990 and then as the B-side to the phenomenally successful "Enter Sandman" single) sounds as if it could have been written specifically for them.

"Gimme the Prize (Kurgan's Theme)"

One of the songs from *A Kind of Magic* to feature in the movie *Highlander* from 1986, "Gimme the Prize" features one of Brian May's most interesting guitar solos, most notable because of the way it utilizes the then contemporary technique of "tapping," something audiences would be more likely to hear on a Van Halen record. May's tapped introduction to this song is technically proficient and in keeping with the dramatic context of the film it was intended to accompany, but it's a rare occasion indeed when we find the guitarist aping the work of another artist quite so blatantly. May did describe Eddie Van Halen's guitar playing as "exemplary" in an interview in 1989, so it's little wonder that the influence showed through.

The rest of the song, too, shows that some thirteen years after the influence of heavy metal first invaded the band's sound, it was still latent within them, bursting forth in May's literally wailing guitar (though less so during the solo where he imitates the bagpipes). Uncorroborated reports that both Freddie Mercury and John Deacon hated this song suggest that this was May's pet project rather than a group move back toward the metal aesthetic.

"I Want It All"

A surprising speed metal interlude during this highlight from *The Miracle* is notable for many things, but especially for Roger Taylor's only recorded use of that heavy metal staple: the double bass drum pedal. Allowing a drummer to effectively double the tempo with the flick of a toe, this is a metal technique more likely to be seen on a Motorhead or Metallica record than on what ended up being one of Queen's most commercial-sounding albums.

On either side of this curveball midsection, the song is heavily reliant on a synthesizer chord progression that runs through the entire song (one that Brian May said had been in his head for months before it was recorded), suggesting that the song was the subject of much workshopping using May's progression as a springboard for different stylistic interpretations.

"The Hitman"

With its nod to the Edgar Winter Group's 1972 sideshow instrumental classic "Frankenstein," the breezy chug of "The Hitman" from *Innuendo* could conceivably have been lifted straight from the *Wayne's World* sound track. That it appears on Queen's final traditionally recorded album indicates that a deep sympathy for metal music and specifically for the guitar riff as a building block of their sound ran throughout the band's career. In a neat parallel with the way "Ogre Battle" came to fruition, the initial riff was Mercury's, becoming a fully formed song only once Brian May had adapted it to fall more comfortably under his fingers and provided the band with a workable and much heavier-sounding demo version.

How Metal Was Queen?

These examples from across nearly a twenty-year recording history suggest a deep connection to heavy metal music in its rawest forms, but the real question is, did Queen merely take on influences from existing work, or were they in fact covert pioneers of the genre? In all honesty, it would perhaps be a stretch to suggest that Queen has some ownership of the metal genre as we know it today, but their ease with stylistic transitions shows their remarkable adeptness for it.

Of the material assembled here, "Stone Cold Crazy" is perhaps the most convincing argument for the band having truly predated or pioneered a certain stylistic movement, namely, the thrash metal explosion of the 1980s, but besides that, it would be more accurate to conclude that metal was simply another area for the band to borrow from, to amend, and to bend to their own songwriting style. It's appropriate that one of the other main cultural movements of the period, punk, was by far the more musically primitive: this kind of "message over delivery" musical maxim was very much not Queen, and they completely ignored it despite magpie-ing their way through countless other musical genres.

So, in short, Queen was fairly metal: simultaneously innovative and consistently reverential to what had gone before them, but for every grunting guitar riff, there was a Mercury vocal flourish waiting to spike the balloon and remind listeners that Queen was still lovably dilettantish. The respect they've subsequently been shown comes mainly from the commercial end of the metal spectrum (the likes of Tony Iommi and James Hetfield are accepted metal denizens but mainstream nonetheless), those who understand and favor the power of a good commercial metal riff.

10

Pop and Circumstance

Queen's Imperial Phase

Goodbye, Sheffield

To the untrained eye, it would appear in early 1975 that Queen was about to have their moment. They'd cracked the charts on both sides of the Atlantic, toured the world, appeared on Japanese television, and announced themselves as one of the most enjoyably deranged creative prospects in pop music, complete with a grounding in dorky folklore. There was nothing like them, and they were now demonstrably able to produce hits and make money.

Now that they had returned from Japan in May 1975, money was increasingly becoming the issue that rendered the band stationary. Their initial management deal with Trident was a good fit for a band desperate to get an album recorded, but now that the band was a proven commercial draw, suddenly the restrictive nature of the agreement meant that their meager salary wasn't increasing in line with the huge financial gains the band as a company was making. In fact, it wasn't increasing at all. John Deacon was unable to put a deposit down on a house with his new wife Veronica Tetzlaff (Mercury turned up at their January wedding wearing a particularly natty feather boa), and Roger Taylor was advised to hit his drums with less vigor in case the band funds couldn't cover replacement sticks and skins. Royalties from *Sheer Heart Attack* (which had now comfortably outsold *Queen II*) and monies from international ticket sales were nowhere to be seen.

There was only one solution: Queen had to break free. Their manager incumbent since 1972, Norman Sheffield (brother of Barry, with whom he opened Trident Studios), was deemed to be the most pressing problem and jettisoned by the band. Prospective replacements were touted, including Led Zeppelin's then manager Peter Grant, but the band eventually settled on John Reid, who counted none other than Elton John among his clients. Reid certainly fit the bill when it came to the band's more extravagant partying habits: in 1974, he spent a month in prison after an altercation with a journalist at a party in New Zealand where Reid was outraged to learn that the whiskey reserves had run dry.

But when it came to Sheffield and the damage he had done to the band's career, it was Mercury who made his feelings most plain. He wrote a song about him titled "Death on Two Legs (Dedicated to . . .)" and made it the opener to Queen's biggest album yet.

"Do You Feel Like Suicide?"

Queen went back into the studio with Roy Thomas Baker once again, but this time the stakes were higher than ever. As it turned out, the stresses of recording *Sheer Heart Attack* with Brian May hospitalized were a comparative cakewalk to making the album that became *A Night at the Opera*. And despite the band having no money themselves, the financial investment made in the album was colossal: reportedly £40,000, at that time one of the most expensive albums ever made, split across lengthy sessions in seven different studios.

Freddie Mercury's approach to spending that money was to settle his personal gripe with Norman Sheffield. "Death on Two Legs" is, on modern reflection, a shockingly bitter document. In its review of *A Night at the Opera*, *Melody Maker* described the song as "heavy metal," but it is far too delicate and English in its expression: like the comedy in the *Carry On* movies of the time, Freddie's camp exuberance in the delivery of the lines made them all the more caustic. He told *Sounds* magazine the following year, "My throat was bleeding, the whole bit. I was changing lyrics every day trying to get it as vicious as possible." The reaction of the band to lines like "Do you feel like suicide?" and its answering backing vocal "I think you should" was initially one of shock. Mercury continued: "They saw the words and they were frightened by it. But for me the step had been taken and I was completely engrossed in it, swimming in it. Wow! I was a demon for a few days." It's difficult to imagine the gaucheness of the suicide couplet flying today, but in 1975, it was explained away as Freddie being Freddie. When the band played the song live, it would be introduced as being written about "some motherfucker I used to know."

Was the ire justified? The song was perhaps a petty revenge for some serious mismanagement, but Mercury's sustained fury and his constant tinkering with the lyrics to make them as vile as possible give a clear indication as to Mercury's reaction when his wings were clipped. Considering that Trident was still the band's management company and an album playback session would inevitably occur at which Sheffield would hear "Death on Two Legs," it was a brazen move to say the least. Sheffield knew instantly that the song was about him and sued Queen and EMI for defamation. The out-of-court settlement that followed implies that Mercury knew the game was up.

Many Studios, Many Sounds

Where *Sheer Heart Attack* had been recorded across multiple studios in a rush to get it written and recorded, *A Night at the Opera* was recorded across multiple studios merely to accommodate the sonic ambition of the band. Sessions took place in London (at Trident, Sarm in East London, the now defunct Round-house, Scorpio near Euston Station, and Olympic Sound in leafy Barnes), but the bulk of the work was done in the Welsh countryside, at Rockfield Studios, the same place as sections of *Sheer Heart Attack*.

The album's crowning achievement and the recording most associated with Rockfield, "Bohemian Rhapsody," is discussed in the next chapter, but it's important to highlight just what an effect this idyllic place had on the sound of the rest of *A Night at the Opera*. The list of artists who recorded there during the 1960s and 1970s gives a fair idea of the esteem in which it was held (Black Sabbath, Hawkwind, Motorhead, Mike Oldfield, Joan Armatrading, and Rush), and the facility itself was technologically fairly unassailable. The residential nature of recording there gave Queen, using the famed "Quadrangle" studio, the necessary time and space to experiment with their arrangements.

More than any other Queen album, it's possible to detect the strikingly deep thought processes and decisions that went into every string plucked or triangle dinged. Mercury sang the vocals for "Lazing on a Sunday Afternoon" into a microphone connected to headphones that were in turn placed in a bucket, making it sound like an outtake from the Beach Boys' psychedelic noodle-fest *Smiley Smile*. John Deacon learned to play the double bass especially for "'39." The band used kazoos to replicate an entire wind and brass section for "Seaside Rendezvous." Brian May turned his guitar into a Dixieland ensemble for "Good Company." Simply put, they threw everything at this album. It became characteristic of Queen to respond to pressure in this way. If the album needed to be a commercial success, there's no way they would've dashed off a breezy couple of singles in the hope of a decent return on their investment; instead, they would make a hideously expensive epic the likes of which had never before been heard.

Taylor Revs, Deacon Evolves

As a result of the huge technical ambition on display, the album is one of the most celebrated in the band's career. It is, for the most part, still Mercury and

May's show when it comes to songwriting, but two of the album's key compositions came from Roger Taylor and John Deacon.

Among ardent Queen fans, Taylor's "I'm in Love with My Car" is a song that divides. On the one hand, it is utterly emblematic of his early songwriting with Queen, but, on the other, it is tonally at odds with where the rest of the band was heading creatively. One reading of the song would accuse it of being sexually unenlightened even for 1975, but a more generous assessment might simply excuse it for its pure silliness. Written by Taylor as a bizarre paean to automotive excess and the potentially rampant sexual innuendo in the surrounding lexicon, it is an exercise in ridiculousness, knowing or otherwise.

The groove of the song is a little looser than previous Taylor compositions, angsty and bluesy in equal measure, and with plenty of Brian May flourishes, but the lyrics are where all attention should be placed: they range from the confusing ("When I'm holding your wheel, all I hear is your gear") to the downright childish ("With your hand on my grease gun, it's like a disease son"), so much so that it's difficult to tell just how po-faced Taylor was when he was chewing his pencil tip. "Get a grip on my boy racer rollbar" is, in its way, the kind of line that sits perfectly on the border between retrograde savant and knowing swipe at masculinity, and it's nearly impossible to tell which one it actually is.

Debate within the band on whether to include the song on the album at all has been the subject of much folkloric speculation (and scenes in the eventual movie dramatization of the band's career), but what we do know is that Roger Taylor was insistent that the song at least be a B-side to "Bohemian Rhapsody."

The B-side to "Bohemian Rhapsody," Roger Taylor's "I'm in Love with My Car."   *Photo by Mark Greban*

His insistence was so strong, in fact, that he locked himself in a cupboard until his reluctant colleagues agreed that it would share a sliver of vinyl with Mercury's masterpiece and, therefore, eventually net Taylor a substantial slice of the songwriting proceeds simply by dint of being packaged with a hit.

John Deacon, on the other hand, demonstrated an almighty songwriting leap on *A Night at the Opera* and managed to get his first top-ten hit out of it as well. "You're My Best Friend" was written for Deacon's new wife Veronica Tetzlaff and is a completely unchallenging listen, a bouncing and nostalgic piece led by the Wurlitzer electric piano, which Deacon had only just begun to learn how to play. While happy to sing the song, Mercury made clear his opposition to the electric piano on several occasions, declaring in a BBC Radio 1 interview, "It's tinny and horrible and I don't like them. Why play those things when you've got a lovely superb grand piano?"

Like "Killer Queen," it is an effortlessly sophisticated song from a technical point of view, the genius of its intricacy completely masked by the apparent ease with which it is performed on record—doo-wop backing harmonies, an unusually efficient song structure, and a restrained Mercury vocal that blends into rather towers above May and Taylor's contributions.

It wasn't released as a single until May 1976, well after the success of "Bohemian Rhapsody" had died down but sharing with that song a music video directed by Bruce Gowers that showed the band surrounded by candles with Deacon sitting at the grand piano. The single's sleeve also shows the band standing rather threatlessly in a park in unusually reserved attire (save for Freddie's ludicrously small gym shorts). Deacon stands slightly to the front, as close to taking center stage and soaking up the applause as he could muster. Everything about the song is polite, amiable, and chaste. In many ways, it is as far away from "I'm in Love with My Car" as a Queen song could be: innocent and sweet, depicting love as a purely emotional experience with not a hint of physical or sexual energy.

The Sound of Ambition

A Night at the Opera captures Queen at their most creatively driven, their most bombastic, and their most refined. The sonic capabilities of Rockwood meant that the band now had twenty-four audio tracks to play with and build up rather than the usual sixteen. Recordings like Brian May's "The Prophet's Song" are not only compositionally adventurous but also sonically inventive. Roy Thomas Baker's role of channeling the band's grandstanding technical ambitions became an ever more important challenge, as he oversaw elements such as a multitracked one-man vocal canon requiring delicate threading into place with disparate koto instrumentals and phased recordings of air-conditioning

The sleeve for the 1984 re-release of John Deacon's "You're My Best Friend."   *Author's collection*

units. Mercury's central vocal canon and the subsequent chorale featuring May and Taylor's voices required extensive planning and mastery of the tape-delay techniques that May had been experimenting with on songs like "Brighton Rock" and "Now I'm Here" from *Sheer Heart Attack*.

"The Prophet's Song" is, in some ways, more technically adventurous than "Bohemian Rhapsody"; it just happens to have far fewer sing-along sections. At over eight minutes in length it's also Queen's longest song to feature vocals. An engineering masterpiece, it represents an apotheosis of the band's studio achievements, a deft and sensitive affirmation of their own prowess. It's as if by recording the song in such an overtly elaborate way, they were simultaneously acknowledging both their history as rock technicians and their current aspirational status of arch-creatives, brazenly aiming to confuse as much as they were to delight.

Talking to *Sounds* magazine in 1976, Mercury confirmed that the studio was an environment of great reward but great stress: "I do enjoy the studio, yes. It's the most strenuous part of my career. It's so exhausting, mentally and physically. It drains you dry. I sometimes ask myself why I do it. After *Sheer Heart Attack* we were insane and said 'never again.' And then look what happens."

Aside from the technical achievements (see chapter 6 for more on "Good Company"), veins of songwriting also diverged on *A Night at the Opera*. "Love of My Life" in particular is the most overt flexing of Mercury's emotional muscle, a song dedicated to Mary Austin, his girlfriend at the time, eventual fiancée, and a constant close friend throughout his navigation of his sexuality. It is a deeply serious song played completely straight, played more so than any other Queen song without any wink to the camera or a knowing instrumental flourish to assure the listener that this was indeed still Queen. The song's strange place in the catalog also turned it into a live favorite as soon as the band incorporated into their set list in 1977 and eventually found a huge audience in Argentina and Brazil when, following huge South American shows, the live version from *Live Killers* managed to stay on the singles charts for most of 1981.

That notion of ambition that allowed them to experiment so widely with sound, song, and execution even extended to the album's sleeve. Designed by artist David Costa as an adaptation of the existing Queen emblem that Mercury had made in the early days of the band, it is simultaneously ornate and technicolor, a tidy summation of everything they were attempting.

Rock Royalty—Finally

With the final strains of Brian May's arrangement of "God Save the Queen" closing the album, the public at large would come to regard Queen as the very thing they'd always wanted to be ever since Freddie Mercury christened the band: rock royalty. The album was mixed in a marathon thirty-six-hour period in early November 1975, just a week before the band was due to head out on the promotional tour to accompany the release.

The tour would see the band tackle a now familiar route around the concert halls of the United Kingdom and North America and an expanded Japanese leg but also eight dates in Australia. At manager John Reid's insistence, rather than playing larger concert venues to more people than on previous tours, the band would simply perform on multiple nights at the same place, an attempt to preserve the power of the shows themselves. Six nights in London, four nights in New York, and two in Tokyo, Adelaine, Sydney, and Brisbane: all designed to show the band at their most effective. Although bigger dates were to come in the years that followed, the shows from the *A Night at the Opera* tour can be considered among the band's most successful.

The U.K. leg of the tour ended with a special show at the Hammersmith Odeon on Christmas Eve 1975, recorded by the BBC and televised as an edition of *The Old Grey Whistle Test* (a live showcase seen at the time as a bastion of pleasingly exploratory leanings in rock music). "Bohemian Rhapsody" was at number one on the singles charts, and television audiences were becoming accustomed to seeing these wing-suited oddballs prancing around the stage in their living rooms.

And the prancing was truly pervasive: in the performance, the sheer ground covered by May and Mercury in particular as they lean, pivot, duel, and lunge

Mercury and May in Zandra Rhodes–designed costumes onstage at the Hammersmith Odeon.
Martyn Goddard/Shutterstock

at the audience with guitar necks and microphone stands as weapons is huge. A crucial document of the band's live craft, the Christmas Eve 1975 show is, by any conventional measure of rock performance, a formidable display. Both May and Mercury were unwell with fatigue for the show, but the adrenaline of television recording rendered any discomfort invisible. Segueing from nuggets of "Bohemian Rhapsody" into an acidic "Killer Queen" and using May's guitar solo to jump straight into "March of the Black Queen" before circling back once again to the closing phrase of "Bohemian Rhapsody," the band's generic flexibility is stunningly apparent.

If they were still viewed in some quarters as geeks rather than rock stars (as one newspaper piece put it at the time, "The four bachelor boys who go to make up Queen are unusual in that they all hold university degrees"), that interpretation of the band was now relenting as the world began to accept them as one of the more prominent acts on the planet. When they returned home six months after they kicked off in Liverpool, exhausted and conquering, Queen was a different proposition. Their grand experiment—their last-ditch attempt to join the upper echelons of rock society—had succeeded. Although for many recorders of the band's history this moment would never be surpassed, it's true to conclude that commercially, critically, and culturally, Queen was now more significant than they had ever been.

11

Is This Just Fantasy?

An Attempted Explanation of "Bohemian Rhapsody"

U ndoubtedly, the song for which Queen will be most widely remembered is "Bohemian Rhapsody," an anomalistic, multilayered collection of unrelated musical nuggets that became a seemingly inexplicable commercial powerhouse. And then, after that, it became a commercial phoenix rising on more than one occasion to top the charts yet again, a byword for epic rock and progressive excess, for operatic silliness and guitar hero grunt. Given that so many analyses of the song have been made in books, magazine articles, and documentaries since the song was released, to offer in this chapter a rehashed amalgam of what's gone before seems somewhat pointless, so the aim here is to provide a deep appreciation and some new perspectives, if indeed there are any left on this most-written-about artifact.

It is ultimately Freddie Mercury's piece, but to call it the product of just one man would be to undersell the contribution of his bandmates, Brian May's guitar solos and Roger Taylor's high falsetto being the obvious elements to point out. But this song, with its accompanying promotional video (arguments abound as to whether it truly is the first music video in history), sold Queen as an ensemble like never before. The reappearance of their lit-from-above "diamond" formation as seen on the cover of *Queen II* was to become the defining image of the band's career, united in presentation and in purpose. It was usual for May to rearrange and reinterpret Mercury's musical ideas by changing the key, the phrasing, or the register. But now, the whole band's efforts were required to correctly interpret the ringleader's demands.

Like Brian Wilson ten years before him as he marshalled the forces of the Wrecking Crew for the recording of his wide-screen pop classic *Pet Sounds*, the music sounded loudest in Mercury's head, and the process of dictating it to other musicians was just as vital as its initial inspiration. Fortunately for Mercury, his bandmates were equal to the task despite the frustrations it caused. Sessions would rumble on from August into September 1975, and, although

The picture sleeve for the "Bohemian Rhapsody" single release.   *Photo by Mark Grehan*

Roy Thomas Baker claimed that the sessions were good natured in character throughout (he called them "a joke, but a successful joke"), it's hard to believe that an element of cabin fever couldn't prevail at times, especially when the band was in thrall to one dervish composer-conductor.

Was the Song Really a One-Off?

Or, in other words, what clues from the band's previous recordings tell us that a song like "Bohemian Rhapsody" was a natural progression? As previously discussed in reference to songs on *Queen II* and *Sheer Heart Attack*, the band's innate kinship with all things musically epic far predates this one song. Perhaps it goes as far back as John Deacon watching Deep Purple at the Royal Albert Hall or the first time Brian May heard Mantovani's orchestra, but what's clear is that this song was not a bolt from the blue, a miraculous composition visited on Mercury by a higher power.

Tracing the band's desire to make "big" music proves that "Bohemian Rhapsody" was the point at which Mercury's technical ambition matched up with the commercial potential of his band. A song with structural intricacy like "March of the Black Queen" from *Queen II* and a song with naked anthemic aspirations like "In the Lap of the Gods... Revisited" from *Sheer Heart Attack* (both Mercury compositions) clearly show that something like this was always in the cards. Of "March of the Black Queen," Brian May told BBC Radio 1's Tom Browne that "all the texture work was there, and the intricate harmonies.... [It was] sort of the precursor of 'Bohemian Rhapsody' in many ways."

Similarly, there are counterpart songs on *A Night at the Opera* that tell us the scale of ambition within the band. Both May's "The Prophet's Song" and Mercury's "Death on Two Legs (Dedicated to ...)" reach for the same level of drama, but neither was deemed suitable singles and so never broke out in the same way, but there is another theory here: could "Bohemian Rhapsody" have been the product of competition? Generally speaking, the band's collegiate creative relationships were presented in interviews as exactly that: collegiate, respectful, even fond and encouraging. Mercury would praise John Deacon's improving songwriting and Brian May's gentle balladry whenever he was asked about it. Brian May's habit of "improving" the material of others by transposing, rearranging, or improvising over it is generally seen to be in that collaborative spirit, but beneath the surface, there was the inevitable broiling tension that comes with four songwriting personalities cooped up in one recording studio.

Outtakes from sessions around the mid-1970s show the band arguing as petty brothers might, ripping into each other's playing habits and bemoaning their less-than-perfect playing. In those recordings, it's telling that Mercury is mostly behind the glass, that is, with the producers in front of the mixing desk rather than in front of a microphone.

For an insight into the competition and jealousies that often go hand in hand with gifted composers, look to Brian Wilson, who in 1976 described "Bohemian Rhapsody" as "the most competitive thing that's come along in ages." What a perfect choice of words: songwriting for Wilson is a competition, one he'd previously held with Paul McCartney and John Lennon when the Beatles' *Rubber Soul* convinced him he needed to up his game with *Pet Sounds* in 1967.

So when it comes to "Bohemian Rhapsody," you can be sure that all four members of the band knew as they were recording it that it was a striking work. Whether they were all on board with it as it was being recorded, however, is a different and thornier question. They had written and recorded things like it before but not with Mercury's role quite so prominent, so dictatorial. Friction would perhaps have been expected if not inevitable. In this way, the song truly was a one-off, although those creative tensions would be placed on the band more forcefully in the following decade.

When Did "The Cowboy Song" Become "Bohemian Rhapsody"?

The roots of "Bohemian Rhapsody" date back to the turn of the 1970s and the days of Smile, the band that would eventually morph into Queen. Chris Smith, a keyboard player with Smile and a member of the same social and musical circle as Freddie Mercury and the rest of Queen, recalled hearing Mercury tinkering at the piano, demonstrating fragments of something he called "The Cowboy Song," which contained the lyrics "Mama, just killed a man, put a gun against his head, pulled my trigger now he's dead."

Other musicians and friends close to Mercury in the early 1970s also claimed to have heard embryonic versions and snippets of elements that would end up in the final song, most commonly the opening ballad section. Roy Thomas Baker relayed the story of hearing the opening played to him by Mercury on the piano before stopping suddenly and declaiming, "Now, dears, this is where the opera section comes in."

"The Cowboy Song" had been knocking around for some time as a self-contained piece before it was connected to the other sections of "Bohemian Rhapsody," which were all conceived by Mercury but subjected to the band's inevitable elaborations. Brian May, for example, described carefully working out what he wanted to do with the twiddling guitar solo that precedes the operatic section. This nugget of a ballad would've survived on any early Queen album, a counterpart to Brian May's "Dear Friends" from *Sheer Heart Attack* or Mercury's own "Nevermore" from *Queen II*: so was Mercury saving it for a grand exposition and development of its own?

Song Elements

The song is generally accepted to contain three or four main segments: an opening ballad leading into a highly elaborate operatic pastiche that then builds to a hard rock section before calming back down into a coda that retools material from the opening ballad. But within those three or four main sections, there are hundreds of individual musical motifs, especially in the middle operatic section, which, unsurprisingly, presented the biggest technical challenges and took up the most studio time. Rather than combing through every second of the song, as previous analyses have done already in forensic detail, it's certainly worth highlighting some of the more pivotal moments from each section and their effect on the song as a whole (in order of their occurrence).

- **"Is this the real life?"** As declamatory and exposed an opening as you could imagine, the first lines of "Bohemian Rhapsody" are, conversely, full of confusion and uncertainty. These dream-like lyrics and the "hanging" nature of the unresolved first chord define the song as a work of imprecise mysticism from the outset regardless of the precision in writing and recording. The importance of the opening statement as a mood setter can't be overestimated: it requires quiet attention in the same way the beginning of a classical work traditionally would as the conductor raises his baton.
- **Guitar solo number one** Brian May's major contribution on "Bohemian Rhapsody" is to link the two main opening sections with a guitar solo. It contains several iterations of May's technical hallmarks (runs that skip deliberately out of time, his "dut-dut-diddly" phrasing), but more broadly than this, it is the tonal bridge, gradually becoming more animated and angular to smooth the listener gently into the completely different musical character of the operatic section.
- **Mercury's piano in the operatic section** For all the mock bluster and multi-tracked insanity of the vocals in the middle section of the song, Mercury's piano remains almost child-like in its simplicity, played with the air of a rehearsal *répétiteur* coaxing ever more extreme renditions of the next line from an exhausted chorus. You can almost imagine him ending each of his quiet solo lines with a yelled "Now *fortissimo!*"
- **Roger Taylor's falsetto** It is customary of Queen's attitude toward studio recordings that no external players be involved, no matter the instrumental or vocal requirements of the song. Unlike, say, Pink Floyd enlisting the vocal talents of Clare Torry on "The Great Gig in the Sky" from 1973's *Dark Side of the Moon* LP, it was against the band's philosophy to look outside the group (until later collaborations in the years that followed, anyway). Consequently, the character of Roger Taylor's high falsetto during the operatic section of "Bohemian Rhapsody" becomes part of the character of the song. It's an act that serves the artist rather than the composition. A more purist approach would include a hired choir capable of hitting those notes comfortably, but it's symptomatic of Queen's "nobody played synthesizer" philosophy to keep everything in-house, their knowing arrogance in assuming all musical roles themselves. It is Taylor's final falsetto note that encapsulates this most effectively. As he sings the "me" of the line "Beelzebub has a devil put aside for me," it slides violently upward in a pastiche vibrato that would've been trameled and decharacterized in the hands of a conventional choir and conductor.
- **Guitar riff climax** Freddie Mercury's guitar riff (performed by Brian May) ends the operatic section and has provided popular culture with a

shorthand for head-banging rock excess. Unusually, it has an almost swung feel in the rhythm, a markedly unconventional move that, generally speaking, only the more "muso" rock bands would attempt to pull off.

- **The Deacy Amp** John Deacon's famed Deacy Amp makes its only appearance on "Bohemian Rhapsody" right at the end for Brian May's closing contribution, a delicately harmonized duet of guitar lines with a sustaining sound that suggests violas in their high register, desperate and straining, yearning to emote.

- **"Nothing really matters"** The nihilistic, fantastical closing couplet "Nothing really matters, anyone can see / Nothing really matters to me" is confirmation that the song's meaning is purposefully meaningless. By its own admission, the song is inconsequential, something one can apply to one's own life and story but not something to which one can attribute specific references. Elton John's "Candle in the Wind" is about Marilyn Monroe and nothing else. "Bohemian Rhapsody" is about nothing and delights in it.

- **The tam-tam** The song could never have a bombastic end, a sudden ensemble crash and choked cymbal. It had to end in a whisper to bring us back to the delicate silence of the opening, that atmosphere of reverence and anticipation. When Roger Taylor strikes the tam-tam, the final note of the entire song, it is not simply the relief of tension: it is the silence that seals the song at both ends.

What Influences Did Freddie Mercury Incorporate?

The chanson tradition in French popular music reached a modern zenith with Belgian singer-songwriter Jacques Brel, who forms a link in a chain of musical influence that connects David Bowie all the way back to the Neapolitan songs of the nineteenth century, songs like Giovanni Cappurro and Eduardo Di Capua's "O Sole Mio." The common thread that links these performers and songs together is drama. When Jacques Brel sang, "My death waits there among the leaves, in magicians' mysterious sleeves" in "My Death," his deft creation of drama is what lingers, not the assumption that everything he sings applies directly to the man singing it. There is a certain detachment in his performance that is characteristic of his work, one despite which Brel is still able to bring that all-important drama, that theatrical power that connects song to listener. Bowie does it all across the imagined interplanetary sadness of his *The Rise and Fall of Ziggy Stardust and the Spiders from Mars* LP, and Luciano Pavarotti does it when he sings the melancholy final verse of "O Sole Mio."

It is perfectly possible and in fact quite tidily attractive to locate "Bohemian Rhapsody" in this lineage. Mercury's mystical narrative within the song's lyrics has been endlessly pored over in countless essays and analyses, but he staunchly insisted that there was no definitive inspiration. Seeing the song as an exercise in dramatic rather than personal expression effectively allows us to look at it without getting sidetracked by what-ifs about the precise genesis of Mercury's "mama" in this instance. Mercury's influences in the composition of "Bohemian Rhapsody" weren't always necessarily musical, but those nonmusical influences were just as important.

Musically, however, the influences are less oblique and a little easier to trace. In his piano work, Mercury most obviously channels the lush textures and defined, stately pace of Pyotr Ilyich Tchaikovsky's Piano Concerto No. 1 or Sergei Rachmaninov's Prelude in C sharp minor. During the operatic section of the song, the style becomes less of the late romantic and more of the late classical, specifically the plinking chromatics of Frédéric Chopin. Mercury studied piano up to grade four (in the United Kingdom, the musical examination systems generally go from grades one to eight) and had studied some elements of music theory, so his influences on the instrument would likely have been of this nature. His studies also explain the general competency of his harmony work and the fluctuations in speed and tempo, the indelible marks of one who has learned too much music theory to unlearn it.

Despite the central operatic section lasting only sixty-five seconds, the influence of classical music and opera on the song are the most prominent. It's generally accepted that this is extreme and sophisticated pastiche, although it is one that does not adhere to any traditional formal boundaries: in other words, it's an impression of opera, speaking in its accent rather than its language. Exclamations of "Mama mia" and "Galileo Figaro" certainly evoke the world of Italian opera, but musically the picture is still more jumbled. The call-and-response nature of the vocals as Mercury is answered by the "chorus" of May, Taylor, and Mercury (again) has more in common with Gilbert and Sullivan than it does with Giacomo Puccini or Giuseppe Verdi: just listen to "When the Foeman Bares His Steel" from *The Pirates of Penzance* for an example of the soloist/chorus dynamic in question.

As the song progresses through to its delicate finale, the more traditional musical influences of Led Zeppelin and Jimi Hendrix show themselves once again in May's rendition of a gargantuan Mercury guitar riff. This is, as we've seen, completely par for the course in the context of Queen's back catalog and their influences, so what's remarkable about it? Specifically, the transitions between these extremely disparate influences are so nimble, making the knowingly ridiculous aspects of the song on a tonal par with the wrought balladry: no single songwriting guise is treated differently, and they are allowed to exist in the same song in a way that no other artist had so far thought to do. Spiritual forebears such as the Beatles' "A Day in the Life" resisted genre tourism, whereas Queen positively embraces and delights in it. Similarly, the Beach Boys' "Good Vibrations" caused as much confusion as it did delight when its tripping excesses hit mainstream radio, but Brian Wilson's composition was more consciously lean (the band's publicist supposedly coined the term "pocket symphony" to describe it). "Bohemian Rhapsody" *knows* it's an excessive song, and it's proud.

Were the Vocals Really All That Perfect?

There are widely available recordings of isolated vocal tracks from recording sessions for "Bohemian Rhapsody," much of which is of interest to anyone with an analytical mind, but aside from the intricacies of building those huge harmonic clusters, it's enough to say that "Bohemian Rhapsody" utilized every possible aspect of the band's collective vocal prowess. Listening to those separated tracks, each thread of a musical line given its supporting part, it's possible to hear Mercury's voice in particular at its very breaking point.

We think of the song as a gem of construction, of precision and discipline, the rigor of which had never before been committed to a commercial rock recording, so it's all the more surprising to hear fluffs aplenty, imprecise lines in Brian May's lower register, and, at one climactic point, a hair-raising vocal crack from Mercury on the word "die." The truth of the recording is that it is littered with "that'll do" moments, but the sheer volume of material and studio wizardry required to assemble them overshadows any inconsistencies. It's a rock journalism cliché to cite Phil Spector's "wall of sound" recording techniques in discussion of audio invention, but the influence is certainly there, although "Bohemian Rhapsody" is perhaps more accurately described as a monolith of sound rather than a mere wall. In addition, Roy Thomas Baker had worked on recordings by the D'Oyly Carte Opera Company (famous for their productions of Gilbert and Sullivan operettas), affording him a sensitivity with the human voice that more generic rock producers simply wouldn't have the instinct to draw on. If it's not too esoteric a comparison to draw, there is a similarity in tone between the opening section of "Bohemian Rhapsody" and Gilbert and Sullivan's "Ah, Leave Me Not to Pine Alone and Desolate" from *The Pirates of Penzance*.

With the band's approach to keeping everything in-house (an approach that was now gradually extending to the business side of Queen), meaning that all vocal duties had to be taken on themselves, the workload and pressure on May, Taylor, and Mercury's voices was huge. As such, the fatigue in the aforementioned isolated vocal tracks is understandable. The vocal gymnastics are indeed remarkable all throughout the recording, but that they are less than perfect makes the band, perhaps subconsciously, a more human ensemble. They strived for perfection and certainly worked hard enough to achieve it, but those imperfections are the whorls in the wood of the song: they make it more organic, less machined.

Where Do the Operatic Lyrics Come From?

Brian May later went on record stating that he believed parts of Freddie Mercury's personal life were bound up in the song. But which specific elements? May qualified his assertion by stating that he believed the lyrics were personal to their author. However, the Capital Radio deejay Kenny Everett (the song's most notable cheerleader in the United Kingdom) claimed Mercury had told him in person that the lyrics of the operatic section were chosen only because they rhymed and that there was no veiled meaning behind any of it. Theories also exist that suggest it was written as a veiled tribute to music publicist David Minns, whom Mercury had been seeing consistently despite his long-term relationship with Mary Austin. With nothing more than inklings as to what the lyrics of the song might concern, as we've outlined, once you accept that "Bohemian Rhapsody" is effectively about nothing (although other interpretations are of course available), it becomes easier to dispassionately piece together the origin of Mercury's words.

At first glance, the whole lyric sheet is a hodgepodge, bringing together a coterie of religious figures, mythical icons, and stock characters from traditions reaching histories as disparate as Italian drama and Persian mythology. Bismillah, Galileo, Figaro, Scaramouche, Beelzebub: all have been well documented and researched in other book chapters and articles about the song, so it's enough to say here that Mercury's reliance on classical dramatic structures, religious figures, opera, and the surrounding tropes of all of these influences was significant. He uses them not as direct narrative markers or directions but more as colors in his palette, chosen and used with precision to create specific tones and shades on his canvas.

Even the song's title reaches for operatic grandeur. Many will be reminded of Giacomo Puccini's opera *La bohème* and its cast of poverty-stricken dreamers, which seems a perfectly apt and Mercurian inspiration given the band's financial issues around the time. The *Cambridge Dictionary* definition of the word *rhapsody* reads, "a piece of music that has no formal structure and expresses powerful feelings," which, again, is a neat fit for the song itself. The structure is through-composed rather than traditionally strophic, and the feelings expressed within it, though unfocused, are indeed powerful in nature.

How Commercially Successful Was the Song?

When the sessions for *A Night at the Opera* were finally finished, attention turned to what single should be the first taste for the record-buying public. There were shorter, leaner candidates on the album than a six-minute experimental album track that no one (surely?) would understand. As it happened, conversations between the band and EMI centered around the song's unsuitability for a single release, simply because the nature of pop radio at the time meant that anything over a standard single running time of only a few minutes would be ignored. Buoyed by the effort they'd expended on recording it and their collective belief that it was in fact a work of genius, Queen held their ground, but they were at an impasse.

According to a 1995 *Sound on Sound* feature, Capital Radio's Kenny Everett (who would go on to become a close friend of Mercury's) was given a copy of "Bohemian Rhapsody" to listen to, a reel-to-reel version handed to him by Roy Thomas Baker after a curry, on the condition that he didn't play it on his show. The double bluff worked, and Everett, a figure synonymous with subversion and impishness in broadcasting, couldn't resist. Over the course of one weekend at the end of 1975, Everett played portions of the song fourteen times. The reaction from listeners was stronger than any marketing campaign could've been, and scores of listeners harassed their local record shop proprietors for copies of a single that hadn't even been printed yet.

John Reid held a crisis meeting with EMI, and it was decided that the single would be printed (with Taylor's "I'm in Love with My Car" on the B-side) as soon as physically possible to meet the potential demand. It went to number one on the U.K. singles chart in the first week of November. It also went to number one in Australia, Belgium, Canada, the Netherlands, and New Zealand, and it reached number nine in the United States. This was the deepest commercial penetration the band had managed so far. It's no overstatement to describe the eventual release of "Bohemian Rhapsody" as the pivotal moment in this story.

Critically, the song was met with confusion. Reviews of the time commended the technical prowess of the song and its performance but were nonplussed, emotionally divested in the song. Queen had suffered their fair share of critical maulings as they struggled to find their audience, so it's to be expected that the song's commercial success was of far more interest than the veneration from the music rags. As Mercury put it to *Sounds* magazine the year after the song was released, "What its success means to the band is acceptance."

The Return of Dietrich

The now iconic video for "Bohemian Rhapsody" jostles with other candidates for the accolade of the first official pop music video, but it is generally accepted to be the most significant early example of the medium. It was created not as part of a grand artistic visionary expression to blend seamlessly with the song itself but actually because the band was due to be playing a concert in Dundee when *Top of the Pops* was recording. As soon as it was known that the single was going to chart, it became obvious that some kind of promotional video would be necessary. The alternative for artists unable to attend the show's recording was either to create a "pop promo," essentially a mimed performance utilizing some local hall or performing space wherever they happened to be on tour or to let the BBC roll out Pan's People, a dance troupe that had only minimal time to prepare a sympathetic dance routine that would be televised as the single recording played out. How different things could have been had Queen not decided to do something different.

Agreeing with the band that something should be put forward to *Top of the Pops* to spare the nation an interpretive dance version of their biggest hit to date, Trident allowed the band to hire a truck on which they could shoot a video, to be directed by Bruce Gowers, who went on to shoot videos for Prince and Michael Jackson as well as live episodes of *American Idol* (where he would eventually run into Queen again in a very different format). Having taken the truck to Elstree Studios, where the band was rehearsing for their upcoming live show, the video was storyboarded by Gowers and the band, with Mercury taking an executive role. Special effects were mooted.

The video shoot took three hours, an astoundingly swift execution that would be unheard of for any major recording artist today (according to Gowers, they began shooting at 7:30 p.m. and had retired to a local pub by 10:45 p.m.). The band's decision to re-create the Mick Rock photograph from the cover of *Queen II* turned out to be one that cemented their iconography in world culture, establishing that single image of the band, the Marlene Dietrich–inspired diamond formation, as the one that could identify them in any territory in the world. Although they appear comically dated to contemporary eyes, the visual effects in the video were the product of a technical wizardry that was simpatico with the band's own approach to do-it-yourself engineering: Mercury's cascading face effect was created by utilizing visual feedback, while the honeycomb-style multiple iterations of the band came simply from fitting a prism on the camera lens.

The mimed performance section of the video, too, works wonders at capturing the chaos of the band's live show despite being filmed in an empty auditorium. When a shirtless Roger Taylor closes the whole piece by striking a huge gong in a possible nod to the famous "topless man striking a huge gong" introduction to films made by the Rank Organisation, it is just another in a line of attempts to make the video iconic in the very loftiest sense of the word. Almost everything in the "Bohemian Rhapsody" video is designed for longevity. Although it is full of complex effects and visual gestures, at its basest level, the aim was to be remembered.

When it was shown for the first time on the *Top of the Pops* on November 20, 1975, it was alongside the rather more pedestrian likes of the Bay City Rollers' "Money Honey" and the Eagles' "Lyin' Eyes" (featuring Pan's People naturally). It was an instant pass into the history books. A promotional video had never looked so singularly curated and intentionally iconic as this. It's telling that still, on the regular occasions when montages of Queen history are shown on television (think the hyperbolic jump cuts that introduce acts on *The X Factor* or celebratory televised award show packages), the first frame is more often than not the Dietrich diamond in silhouette, an immediate signifier to a mass audience of exactly who they're about to encounter.

What Makes It Special?

The impressions made on a modern listener when reevaluating "Bohemian Rhapsody" mark it out as an early example of something to which we're now quite accustomed: the event track. Examples of this could include songs as seemingly disparate as Bill Haley's "Rock around the Clock" and Childish Gambino's "This Is America," songs that by their cultural resonance draw a line across pop history. Michael Jackson's "Thriller," the Beatles' "A Day in the Life," Beyoncé's "All the Single Ladies," Whitney Houston's version of "I Will Always Love You": once these songs affected society and become part of the cultural conversation, it was impossible to consider pop music as a whole without reference to them. With that in mind, "Bohemian Rhapsody" certainly qualifies as an event track of the highest order.

It reached the top of the U.K. singles charts on two separate occasions: once on its original release, where it stayed for nine weeks and sold more than a million copies, and a second time in 1991, shortly after the death of its composer. Cover versions of the song are so numerous that it's nearly impossible to catalog them all. As of December 2018, it is the most streamed song written in the twentieth century.

When we talk about "Bohemian Rhapsody" today, it's always to measure the song's extremities: it's so *long* for a single release, the rock section is so *heavy*, the video is so *groundbreaking*, the lyrics are so *weird*. The song can be taken purely in this fashion, as a celebration of excess and gaudy technical prowess, but beneath it, there is still, to this day, enough mystery surrounding it to render it an object of perennial fascination, seemingly inexhaustible in analysis. Now that it has become lodged fast in the collective cultural consciousness, it will continue to outlive its composer and its custodians long into the future, a "successful joke" to which we already know the punch line and that we never tire of repeating.

12

Day Follows Night

Queen Coasting

Q ueen had scaled a peak. "Bohemian Rhapsody" had chanced them into the big leagues, effectively sold an entire concert tour, and confirmed that, when it came down to it, they really needed only one thing: more songs.

Looking at the set list for a huge free show in London's Hyde Park in September 1976 (attended by 150,000 people) shows a collection of songs that had been in the band's live repertoire for around four years. Songs from *Queen* and *Queen II* were still lingering, as was the medley of rock 'n' roll covers like "Jailhouse Rock" and "Big Spender." In short, despite the huge commercial power the band now had, the pressure was on once again to maintain their position.

Sessions for Queen's fifth album, *A Day at the Races*, began in July 1976 and encompassed the Hyde Park show (as well as three other big summer shows in Edinburgh and Cardiff), catching the band at a strange time: there was no album to promote yet, but the desire among Queen fans to see their now infamous stagecraft on a large scale was too tempting for them to put off. As such, the only new material performed at Hyde Park as a short recording of the overture to *A Day at the Races* and a new Mercury ballad: "You Take My Breath Away."

It mattered little: although attendees at the front of the throng had a decent view of the band, the stage was woefully small, and a large portion of the audience couldn't see. After volleys of bottles and cans flew forward, the band was told to attempt to control any further misbehavior. Mercury entreated the audience from the stage to stop throwing things, "tin cans or whatever." The onstage delay failed during "The Prophet's Song," meaning that Mercury had to improvise a raw version of the multitracked middle section. The show drastically overran (maybe due in part to Brian May's seven-minute guitar solo during "Brighton Rock"), almost landing the band with a hefty fine and resulting in Bob Harris, host of BBC television's *The Old Grey Whistle Test*, having to nervously inform the crowd that the evening was indeed over and that no encore would be forthcoming.

Bootlegged footage shows the concert to be reasonably spectacular but with a very palpable feeling of the same muscles being flexed once again. The band was so polished despite the technical hiccups that the life had begun to drain from their material. It was time to hit the studio—and quickly.

A Poor Man's *Night at the Opera*?

It's not only the title stolen from the Marx Brothers' comedy that earmarks *A Day at the Races* as a more slapdash companion piece to *A Night at the Opera*. As a collection of songs, it treads similar musical ground with a few new experiments thrown in for good measure, a grab bag of new singles and set fillers that they could take on the looming world tour set to kick off in January 1977. It was also the first album that Queen produced alone, meaning it was the first not to feature the studio expertise of Roy Thomas Baker. So developed and honed was the band as producers as well as musicians that it was barely noticeable that the personnel had changed.

Perhaps symptomatic of the album's status is "Tie Your Mother Down," both a very old song by Queen standards and one that found its home in live performance rather than on the singles charts (it managed to get to number thirty-one in the United Kingdom). The initial riff was developed by Brian May in 1968 while vacationing in Tenerife, and it became a staple of live sets for the rest of the band's career.

"The Millionaire Waltz" was, after "Death on Two Legs," the second song Mercury wrote about a Queen manager: in this case, John Reid, who fares an awful lot better than Norman Sheffield did when exposed to Mercury's acid pen. The song extends some of the techniques and classical influences displayed on "Bohemian Rhapsody," most notably allowing Brian May's guitar room for its most extensive orchestrations yet. Layers on layers of May's guitars adorn the song, which cycles through several sophisticated harmonic changes very quickly. The lyrics are surprisingly tender, suggesting that Mercury's connection with Reid was far more fond and convivial than the average artist–manager relationship.

The album is remarkable for its curios, however: John Deacon's "You and I" is a deceptively simple jangle-pop number, while Roger Taylor's "Drowse" is at the most psychedelic end of his blues-rock shtick.

"Can Anybody Find Me . . . ?"

If one of the main goals for *A Day at the Races* was to furnish the band with at least one monster single, then it was achieved thanks to Mercury's "Somebody to Love." Now seemingly ticking off genres as he went, this gospel-inflected paean to desperate loneliness is perhaps the most significant Queen song where the main musical lineage can be traced to a nonwhite vocal tradition. Mercury's love of Aretha Franklin (as discussed in chapter 2) dominates the song as he casts himself as the soloist in a fabricated gospel choir formed of himself with May and Taylor.

The song also gave the world one of the most recognizable examples of Mercury's vocal virtuosity, specifically with his closing a cappella iteration of the song's title. Holding the word "to" for the full wringing of its potential before cascading down throughout "love," Mercury created a musical cell that singers have been trying to replicate since. Listening to outtakes from the recording session for the song (available to hear online), it's clear that there were many alternative versions of the song's climax, ranging widely in register and delivery, presumably all jettisoned in favor of Mercury's more iconic falsetto.

A promotional video for the song (now standard practice for the band) was cut together from a mimed in-studio performance at Sarm East during sessions for the album and also from live footage of the band's Hyde Park show. Interestingly, it shows John Deacon standing with the rest of the band around a single vocal microphone for the final choral section, even though he never sang on the recording itself. Also noteworthy is just how casual the band seems: dressed in woolly jumpers and loud shirts rather than any kind of coordinated wing-suit affair (this "at-ease" guise would return in later videos for some of the band's straighter singles).

As was now the expected scenario, the single charted comfortably at number two in the United Kingdom and number thirteen on the U.S. *Billboard* "Hot 100" on its release in early November 1976: a success.

Freddie Goes Romancing

Equal in craft to "Someone to Love" is Mercury's "Good Old Fashioned Lover Boy," which incorporates Queen's peculiarly British end-of-the-pier influences into one of his purest pop compositions. Musically, it's a curious mix of John Philip Sousa–derived oompah silliness and Motown backing vocals (watch out for a perfectly silly "one-two-three-four-five-six-seven-eight-nine o'clock" toward the end), rounded out by a May guitar solo that apes the reedy sound of Glenn Miller and His Orchestra. It is playful yet sincere, in other words, exactly how one imagines a Queen love song to be.

But it's the lyrics on this song that show Mercury to be playing ever more daring games with the public status of his sexuality. Now a few years after he first began to degender the band's cover of "Big Spender" ("I don't pop my cork for every*one* I see"), Mercury is comfortable enough to address this song directly to another man or at least allow that interpretation to register: "Lover boy, whatcha doin' tonight?" Key in this non-heteronormative interpretation of the song is the fact that there are no precise descriptions of the object of the narrator's desire, just the fact that it could very well be a man.

The relationship in the song is disarmingly pure, chaste even (although there is the odd Taylor-esque wink at the camera in Mercury's reference to his hot seat of love), capturing Mercury in the mode of a wide-eyed romantic. Only ten years had passed since the decriminalization of homosexuality in the United Kingdom: there was no template in society for a domestic or even vaguely conventional romantic relationship between two men, but there is a case to suggest that "Good Old Fashioned Lover Boy" was working toward something like it.

"You're Singers . . . Fuckin' Sing!"

These words were barked at May, Mercury, and Taylor by none other than Groucho Marx as he hosted them at his home in Los Angeles in March 1977 while the band rolled through America for the *A Day at the Races* concert tour. Just a matter of months before his death from pneumonia, the oldest Marx brother had gotten wind that the band had named their last two albums after two of the most successful Marx movies and invited them over for a spot of light entertainment. The message he sent them congratulated them on their "sage" choice of album title and, according to some sources, concluded by claiming that his next movie production would be titled "The Greatest Hits of the Rolling Stones."

Roger Taylor's recollection of the meeting years later was that Marx sang songs for the bemused trio (John Deacon, ever nervous of the spotlight, declined to attend) before demanding that they repay the favor. A Spanish guitar was located and handed to May, and they sang him a rendition of "'39" from *A Night at the Opera*. The Groucho Marx episode is a good gauge of the band's star power during this period. Just a couple of years earlier, the band had been sitting in Rockfield Studios watching Roy Thomas Baker's VHS copy of *A Night at the Opera*, and now they were being told to "fuckin' sing!" by the man who created it.

"They Sang Every Note of Every Song"

After a launch event for the album held at Kempton Park Racecourse (a special horse race titled "The Day at the Races Hurdle" was run to mark the occasion), it was time to head back out on the road. A realization occurred during the U.K. leg of the live schedule: after countless shows in the same venues around the country, the fans had begun to know the songs. It sounds like an obvious point, but the band found their insistence on singing the words back at the band confusing, annoying even. It removed spontaneity, and it removed the thrill of surprising an audience with material they couldn't yet understand. At Bingley Hall in May 1977, May and Mercury turned to one another. According to May's recollection in *Classic Rock* magazine in 2015, they decided that "something's happening here. We've been fighting it, and we should be embracing it. That's where 'We Will Rock You' and 'We Are the Champions' came from."

The realization is yet another turning point in a whole mid-1970s series of turning points for the band. The final two shows of the tour were at Earls Court in London on June 6 and 7 and were heralded by the use of a new lighting rig, known as the Crown, costing approximately £50,000 and weighing two tons. The Crown would also ascend and descend as the band entered and left the stage, itself a feat of engineering so impressive that the Electric Light Orchestra ended up buying it off them and turning it into a UFO for their stage shows.

Those final two shows were ebullient in character, as vivid and striking as Mercury's jester-esque checkered catsuit. They were dubbed the "Jubilee" shows because they happened to coincide with Queen Elizabeth II's Silver Jubilee celebrations. Their new set was now marbled with songs from *A Day at the Races*, and the band tore through a career-encompassing program that included in its encore a bracing cover of Elton John's "Saturday Night's Alright for Fighting," a move that must have pleased John Reid.

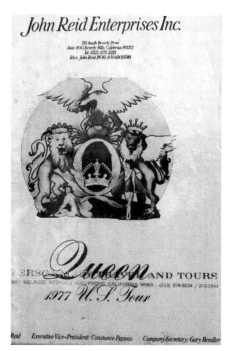

A tour schedule for the band's 1977 U. K. jaunt,
very definitely issued by John Reid Enterprises.
Martin Skala, QueenConcerts.com

As fitting and strong a send-off to the album as these enormous shows undoubtedly were, a precedent had now been set. Albums were getting more expensive, tours longer, and TV appearances more grueling and stressful. Having entered an imperial phase of sorts, Queen was duty bound to try to stay there for as long as possible. As always, the next album really needed to be "the one."

13

Spread Your Wings

When Did Queen Truly Conquer?

In 1953, the American artist Frank Kelly Freas painted the cover of *Astounding Science Fiction* magazine. It was an image of a bewildered-looking robot, rendered in the beautifully kitsch sci-fi style of the mid-century, holding the corpse of a man apparently killed by the same robot. A dab of red blood colors the end of the robot's finger, confirming his guilt. The caption reads, "Please ... fix it, Daddy?" The artwork was commissioned to accompany a story called "The Gulf Between" by Tom Godwin, an emerging science-fiction writer on his first assignment for the magazine. It is an effectively charming and chilling piece.

Twenty-four years later, Freas was contacted by Queen. Roger Taylor had found himself in possession of the October 1953 issue of *Astounding Science Fiction* and wanted Freas to replace the dead man in the image with that of his bandmates so that they could use it for the cover of their new album, which was guaranteed to sell in the hundreds of thousands. A skeptical Freas agreed but didn't listen to a single note of the band's music until the retooled artwork was completed. When he finally did give them a go, he liked "Killer Queen."

There's a peculiarly Queen-ish homespun joy to this process: their collective adolescent enthusiasm for science fiction and fantasy was still strong enough to pursue a legend of the genre so that they could be closer to it, even envelope themselves in its history. Indulgent and arrogant, perhaps, but the results were undoubtedly arresting.

I Ain't Gonna Lose: Queen Accepts Their Megastardom

Indulgent, arrogant, and arresting: this could also be applied to *News of the World* in its entirety. And this being Queen, it's also perfectly possible for those first two adjectives to be wholly complimentary: this was indulgence and arrogance not in musical excess for once but in posturing and grandstanding. Hit

The cover of the October 1953 edition of *Astounding Science Fiction*, featuring the Frank Kelly Freas artwork that was adapted for the cover of *News of the World*.

singles and world tours were now bread and butter, limousines their preferred method of transport. Whether they were partying with Aerosmith or clutching a series of platinum discs in a bizarrely formal ceremony in Japan, everything the band did was now officially the behavior of cultural icons, the behavior of megastars. Megastars do not sing songs about Richard Dadd paintings. Megastars do not sing songs about ogre battles. Megastars do not sing songs about merely "Doing All Right."

With *News of the World*, there was a conscious shift in the band to acknowledge and play on their role as arena fillers. The audience was to become part of the show, part of the band itself. An opening couplet of songs, May's "We Will Rock You" and Mercury's "We Are the Champions," immediately became definitive, emblematic of this new version of Queen who would no longer stare at the audience in disbelief as they sang along. The stomp-stomp-clap of the former is this version of Queen distilled in two seconds: communal, rallying, direct. Although sketches for "We Are the Champions" dated back to 1975, its release as a single at this point in the band's career only solidified their new guise further. A music video was produced at the New London Theatre, starring the band and hundreds of members of the official Queen fan club. Each attendee was given a limited-edition copy of the single and were treated to a free live show after filming had wrapped, as if to cement the fact that Queen now knew how important their audience was. The song is Queen's "My Way," their attempt at immortality, the song sung most loudly in sporting stadiums across the world forty years after its composition.

Simon Ferocious Drops In: What Happened When Queen Met the Sex Pistols?

One of the most delightful apocryphal stories about Freddie Mercury is possibly so alluring because it plays into everything fans and devotees fondly remember about his character: caustic wit, playfully delivered. Conversely, it quite ably demonstrates Queen's willful immunity to, perhaps even ignorance of, whatever might be happening in popular culture outside of their own work. During recording sessions for *News of the World* in August 1977, the gobby rage of punk was tripping through the nation and causing little short of a musical social revolution, democratizing pop so that anyone with enough confidence could theoretically sell out the 100 Club on Oxford Street if they could string a few chords together. The lead proponents of this movement were the Sex Pistols, who just so happened to be recording an addendum track for their debut album, *Never Mind the Bollocks, Here's the Sex Pistols* in Wessex Studios at the same time that Queen was knee deep in their own album sessions.

Sid Vicious, bassist with the Pistols, represented many things opposite to Queen: musical economy, efficiency, and antiestablishment anger. As such, with confrontational verve, he burst into the studio where Mercury had been working and challenged him: "Have you succeeded in bringing ballet to the masses yet?" Mercury challenged him back and called him "Simon Ferocious." Mercury recalled later, "He didn't like it at all." Further flurried exchanges between the two didn't quite come to blows, but the way Mercury told it suggests that it was at least a partial defeat for Vicious.

Strangely, Roger Taylor's main songwriting contribution to *News of the World*, "Sheer Heart Attack," is the most punk-sounding song the band ever produced. But, as the title suggests, it was originally conceived for the earlier album of the same name in 1974. Taylor's lyrics for the song are a quite clear aping of the punk style, whizzing through references to TV, DNA, disaffection, and being brain-dead ("I feel so inar-inar-inarticulate"), while musically, the guitars and drums (both played by Taylor—John Deacon doesn't feature on the recording at all) are deliberately a simplistic chug. The similarity to the punk sound was in line with the more melodic U.S. wave of acts like the Ramones rather than the Sex Pistols, but it still wasn't lost on Roger Taylor, who commented at the time that "it really fit into that punk explosion that was happening at the time."

Making "Sheer Heart Attack" even more anomalous on the album is the song that follows it in the track listing. John Deacon's melancholy anthem "Spread Your Wings" is his first attempt at narrative songwriting. With the same sense of bombast as "We Are the Champions" but shot through with existential sadness and a desire to burst the shackles of mundane employment, it's another strong Deacon effort that prefigures themes he would revisit in "I Want to Break Free."

The "Good Old Fashioned Lover Boy" Is Dead

Around the time of the album's recording, the band's rampant offstage partying was becoming legendary. Although it wasn't quite at the level it would achieve in later years, it was still beginning to show through in Mercury's songwriting in particular. On *A Day at the Races*, he had coyly invited a suitor to "Let me feel your heartbeat go faster" during "Good Old Fashioned Lover Boy," but on "Get Down, Make Love," he conjures pure hysterical filth rather than anything traditionally romantic. Along with Taylor's "Fight from the Inside," the song marks a step toward the influence of funk and disco, albeit in a still-embryonic form and juxtaposed with blues-bar rock. Musically, "Get Down, Make Love" revolves around repetitive riffs on the piano and a very ripe bass tone, while Mercury's lyrics are pushed to the front: "You take my body, I give you heat / You say you hungry, I give you meat" is one of the more eyebrow-raising lines, but the whole piece is a paean to sex and the rambunctious desire for its practice. It features a significant instrumental section in which the sound of Brian May's guitar is extensively manipulated using an array of effects (guitar effects, to be clear—still no synthesizers) and mingled with the delayed reverberations of Mercury's joyous moanings, while Taylor's whirling drums are expanded to incorporate Latin instruments. It is a genuine musical departure for the band, on the one hand directly related to the band's increasingly debaucherous manner outside the studio but on the other a precursor to more soundscape-indebted work still to be produced on the band's sound track album *Flash Gordon*.

As established, this is a long way from the bombastic nerdiness of "Ogre Battle" or the plaintive balladeering of "Nevermore": "Get Down, Make Love" is Queen's first direct incitement to experience the real world of adult relations, and there would be many more examples to follow.

Now the Party's Over

For all the bluster of the front end of the album (and songs like "It's Late" toward the finish), *News of the World* still shows evidence of the doodling nature of the band's rushed songwriting conditions. John Deacon's "Who Needs You" is reminiscent of his "Misfire" from *Sheer Heart Attack*, an almost gratingly upbeat and bouncy burst of cod-Spanish influences in which Mercury is heard to address his bandmates as "muchachos" and exclaim, "I like it, I like it!" in a nondescript Latin accent. The lyrical paucity of the song also shows through when Mercury is forced to repeat the word "so" twice to plug syllable gaps in the metronomic structure of the final verse, a problem that would easily have been solved with a few hours' more honing.

Whereas "Get Down, Make Love" declared excess and sexual freedom as Mercury's newest personality traits, his "My Melancholy Blues" provides the necessary balance. Written to nestle between the velveteen curtains of a smoke-filled jazz bar, Mercury is the *chanteur* recounting his slide into the depression that comes "now the party's over." Deacon plays a fretless bass to allow for a looser delivery, and the most we hear of Taylor is the brush of his feathered sticks on the ride cymbals. It is, in tone and delivery, the counterpoint to the excess that the band knew they relished a little too much.

"Breaking Up, When We're Doing So Well?"

Queen's habit of quite vocally arguing their differences into solutions was well known in the press and, as such, made for column inches. Rumors of blowups and contretemps followed them as the band traipsed yet again around the United States and Europe into 1978. Asked directly about an article in the *New*

Musical Express (*NME*) that had apparently confirmed their intention to split the band up because they simply couldn't stand each other anymore, Mercury told the BBC's Bob Harris, "Breaking up, when we're doing so well? You must be kidding." Mercury was sitting between Taylor and May as he said this, stroking the head of a porcelain bulldog during a filmed interview for *The Old Grey Whistle Test* (Deacon is next to May sucking on a large Heineken), and it is possible to see tension on May's face in particular as he answers humorlessly, in contrast with the rest of the band. Elsewhere on the *News of the World* tour, the band took measures to ensure a degree of sibling harmony. Although they would travel separately in four limousines, all four band members would still dress together in large, communal rooms at whatever arena they happened to be playing; swan around backstage in kimonos; and tear through plates of sandwiches and crates of lager tended to by male stylists wearing T-shirts emblazoned with slogans like "Ladies in Waiting."

The rows, though, would still happen. In sound checks and rehearsals, often the only time available for musical discussion, tempers would fray. Studious but highly strung May, retiring Deacon, and a pair of firebrands in Taylor and Mercury did not make for the easiest or most balanced working relationship. The monotony of the road, too, began to take its toll. It is almost expected in the story of the traveling rock band for boredom to set in and distractions to become all the more welcome in the form of drink and sex.

Looking at the U.S. leg of the *News of the World* tour and the mix of petty interpersonal drama and complex rock theatrics, it's possible to see from where the inspiration for Christopher Guest's *This Is Spinal Tap* mockumentary may have come: shows on this tour would begin with "We Will Rock You" performed first by Mercury and May singing and playing along to a backing tape before a gargantuan explosion sound effect heralded the raising of the infamous Crown lighting rig (a slightly smaller version constructed in Boston). They would then repeat "We Will Rock You" in a full-band rendition and at a much faster clip, literally telling the audience what they were in for during the coming two-hour set. This, more than anything in the *News of the World* era, captured the band at its strongest: declamatory and confident onstage with the full muscle of the music industry behind them despite swirling insecurities behind the scenes. There was a constant pressure for the band to get their business affairs in order, to unpack and begin again the process of collaborating creatively after six years of relentless album/touring cycles.

More than anything, it was time for a break, a vacation of some kind. But when you're the biggest rock band in the Western world, there's really no time for that sort of thing.

14

Greatest Hits

Queen as a Singles Band

Ignore Brian May: Queen *Is* a Singles Band

Brian May once declared that Queen was anything but a singles band, that is, an act dedicated to hitting the highest possible singles chart positions with short, accessible popular songs as likely to be piped into supermarkets as they are to be pored over by obsessive fans in the home. Chic was a singles band, Led Zeppelin was an albums band. ABBA was a singles band, Pink Floyd was an albums band. The effort put into creating albums that hung together in a thematic sense, especially in the early part of Queen's career, was, for May, simply too great for them to be considered a singles band. Asked in 1978 what was left on his list of possible achievements for Queen in the future, May suggested that a number-one album in the United States would be nice. For him, the scrap to reach the top of the album charts was *always* more important than the singles chart.

However, it is perfectly possible to refute May on this one. Queen was a singles band in the classic sense of the phrase despite protestations of their being an albums band through and through. When Queen's first *Greatest Hits* compilation was released in 1982, it served as a reminder that, eight years into their career, they had amassed a collection of charting singles that any albums band would be utterly flabbergasted to count among their back catalog, such is the consistency of hits:

1974   "Killer Queen," Mercury (U.K. #2, U.S. #12)
1974   "Now I'm Here," May (U.K. #11)
1974   "Seven Seas of Rhye," Mercury (U.K. #10)
1975   "Bohemian Rhapsody," Mercury (U.K. #1, U.S. #9)
1975   "You're My Best Friend," Deacon (U.K. #7, U.S. #16)
1976   "Good Old Fashioned Lover Boy," Mercury (U.K. #17)
1976   "Somebody to Love," Mercury (U.K. #2, U.S. #13)
1977   "We Are the Champions," Mercury (U.K. #2, U.S. #4)

1977   "We Will Rock You," May (U.K. #2)
1978   "Bicycle Race," Mercury (U.K. #11)
1978   "Don't Stop Me Now," Mercury (U.K. #9)
1978   "Fat Bottomed Girls," May (U.K. #11)
1980   "Another One Bites the Dust," Deacon (U.K. #1, U.S. #1)
1980   "Crazy Little Thing Called Love," Mercury (U.K. #2, U.S. #1)
1980   "Flash," May (U.K. #10)
1980   "Play the Game," Mercury (U.K. #14)
1981   "Save Me," May (U.K. #11)

Was There a Golden Age of Queen Singles?

Simply speaking, it's no coincidence that Queen's first *Greatest Hits* volume was released at a time when they weren't consistently lighting up the singles charts. In fact, *Greatest Hits II*, which was released in 1991, doesn't contain any material from before 1984 (specifically Roger Taylor's "Radio Ga Ga"), neatly demonstrating the comparatively fallow period that began in 1980. If we were to suggest a golden age of Queen as a singles band, it would be almost precisely the period covered by *Greatest Hits I*, perhaps sneaking in "Under Pressure" from 1981 as well. The sheer hit rate in this period is impressive: eleven top-ten U.K. singles between 1974 and 1981 isn't on quite the same scale as, say, ABBA, who managed nineteen in the same time frame, but for a rock band who stuck to the traditional album-tour cycle rather than spending all their time exclusively honing chart toppers, it's certainly competitive.

That fallow period between 1981 and 1984 can be put down to one thing: *Hot Space*. Although it's explained more fully in chapter 23, the effect of this album on Queen's commercial power shouldn't be underestimated. It was as if they were, for the first time in their career (but not the last), lagging behind a cultural consensus to which they had previously paid no attention.

Did Later Singles Struggle?

Struggling to make a dent in the singles charts is something most artists with a sizable sales history have experienced, and Queen is no different. The consistency of the hit rate is definitely skewed toward the first half of the band's career, but it's important to note that they were simply releasing fewer singles in those early years. An accruement of album sales and their ever-increasing popularity as a live act certainly meant that there was little risk in releasing singles that didn't chart from the mid-1980s on, and as such, there are examples of albums where most of the track list was given a single release (seven out of the nine tracks on *A Kind of Magic* were released as singles, for example, with only three of them charting in the United Kingdom).

As the band became more of a staple in the musical life of their home country and across Europe (their singles chart history in America contained triumphs but was in general a more volatile sales territory), it followed that their output of singles would increase, making Queen a comfortable fixture on the chart rather than a blinding feature of it. The penetration of Queen singles into the U.K. singles chart does, superficially, appear to be characterized until 1981 by fewer but more potent releases, while from around 1984 on, their singles are a shallower but ultimately more consistent presence.

Late-Period and Post-Freddie Singles

Singles from *The Miracle* and *Innuendo* albums charted competitively, with the likes of "The Show Must Go On" and "I Want It All" ensuring that the band received plenty of radio airplay. Given the rumors swirling around Freddie Mercury's health toward the end of his life, songs loaded with poignancy and farewell sentiments naturally fared well. The title track from *Innuendo* (discussed more fully in chapter 28) could be argued to have reached the top of the singles charts due to the unique confluence of events in the band and musical events in the song itself. Like "Bohemian Rhapsody" before it, "Innuendo" is, on paper, chart Kryptonite: more than six minutes long (a full half minute longer than "Bohemian Rhapsody"), segmented and indebted to progressive rock in its ambitious structure, and featuring a lengthy instrumental section courtesy of Yes guitarist Steve Howe. Again, it's a testament to the power of Queen's presentational uniqueness that the single was such a success. Without a back catalog made up of songs that announced the artist immediately, it's debatable whether a song like "Innuendo" could have any life of its own on the singles charts.

After the death of Freddie Mercury, there was a natural desire among Queen fans and the music-buying public in general to mark his passing. On December 9, 1991, just two and a half weeks after he finally succumbed on November 24, a double A-side single of "Bohemian Rhapsody" (a rerelease of the original recording) and "These Are the Days of Our Lives" (from *Innuendo*) was rushed out. Following four charting singles released from *Innuendo* throughout 1991, the double A-side shot straight to the top spot. On a purely analytical level, the unique combination of public grief, nostalgia, and the evocative promotional video for "These Are the Days of Our Lives" made the release one of the band's most notable singles chart successes.

Once the acute effects of Mercury's death on the record-buying public had subsided, successful single releases from the band's *Made in Heaven* album can be attributed in part to the lingering emotional attachment to the band's demise and, again, the poignant nature of the record's release. Cynically, it could be suggested that the musical worth of these singles could never have been a factor in their success: surely, the residual goodwill among Queen fans would've sent any release into the charts. The reworked version of Roger Taylor's "Heaven for Everyone" (originally recorded with his band the Cross) was the lead single from *Made in Heaven* and reached number two in 1995 and was released in a number of configurations (one version of the CD single also included three 1970s-era Queen singles as bonus tracks).

As late as 1997, though, the remaining members of Queen were working to commemorate Mercury's death in song. "No-One but You (Only the Good Die Young)" was the final Queen recording to feature John Deacon and the last to be released under the band's name without additional billing (e.g., Queen + Paul Rodgers) until the *Queen Forever* compilation arrived in 2014. Similar in tone and delivery to "These Are the Days of Our Lives," "No-One but You" trades successfully on those key tenets of poignancy and nostalgic reflection but didn't manage to climb higher than number thirteen on the singles chart. May and Taylor take lead vocal duties rather than retooling old Mercury tapes (such as on *Made in Heaven*), which makes it unique in the Queen singles catalog: it could be suggested that the song's tepid commercial performance was due to this lack of a Mercury vocal or the increasing amount of time between the song itself and the tragic event it was commemorating.

Who Wrote the Most Top-Ten Hit Singles?

Freddie Mercury comes out on top: no fewer than eight of Queen's twenty-three top-ten singles on the U.K. charts were solo Mercury compositions (i.e., not including songs credited to more than one writer or communally credited to the entire band). It's interesting to note that Roger Taylor is responsible for writing precisely zero songs from *Greatest Hits I*, but the sudden development of his songwriting as the 1980s wore on into the 1990s meant he ended up with three ("Radio Gaga," "A Kind of Magic," and "Heaven for Everyone"). John Deacon proved himself to be a reliable hit maker, also with a hit rate of three, including the band's only U.S. number one: "Another One Bites the Dust" (he also penned "You're My Best Friend" and "I Want to Break Free").

Given the prolificity he displayed in the band as a songwriter in general, it's perhaps surprising to discover that Brian May was the sole composer of only two of Queen's U.K. top-ten singles. Both "We Will Rock You" and "Flash" are somewhat anomalous in May's songbook, far more direct in style than much of his album-only material. The unwritten policy of making the introduction to each single as iconic as possible as quickly as possible didn't come as naturally to May as it did to the other members of the band: looking at the May-penned singles that fared less well, it's telling that they tend to take longer to "hit" than "Flash" and "We Will Rock You." "Tie Your Mother Down" charted at number thirty-one in the United Kingdom and is notable for its comparatively nondescript opening, which is, on first casual listen, a simple bluesy strum that could've belonged to any number of competent rock bands. Similarly, "Las Palabras de Amor" lingers for a full thirty seconds in circulatory synth riffs before a single word is sung.

This is not to decry May's aptitude for writing hit singles because he demonstrably was able to conjure up several impressive sellers. But compared with the hit rate of his bandmates, it's prudent to note the difference in songwriting approaches: May's less direct natural style works on what might traditionally be called "album tracks," songs that are supposedly prone to deeper analysis, more than it does on the singles.

What Made Their Singles So Popular?

The story has been told by Brian May and Roy Thomas Baker of the sudden realization of the power of a song's introductory phrase. When both "Keep Yourself Alive" and "Liar" failed to grace even the lower echelons of the singles chart, it was mooted that Queen's singles perhaps took too long to get going. As a reaction to this, Mercury's "Seven Seas of Rhye" announces itself in barnstorming style with a short introduction that features plenty of the band's hallmark sounds, mainly Mercury's athletic piano and May's whirling Red Special, the immediacy of which did enough to hook the song in the ear of the nation and score the band their first top-ten single in the United Kingdom.

Since then, the band more or less stuck to this maxim, sometimes with key elaborations along the way but essentially endeavoring to announce themselves and their sound within seconds of pressing "Play" ("Bohemian Rhapsody" is perhaps the exception here because, as discussed in chapter 13, its proper deployment ideally requires silence). Each single aims to be iconic in its opening. Some examples: "Killer Queen" begins with finger clicks, Mercury's a cappella vocal in "Somebody to Love" starts with one simple yet characterful note before the entire band swoops in with choral splendor, and "Crazy Little Thing Called Love" jangles through Mercury's simplistic guitar riff before, again, the entire band arrives.

There are exceptions besides "Bohemian Rhapsody," however. "Don't Stop Me Now" is rare among Queen singles in the way it feeds the listener quite a lengthy introduction before getting to the main business of the song (via an exhilarating increase in tempo). Similar to the bookended nature of "Bohemian Rhapsody," "Don't Stop Me Now" ends with a reiteration of the opening slow section, as if circling back to a sleepy version of itself, a tune the listener now knows and for which, after just a few minutes of upbeat piano hedonism, they feel wistful nostalgia.

As the band entered the second half of its life as a successful singles act, the formulas behind chart success became only more precise. The introduction of each of their big sellers is recognizable after only a few seconds, a deliberate tactic that aligns songs as disparate as "It's a Hard Life," complete with Mercury's operatic vexations on full display, and "Hammer to Fall," the two-chord guitar riff of which could have come from only one man's guitar.

15

"Is This Man a Prat?"

Queen and the Press

Queen's relationship with the press in general tends to be characterized by a strange mix of playful indulgence that morphed into outright hostility as their career progressed and their profile grew. There were several occasions on which all members of the band would claim unfair and dishonest treatment at the hands of the music press or tabloid newspapers, but particularly in Mercury, they had a ready-made press performance artist. Always ready with quips and barbs aplenty, he became known for his easy and appealing copy.

As the band was in its popular ascendancy around the release of *A Day at the Races*, the *NME* printed an interview with Mercury under the headline "Is This Man a Prat?" This was in June 1977, when the wildness and energy of punk rock was making its leaden forebears of progressive rock and pub rock look less fashionable than ever. Led Zeppelin, Pink Floyd, and the Who were suddenly uncoolness personified, as a generation of nerds and ale-drinking, long-haired, mac-wearing blokes (and it was mostly blokes) were usurped by a genuine subculture the likes of which hadn't been experienced on a national scale since mods dictated the culture a decade before. As such, the *NME*'s self-imposed remit to challenge anything they deemed unfashionable meant they were duty bound to stick a pin in the perceived pomposity of the band— and Mercury in particular.

How Brutal Was the *NME* Interview?

Tony Stewart was the journalist tasked with bringing Freddie Mercury down a peg or two with his "Is This Man a Prat?" piece. In the feature, which has since passed into the realm of Queen lore, Stewart takes an aggressive line of questioning that apparently has Mercury on the ropes, hurling out insults at Stewart in an attempt to deflect from what he sees as an album (*A Day at the Races*) that, according to Stewart, "was mostly bland and insubstantial, musically and lyrically."

Having already given the band a negative, live review of a show in Hamburg, Stewart was perhaps only slightly shocked to see that for his encounter with Mercury in John Reid's patio garden in Kensington, a burly security guard was to keep an eye on the proceedings. The two sparred.

"It was obviously quite a staged interview," said Stewart in an interview for this book. Mercury was "patronising" and upbraided the journalist for not having progressed further in his career. Any notion of Mercury being playful or cheeky with Stewart was quashed such was the sharpness of his performance. "He was being a prat," maintains Stewart, "and he knew it, and he didn't really care. . . . You're not going to be a huge star in the rock world without having that aura about you." Just the same as careening around the stage in a leotard, this was a performance—and a sincerely heartfelt one at that. The band was accessible to the press and cooperative in organizing interviews, suggesting that they were collectively complicit in courting journalists to fill column inches, positive or otherwise. As Stewart puts it, "They realized the music press was a necessary evil."

Stewart's "Is This Man a Prat?" feature may be legendary to the contemporary enthusiast, but that particular article didn't even get Queen on the magazine's cover (in that issue it happened to be the Stranglers, with mentions both for the Damned and for the news that Steve Hackett had left Genesis). The fact is that although they were doing well at the time, the wider press hadn't yet seen them as anything more than objects of curiosity. There was no portentous sense that this would be a band to last decades despite their obvious uniqueness. Stewart's piece and Mercury's complicity in making it so incendiary are, in a way, evidence that Queen needed this exposure. Mercury's entertaining sourness was not just true to his mood that day but also an attempt to net the band coverage. In other words, he knew exactly what he was doing by speaking to an *NME* journalist in such a way, and he knew exactly what the results might be. That these results were printed can in no way have been a surprise: Mercury may even have been delighted at what little hoo-ha it caused at the time.

What Was Queen's Attitude toward the Press?

Despite the short shrift afforded the music press by the band, they did go through short periods of genuine critical adulation early on. None other than *Rolling Stone* magazine, high denizens of popular rock criticism, gave the band's debut album a cozy reception, praising all the members individually but most memorably describing Taylor and Deacon's rhythm section as "a colossal sonic volcano whose eruption maketh the earth tremble." (Generally speaking, the early albums were received better in the U.S. than they were in the U.K. press.)

The *Phonograph Record* review of *Sheer Heart Attack* pokes holes in Brian May's perceived attempts to ape Jimi Hendrix and the obnoxiousness of the production techniques and arrangements: "The production effects they pile on with so little restraint and their apparent phobic dread of ever over-dubbing fewer than thirty-five guitar parts on anything combine to smother the actual songs, to which they seem to be paying less and less attention." Criticism in this early phase of the band's recording career tends to focus on those elements of excess, an angle that dogged the band and intensified through the emergence of punk. The perception was only intensified by the band's apparent disdain for the magazines and newspapers that continued to use the band as a convenient punching bag when the cultural climate changed around them. Later, Mercury would sum up his attitudes to bad reviews in typically succinct style: "What do I think of critics? I think they're a bunch of shits."

Early magazine and newspaper features were, despite the mixed album reviews, broadly encouraging, treating the band as a lurid curiosity, an anomaly on pop's otherwise blightless horizon. But as the profile of the band began to soar ever higher with successful albums and debauched tours, the inquisitiveness of the press turned to direct attacks on an act about which it was becoming increasingly easy to write salacious copy.

It's perfectly possible to see the band's collective enthusiasm for fighting back at the press simply as further confirmation of their bitterness toward it. However, the frequency and pointedness of their responses does also suggest that they were personally hurt by the slings and arrows. In 1981, Roger Taylor sent a spectacularly grumpy letter to *Rolling Stone* magazine (handwritten, as the editor noted on printing it in the following issue, on an airsickness bag) after they gave a less-than-favorable account of a show in South America. It concludes, "Grow up. You invented the bitterness. I pity you. You suck. You are boring and you try to infect us." The act of retaliation confirms that these are the words of a man who had been gotten at.

The video for 1989's "Scandal," taken from *The Miracle* album, shows the band performing on a huge stage made to look like a tabloid front page. Brian May wrote the song specifically to comment on his treatment at the hands of the tabloid press during his divorce from his first wife Chrissie Mullen and subsequent relationship with Anita Dobson, the circumstances of which were subject to much public speculation. But the video extends the meaning further still to include tabloid scrutiny of Mercury's lifestyle and rumored AIDS diagnosis. Headlines whizz past the screen, extras dressed as old-fashioned press photographers harass an angry couple, and Brian May performs his guitar solo in a rainstorm of ripped-up newspapers. The message and its execution could not have been less subtle.

The inevitable and tragic irony of the "Scandal" video, however, was that Mercury's notably wan appearance only fueled speculation around his health even further, turning Queen's attempted grand statement about the ethics of tabloid journalism into an unintentional example of its perpetuation.

Appearing live on the cozy breakfast TV show *Good Morning Britain* in 1992, Brian May ripped up a page of the *Daily Mirror* (containing an article that suggested he may be nervous about releasing his first album as a solo artist) during an interview with slightly bemused host Kathryn Holloway, a gesture that leaves little mystery as to whether his attitude toward the printed press had changed over the years. More poignantly, during an earlier appearance on *TVAM* just a week after Mercury's death, both May and Taylor forlornly decried the actions of the tabloid press in the months before their bandmate's passing, with May in particular at pains to emphasize his hostility (in fact, it was precisely 8:57 a.m. when he described the tabloid reporting as "all crap"). It certainly didn't add to the reverential air when popular TV magician of the day Paul Daniels was hauled in to offer his opinions on the very recent death of a musician about whom he quite clearly had very little knowledge or enthusiasm.

Even as recently as 2019, Brian May has been actively engaged in attacking those who criticize him or the band's ongoing work. After the biopic *Bohemian Rhapsody* took home four Academy Awards, May used his Instagram account to unfurl a florid rejoinder to those outlets that showed temerity enough to criticize the movie (or, indeed, any movie that was nominated), describing their activities as "a kind of vindictive sickness that seems to have gripped public life."

Pop culture history is full of entertainingly fraught artist–press interactions, especially through the medium of the print or filmed interview. From Lou Reed's habit of intimidating his interviewers with intense silence to Jerry Lewis's utterly humorless but somehow-still-hilarious refusal to accept anything other than a perfectly direct question, it's a dance between two adversarial parties, both of whom have something to gain from packaging difficulty as entertainment. With Queen, that dance has only very rarely taken place in the context of a direct interview, with Tony Stewart's 1977 *NME* feature being the most striking example.

Since then, it's possible to see a straight refusal to engage other than in circumstances where responses can be completely curated and controlled (Taylor's letter to *Rolling Stone* and May's Instagram post being prime examples). The clear resentment toward the tabloids only grew with the band's profile, and, as a result, so did the band's desire to control their interactions with them.

That there are so many recent examples of May and Taylor continuing to protest their treatment at the hands of critics and journalists is symptomatic of their fierce streak of autonomy, the desire to keep all affairs in-house and to effectively raise the drawbridge of Queen as a brand.

16

Jazz, Not Punk

W hat do you do when you're one of the biggest rock bands in the world but you're out of ideas? You've already released albums that traverse genre on a song-to-song basis, you've sold out arenas across the world, and you've effectively invented music videos and redefined rock decadence for future generations. So what now?

As we've established, Queen was comfortable hopping genres but in a way that completely ignored the zeitgeist. Punk, then, slipped uncomfortably past the band with only a brief acknowledgment in the form of Roger Taylor's "Sheer Heart Attack" from *A Day at the Races* and Freddie Mercury's legendary spat with Sid Vicious. Simply put, punk had nothing to do with Queen. Jazz, however, very much did. *A Day at the Races* ended with Mercury re-creating the environs of a jazz club with "My Melancholy Blues." The band's instrumental proficiency was bordering on the virtuosic. Their musical experimentation was beginning to resemble a mass improvisation across the span of several albums as they leapt between characters.

So the answer is, you release *Jazz*.

Why Did Queen Leave the United Kingdom?

The sessions for Queen's sixth album, *Jazz*, took place for the first time at Mountain Studios in Montreux, Switzerland, and also at Super Bear Studios in the French Alps. Mountain Studios would go on to become a key location for the band in the years that followed, but their sudden move outside of the United Kingdom for recording sessions had a far more pragmatic logic behind it than simply providing a comfortable and inspiring location. Due to the band's now impressive wealth (which they no doubt felt was a long time coming after so many years handing revenue straight to Trident), a surefire way to sidestep hefty taxation was to flee the country for a year.

Although the location was different, one blast from the past undoubtedly made the sessions feel like the old days. Notable by his absence on the previous two records, producer and creative galvanizer Roy Thomas Baker made his return to the Queen fold for the final time and encouraged the band's wilder creative impulses. Musically, *Jazz* shows Queen at their most impetuous and impish. As such, we hear songs that bear no relation to anything else in the band's catalog. Mercury's howling hymn to his Farsi upbringing "Mustapha" features his longest unaccompanied vocal in the introduction, a series of multi-lingual ululations with roots in Arabic and Persian phrases. To begin an album titled *Jazz* in such a fashion is the tip of the iceberg, the first inkling that Queen's elaborate genre joke might be one of the wildest records they ever released.

The experiments continue throughout the record, from the strutting choral-country rock of "Fat Bottomed Girls" to the proto–hair metal of John Deacon's "If You Can't Beat Them." Without doubt the most significant dabble in another genre comes, surprisingly given his track record, from Roger Taylor. "Fun It" has the same lazy funk gait that Michael Jackson would utilize on "Billie Jean" four years later and is the band's first major foray into the club sound and music specifically written with dancing in mind albeit with Taylor's lead vocal in the verses sticking doggedly to his grizzled rock stylings. Interestingly, given the band's previous reticence with any kind of synthesized instrumentation, Taylor also used electric drum pads to create the dry and deadened sound in the percussion. "Fun It" also marks a continuation of the band's lyrical development, cementing them as lusty hedonists focused on having a good time, a character that would come to dominate much of albums like 1982's *Hot Space*.

Adding to the air of reckless pleasure seeking is Mercury's "Let Me Entertain You," which makes reference to the band's real-life tour manager Gerry Stickells in the line, "If you need a fix, if you want a high, Stickells will see to that." (Interestingly, the same song even goes so far as naming the band's record labels in the strangely industrial boast, "With Elektra and EMI we'll show you where it's at.")

Similarly, one of the album's big singles, "Don't Stop Me Now" (which reached number nine on the U.K. singles charts), is, lyrically, utterly fixated on the carnal pleasures for which Mercury was now becoming notorious. No single line in the song doesn't refer to promiscuity and hedonism, whether directly or through the liberal deployment of hilariously illogical similes ("I'm a shooting star leaping through the sky / like a tiger defying the laws of gravity"), and Mercury's addressing of both supersonic men and women in the song fits the more overt fashion in which he was expressing his bisexuality. There is also a musical purity in "Don't Stop Me Now" that isn't exactly rare in Queen songs but in this case is far more simply expressed: it is a song of abandon and joy, with no thought to consequence or even emotion. The absence of any jeopardy or antagonism in the song is what makes it unique in the catalog.

While individual songs gave the band a continued singles chart presence, the musical ambition and willful dexterity proved a costly critical mistake (see the next section for the extent of the ire), but it's hard to imagine any of that registering as the four of them watched sixty-five naked women cycling around Wimbledon Stadium at the promotional video shoot for "Bicycle Race" or indeed as the album hit number two on the U.K. album charts.

Flaccid Jazz?

If there was a defining image for the *Jazz* period, it would be the one displayed on the gatefold vinyl album's inner sleeve, which depicted in detail the video shoot for the double A-side single release of "Fat Bottomed Girls" and "Bicycle Race" (the only double A-side single the band ever released until the death of Freddie Mercury prompted a rerelease of "Bohemian Rhapsody" and "These Are the Days of Our Lives" in 1991). The inner sleeve caused the album to be repackaged on its second pressing, this time without the offending image of a fleet of nude women atop rented bicycles for its U.S. release but instead with an order form that could be sent off in exchange for a hard copy of the poster if desired.

The double A-side itself forms a uniquely intertextual piece: "Bicycle Race," itself a mélange of pretty radio-friendly rock and hard funk, actually references the song it shared a single release with ("Fat bottomed girls, they'll be riding today"). Interestingly, in the call-and-response verses, Mercury also makes explicit reference to the band's status as tax exiles ("Income tax? I say jeez!"), not liking *Star Wars*, and Vietnam and Watergate. The promotional video for the song shows the aforementioned fat-bottomed girls and their bicycle race around Wimbledon Stadium in the kind of detail that would render the video unshowable in most territories were it not for some obscuring visual effects. On learning the nature of the video, the retailer that loaned the bikes to the band, Halfords, demanded that the band pay for the saddles. The video was a passé expression given the impact of second-wave feminism on key U.S. markets for the band, but it didn't seem to have any major adverse effect on the single's commercial performance.

Combined with the offense caused by their promotional antics, the critical consensus on *Jazz* was less than positive. Mitchell Cohen's review for *Creem* magazine in 1979 was particularly chippy, including the memorable attack on Mercury's songwriting: "even his cock-rock, like 'Don't Stop Me Now,' is flaccid." *Rolling Stone* also gave it an elaborate booting, grandly declaring that "Queen may be the first truly fascist rock band" due to the alienating nature of their engineered and superior character.

Who Was Miami Beach?

During the restrictive period in which Queen was managed by Norman Sheffield and Trident, one man worked tirelessly behind the scenes to effectively wangle and wrangle their way out of the agreements they had in place. In 1975,

Jim Beach was a lawyer plowing through the knots of the music department at the Harbottle and Lewis law firm when he was taken on to look after the band's affairs and to pay particular attention to the Trident situation. When the band finally shook Sheffield, they signed a three-year contract to be managed by John Reid, at the culmination of which they opted to have Beach (rechristened "Miami" by Mercury) grab the reins.

After an amicable handover from Reid, Beach never looked back and remains the manager of the band's affairs decades later. The band's collective desire to quietly bring all of their business affairs in-house may have showed them to be unusually demanding clients, but their relationship with Beach was ostensibly based on trust: Beach's role was to react to the whims of the band, creative or otherwise, with the minimal amount of fuss and the maximum amount of results. The result of this relationship was that the band became harder to reach. Journalists would be invited to spend time with the band rather than the other way around, and music industry figures on the periphery of the band's existence would be treated as outside contractors, a gradual internalization of all the band's affairs that would and still does characterize their activity.

Beach's role in the Queen story would be to fortify the walls built around the band, sometimes to the detriment of the working relationships with the wider music industry (not that anyone in the band would've wanted it any differently). He also went on to manage Taylor and May in a personal capacity after the demise of the main life of the band and picked up other notable clients, including the individual performers in the Monty Python comedy troupe, masterminding their huge reunion shows in 2018.

Killers Need to Change

As their new status as tax exiles ensconced the band in mainland Europe, so their tour schedule for *Jazz* kept them out of their home country. The tour took them through their usual North American haunts from the end of October through to Christmas 1978, most notably a Halloween date at the New Orleans Municipal Auditorium, the concert providing an elaborate precursor to the album's official launch party held at the city's Fairmont Hotel. The night itself has become the source of much Queen lore around the extremity and lavishness with which the band and Mercury in particular partied (discussed in more detail in chapter 24).

After America, their exile meant a longer-than-usual ten-week sojourn in mainland Europe, providing plenty of opportunities to record material for the band's first-ever live album: *Live Killers*. With a track list made up of songs from a smattering of shows in Lyon, Rotterdam, Frankfurt, Barcelona, and more, it's an interesting document of the band's live sound at a time when a significant musical change was just on the horizon. They'd efficiently refocused their live set thanks

Program for the 1978 *Jazz* U.S. tour.   *Martin Skala, QueenConcerts.com*

to several stand-up stadium anthems from *A Day at the Races* and *Jazz*, so the performances are instinctive and honed. Even the rock 'n' roll covers medley finally seems to have been jettisoned, and there are surprising configurations, such as the "Mustapha" introduction nailed to the opening of "Bohemian Rhapsody," but ultimately *Live Killers* captures the band on the verge of something else.

As the first half of 1979 slipped past the windows of the limousines that ferried the individual members between Japanese "enormodomes," Queen was displaced yet inexorably drawn toward something new. Onstage, Mercury's attire had shifted ahead of the style of their music. Gone were the harlequin-print jester outfits and cropped white jackets in favor of cap-to-boots black leather: the embodiment of the disco aesthetic and a hallmark of the burgeoning U.S. gay cultural scene (an obvious comparison is Glenn "Leatherman" Hughes, who with his group the Village People topped the charts the previous year with "YMCA" and popularized the look).

Freddie Mercury in full leather garb, a sign that his image was becoming ever-more dictated by his sexuality.   © *Peter Mazel/Sunshine /ZUMA Press*

Queen couldn't release another album like *Jazz*, something so confusing and disparate on a song-to-song basis, even though it managed to keep them riding high on the U.K. charts. The United States, however, had begun to tire of the band. *Live Killers* failed to make a dent, and, while their live shows remained successful, they had slipped into the mid-tier. A stinger of a review from *Rolling Stone*'s David Fricke in June 1979 dismissed the live album as "ersatz Led Zeppelin," a criticism that had dogged the band from their very earliest recordings. If ever there was a time in Queen's history when they really needed to change tack, this was it.

17

Mountain Studios

Queen's Sanctuary

On the banks of Lake Geneva stands the Casino Barrière de Montreux. Otherwise known as Montreux Casino, it was and is a popular gambling haunt for the wealthy that doubles as a concert venue. In 1971, it burned down during a show by Frank Zappa and the Mothers of Invention when an overenthusiastic fan pulled the trigger of a flare gun indoors. The incident was memorialized the following year by Deep Purple, whose signature song "Smoke on the Water" gives a surprisingly lucid and detailed account of the night in question. Deep Purple was booked to record their new album at Mountain Studios, which was housed within Montreux Casino at the time, but due to the fire, they were both unable to get started and provided with the inspiration for their most perennial tune. On a bootleg recording of the show, it's possible to hear the moment the concert stopped as the audience and band realized the severity of the situation, including a shout of "Arthur Brown, in person!"

This occasion in rock history marks Mountain Studios out as a place at the intersection of high drama and legendary personnel. David Bowie, Emerson, Lake

The exterior of Montreaux Casino as it appears today, the original site of Mountain Studios.

Cabana / Shutterstock.com

& Palmer, AC/DC, Iggy Pop, Yes, the Rolling Stones, and more recorded notable albums on the original site, and the casino venue itself was the longtime base of the Montreux Jazz Festival. But a glance at the handwritten graffiti tributes all around the outside of the original entrance to the studio would suggest that there was really only one artist who recorded at Mountain Studios: Freddie Mercury.

Despite the rich rock history, Mountain Studios will forever be associated with Queen and its front man. When the band first arrived there with Roy Thomas Baker in 1978 to record the bulk of *Jazz* (the festival provides another possible explanation for the album's title), it was to be the beginning of a relationship and effective residency that lasted until 1995 and still continues today in a more symbolic capacity, not least because of the statue of Mercury that now stands a short walk from the casino, iconic in an arm-aloft pose, facing the lake that inspired so much of his later work.

When Did It Become Queen's Studio?

Mountain Studios had been cofounded and owned by the hugely prolific singer and composer Anita Kerr (of the Anita Kerr Singers) and her husband Alex Grob in the early 1970s after they relocated to Switzerland and throughout the 1960s and 1970s was a popular choice for artists looking for somewhere to record their next masterpiece in idyllic surroundings, sheltered from the glare of the media. Decorated with a goat logo, an advertisement placed in the middle of a celebratory feature about Kerr in a 1979 issue of *Billboard* read, "It makes good sense to record in beautiful Switzerland." But in 1979, after *Jazz* had been recorded and *Live Killers* had been tinkered with, the band decided that simply recording there was not enough: they enjoyed the experience so much that they bought the place.

It's hard to overestimate the sheer financial and logistical power required to pull this off. Jim Beach, by this time firmly ensconced in the Queen fold as their former lawyer and now manager, was able to push the deal through, keeping the studio running effectively as it had done before: it just happened to be the band's names on all the paperwork. There's no doubt that a band owning its own recording studio in a picturesque location has its artistic advantages, but there was an ulterior motive. The driving force behind their tax exile status, Queen had been stung with a huge bill from the U.K. Inland Revenue for taxes unpaid and was presented with a choice: return home and pay up or buy a studio so they didn't have to return home and pay up. It was obvious, really.

While countless artists rolled through the studio in the decades that followed (many of them were fellow tax exiles, such as Led Zeppelin), Queen was always able to return to Mountain Studios to record in solitude, becoming familiar faces in Montreux to the point where their appearance there felt natural, uncommented, and free.

The famous statue of Freddie Mercury, which looks out across Lake Geneva.

Victor FlowerFly / Shutterstock.com

The location even inspired particular songs: when the Tour de France cycling event rolled through Montreux in 1978, it inspired Mercury to write "Bicycle Race," which in turn bore the entire marketing angle for *Jazz*. In more somber times during the recording of Queen's final album, *Innuendo*, the location made a gravely ill Mercury's work on the album possible without the constant interference of prying paparazzi lenses. Although it wasn't until 1982's *Hot Space* that the band would record a full album there, the studio defines the second half of their recording career. The musical evolution experienced by that band within that one building makes Mountain Studios to Queen what Abbey Road was to the Beatles.

Who Owns Mountain Studios Now?

After the death of Freddie Mercury, the studio continued to operate as it had done previously, with a string of artists passing through to work in relative seclusion. David Bowie, for example, went to Mountain to lay down his own sound track to a television adaptation of Hanif Kureishi's *The Buddha of Suburbia* and his nineteenth studio album, *Black Tie White Noise*, in the early 1990s. But after the remaining members of Queen returned in 1995 to assemble the *Made in Heaven* album with their longtime coproducer David Richards, it was no longer a place the band needed to keep as part of their business interests or as part of their creative lives together as Queen.

In 1995, David Richards bought Mountain Studios from the band and managed it until his death in 2013. The studio facility itself eventually moved locations in 2002 five miles down the road to a new site in the town of Attalens. Information on the current status of the studio is hard to come by, and the official website appears to have expired, so it's hard to say exactly how active it is since its most recent notable proprietor passed on. Meanwhile, the original location within the casino eventually became Queen: The Studio Experience, a tourist attraction operated by the Mercury Phoenix Trust. It was officially opened in 2013 with none other than Brian May on hand to cut the ribbon and open to the public a collection of Queen memorabilia and interactive exhibits. It's proof that, while Montreux and Mountain Studios itself began as an escape from the tax man, they became so much more than a mere convenience: it was home.

18

Winning the Game

Queen on Top of the World

Munich and the Moustache

During stretches of time in New York around the release of *Jazz*, Freddie Mercury and his personal manager Paul Prenter (a figure habitually cast as the villain of the Queen story, the conniving Yoko Ono to Mercury's John Lennon) were systematically partying their way through the gay scene in a fashion that could be described only as voracious. Prenter later made claims about the number of Mercury's sexual partners going well into the hundreds, and the bulk of this activity most certainly began during their time in New York at the end of the 1970s.

Mercury adopted the fashions of the scene and proudly donned his leathers for the *Jazz* tour. Stylistically, this was the most public admission of his own homosexuality yet: although it seems obvious to contemporary eyes, his previous flamboyance had been interpreted as mere campery, perhaps a sort of omnisexuality that was pumped up for the sake of publicity (Mercury once claimed in an interview that he'd sleep with men, women, cats, or anything that moved). The changes in image, including the gradual shortening of his hairstyle, ushered in the beginning of a new era of the band's aesthetic both visually and musically.

With the shifting of Queen's business and creative affairs out of the United Kingdom and over to mainland Europe, the city of Munich also became a vital place for Mercury, a welcoming and experimental city for any pleasure seeker. Mercury and Prenter became familiar faces in the city's Deutsche Eiche (literally "German Oak") complex with a flurry of friends and acquaintances in tow. And so, with this lifestyle of unchecked and joyous abandon in full flow, the kind of lifestyle befitting a sex machine ready to reload, Mercury made a stylistic move that became emblematic—more emblematic, even, than the winged crest he designed to be the band's logo nearly a decade before. It seems ludicrous to afford such gravity to the arrival of some hair on someone's upper lip, but make no mistake: Mercury's moustache meant everything.

The first glimpse the world got of the moustache was in the music video for "Play the Game," the second single from *The Game* (more on the first single later), and on the accompanying single sleeve. In the video, Mercury is also wearing his soon-to-be-trademarked "Flash" T-shirt (at this point, the band had already completed the first sessions for the sound track to Mike Hodges's movie version of *Flash Gordon*), and the rest of the band are more soberly clad: Deacon again in his shirt and tie, May sporting a waistcoat.

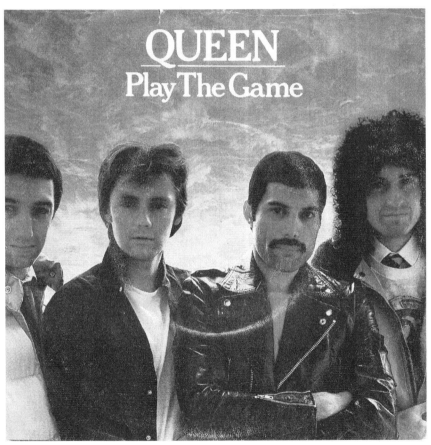

The single sleeve for"Play the Game," introducing the world to Freddie Mercury's moustache.
Photo by Mark Grehan

Reaction to the moustache among Queen fans was vociferous. Those who had initially gravitated toward the band as a kind of theatrical progressive version of Led Zeppelin were alarmed by this very open embrace of gay culture, and there are anecdotal accounts of razors being thrown onto the stage in the early 1980s in an effort to convince Mercury to remove the newly acquired fuzz.

A prevailing narrative in the Queen story is that Mercury was somehow ashamed of or reticent about public acknowledgment of his sexuality, but looking back with contemporary eyes, it's quite impossible to conclude that he was in any way worried about his perception. The moustache, the leather, the lyrics: it couldn't have been clearer, but, so dictated the social norms of the time, to label Mercury as anything other than performatively camp would've been an invitation for endless controversy, debate, mudslinging, and almost certainly a loss of fans.

Internally, too, Mercury's increasing toe dips into public acknowledgment of his sexual status and his extreme financial extravagance (he would routinely go on spending sprees to fill his Kensington home with various international objets d'art) were met with some difficult reactions. In a *Rolling Stone* interview in 1981 as the band prepared for their huge outdoor South America concerts, Deacon admitted, "Some of us hate it," letting on perhaps a little more than he intended about the state of the band's personal relationships with one another as Mercury's star burned so much brighter in the public than anyone else's.

In the same *Rolling Stone* interview, Mercury seemed to acknowledge that he was now a follower of fashion rather than an aspiring trendsetter: "I went through this period where I thought I was making an impact on the fashion world ... then I thought, 'Oh, grow up.'"

The moustache was a symptom of something bigger: Queen was becoming collegiate in the strictest sense of the word as their personalities drifted away from one another. It would be too strong to characterize relationships as acrimonious, but there was, after nearly a decade of the band existing in one form or another, the natural erosion of good feeling. Taylor and Mercury would party with willful glee and silliness (Taylor claimed around the time that he would love to own and operate a whorehouse, seeing it as a delightful way in which to make a living), while Deacon, for example, would slope off whenever he could to see his wife and children. You might stereotypically suggest that this was just their Britishness on display, but there were no flare-ups, no punches thrown, and no champagne glasses flung: just a gradual, awkward evolution, the unease that develops over time spent together doing far too much and far too little.

Which Queen Song Was Written in the Bath?

Surprisingly far in advance of Queen's next album, *The Game*, they'd already delivered a hit single. Arriving in Munich in June 1979 to work with their new producer Reinhold Mack at disco pioneer and pop polymath Giorgio Moroder's Musicland Studios, Mercury found himself resident at the Bayerischer Hof Hotel and, more specifically, soaking in the tub with an acoustic guitar draped across his midriff (though Mercury later admitted he couldn't play the guitar "for nuts"). Pinging out the simple introduction and following it wherever it meandered, Mercury claimed to have a whole song written inside ten minutes.

There's a certain joy in the thought of Mercury then springing out of the bath and into the studio where Deacon and Taylor were ready to record the basic tracks for what became "Crazy Little Thing Called Love." May was absent for this particular session, and, according to Mack's reminiscences, Mercury was keen to polish the song off before the guitarist arrived such was his confidence that he would disapprove.

When May finally did make it to the studio, all the hard work had been done. Indebted to Elvis Presley at his most tremulous and shuffling, the song was lean and efficient, everything that went against May's tendency for elaboration. To deepen May's mistrust of the new song, Mack had him record a guitar solo on an instrument that was *not* the Red Special. Instead, with the aim of capturing something of the early rock 'n' roll feel the song was reaching for, May recorded his part on a Fender Telecaster, a distinctly off-the-peg instrument known for its heritage and brilliant versatility but about the most generic and peaceable electric guitar available—in other words, very much not May's type of instrument.

The recording sessions weren't supposed to be for any album in particular, but "Crazy Little Thing Called Love" was deemed good enough and different enough for a single release, attached to no particular album. It was an instant success, giving Queen their first-ever number-one single in the United States in early 1980, a territory that had been tiring of the band. Before that, it also managed to hit number two in the United Kingdom: confirmation that a certain brevity of approach was working. Buoyed by the success, the band's first U.K. tour in eighteen months was booked for a series of sub-two-thousand-seat venues, smaller than they were used to. Rather than calling to mind the scene in *This Is Spinal Tap* where the band's manager Ian Faith explains the smaller venues away by claiming their audience was merely "becoming more selective," Queen's downsizing was a necessary step in their imminent reinvention.

The "Crazy" tour ended with a series of London dates in various venues across the city, from the Lewisham Odeon to their old stomping ground of the Rainbow, culminating with a Boxing Day Hammersmith Odeon show organized by Paul McCartney, the first of his Concerts for the People of Kampuchea, which also featured headlining shows for the Specials, the Clash, the Pretenders, Wings, the Who, and several more. Footage of Queen's opening night of the series shows them in transition: Mercury is topless save for a red leather necktie, while both Deacon and Taylor sport buttoned-down looks that wouldn't be out of place on a Kraftwerk album cover. "Jailhouse Rock" found its way back into the set list for some shows, a knowing nod to the inspiration behind their latest hit.

Program for the fundraising Concerts for the People of Kampuchea. Queen opened the series.   *Martin Skala, QueenConcerts.com*

It's Gotta Be Mack

Having already clicked with their new producer Reinhold Mack in the summer of 1979 and through early sessions for *Flash Gordon*, Queen returned to Music-land Studios in Munich in February 1980 to add more songs to those they'd already assembled (by this point, "Crazy Little Thing Called Love," "Sail Away Sweet Sister," "Coming Soon," and the May-penned single "Save Me"). What characterized these sessions with Mack (who usually went only by his surname) was the efficiency with which they were conducted. Whereas Roy Thomas Baker would indulge the band and encourage them to luxuriate in their arrangements, bending technology to their songwriting whims, Mack favored precision and brevity. It's no coincidence that *The Game* is one of Queen's shortest albums at just under thirty-six minutes in length.

As a close associate of Giorgio Moroder, Mack spent most of his early professional career at Musicland working as coproducer on albums by Deep Purple, Electric Light Orchestra, T Rex, and a string of Rolling Stones releases. In other words, his credentials were sufficient to work with Queen, and, on paper at least, he was stylistically on the same page. But there was immediately a creative friction between producer and band. Mack's efficiency and stereotypically Teutonic approach to recording was diametrically opposed to Queen's methods of old, which usually consisted of endlessly and angrily debating ideas until either a vague middle ground was found or three-quarters of the band were steamrolled into submission.

The advantages of this character dissonance between the two parties quickly became apparent, as the previously flamboyant and decidedly barrierless band became suddenly contained, restricted even. From the introduction of "Crazy Little Thing Called Love," constrained by Mercury's admittedly unskilled guitar playing, to the pop-rock efficiency of Taylor's "Rock It (Prime Jive)," there was in the recording of *The Game* a slickness that Mack had honed with his previous work and applied to one of the most musically outgoing rock ensembles in the world.

In keeping with Queen's occasional habit of referencing various behind-the-scenes characters in their lyrics, Mack even made his way into Brian May's "Dragon Attack," confirmation that his influence was not only invigorating to the band but also completely welcome. "Gonna use my stack, it's gotta be Mack," Mercury sings, over a singular riff that dominates the whole song in a way that the band had hardly attempted before, the relative simplicity evoking the atmosphere of a studio jam rather than a polished composition. May admitted as much in an interview a few years later, describing the riff as having arrived "very late one night probably to the morning, probably very drunk." That the song was left as it was with little to no histrionics and no fireworks to speak of, just the raw power of a louche and addictive riff, is testament to Mack's influence on the whole album.

. . . And *Someone* Played Synthesizers

The first audible sound on *The Game* does not come from any detectably "human" musical instrument. Instead, the shimmering, metallic whir that begins "Play the Game" comes from an Oberheim OB-X, a synthesizer favored by Prince and Jean-Michel Jarre and the very first synthesizer to be used on a

Queen record. Although the band stopped obsessively referencing their opposition to using synthesizers on album sleeves some years previously, this was still a major musical development and an ideological about-face.

Announcing their new album with this confusing and enveloping sound could have sent them in any number of stylistic directions with "Play the Game" as a song, but it's a charmingly Queen-esque decision to then launch into one of the most beautifully accessible pop songs in their canon. Wide-eyed and sweet, in the main it's a close cousin to John Deacon's "You're My Best Friend" but with one more statement of synthetic intent: the Oberheim OB-X returns in the middle eight to remind us that when Queen makes a musical decision, they really commit to it, dueling in direct opposition with a heavy metal riff from the rest of the band.

Could this be an acknowledgment that they had been battling with synthesizers or that Deacon, Taylor, and May had been battling with Mercury, who actually prodded the buttons on the Oberheim? "Play the Game" is, on the face of it, a gorgeously simple song executed with the band's trademark tightness, but it's also the beginning of a major new musical phase. Synthesizers also crop up on "Rock It (Prime Jive)," adding a somewhat motorik element, and in the hymnal chords that accompany May's "Sail Away Sweet Sister," a thread that runs gently through the whole album.

Embracing Pop

There was more going on that just the synthesizers, though: there was a decisive shift in genre as well. While previous albums certainly showed an awareness of pop convention, Queen's natural mode was not to embrace it but to manipulate it. Singles were surprising successes not because of their tight formulaic adherence to what a pop song "should" sound like but because of their flouting of the conventions, their pastiche of its tropes. That's how, for example, a five-and-a-half-minute mini rock opera made it to number one on the singles charts and how a choral hymn to arrogant superiority became a fixture at international sporting events.

But with the songs on *The Game*, Queen made a deliberate attempt to follow the rules of pop, with most songs clocking in around the optimum length for single release. There was also, for the first time, a regimental approach to songwriting: Mercury decreed that he and May would be afforded three songs each, while both Deacon and Taylor would be responsible for two. There is no thematic governance to the record, no self-referential medley section such as we saw on *Jazz*: the only unifying trait is efficiency of expression.

As a result of this new approach, songs are catchier, simpler, and cleaner. Aside from the major singles from the album, the directness is arresting.

Deacon's "Need Your Loving Tonight" would sit happily alongside Journey or Boston on a compilation of driving anthems, as could "Rock It (Prime Jive)." May's closing "Save Me," too, is notable as another example of that customarily perfect execution of a pop idea, a gentle ballad of regret written in an unusually straight and serious emotional character, though May kept his distance: he based the lyrics on the story of an acquaintance's breakup rather than his own life.

There are quite incredible missteps along the way, however, most notably Mercury's "Don't Try Suicide." Although it suffers more as a song when viewed with contemporary eyes, it still says something about Mercury's arrogance as a songwriter that he felt the most appropriate way to tackle the subject of suicide was a jaunty rockabilly pastiche with such toe-curling lyrical howlers as "Think you're gonna slash your wrists this time? Baby, when you do it all you do is get on my tits."

Deacy's Hit

One of John Deacon's two allocated contributions to *The Game* also happens to be the most popular song Queen ever released and their second U.S. number-one single: "Another One Bites the Dust." There's a fuller discussion of this landmark song in the following chapter, but its impact on the life of the band can't be overstated. During downtime from Queen, Deacon found himself in a perhaps unlikely situation for a middle-class kid from Leicester: in the studio with Nile Rodgers and his legendary disco outfit Chic as they recorded their album *Risqué* in Hell's Kitchen, New York.

It's not clear exactly if Deacon played anything more than a spectator's role, but both Rodgers and Chic cofounder Bernard Edwards confirmed that he was present for the sessions for "Good Times," the disco staple and song that launched countless hip-hop careers as the culture of sampling began to emanate from the city's underground musicians. The influence is obvious and fond. Indeed, "Good Times" and "Another One Bites the Dust" share that same thudding bass motif, precisely engineered to encourage dance floors across the world to swell to their capacities. Deacon later claimed to be the only Queen member really interested in commercial "black music," as he termed it, which would certainly explain the more tumultuous sessions that followed for Queen's *Hot Space* album, their most funk and disco–inflected record.

Confusingly, considering the pronounced shift toward synthesizers on *The Game*, "Another One Bites the Dust" features only the core electric instruments the band was accustomed to using: all the nightmarish swirling sounds that slither across the quieter sections were created by Brian May's guitar and limited effects work.

The Carmen Miranda of Rock 'n' Roll: Queen Takes South America

This is how Freddie Mercury described himself after being pictured with a basket of fruit on his head onstage in Japan. But what better person than the Carmen Miranda of Rock 'n' Roll to play a show to the biggest crowds the continent had ever hosted for a cultural event?

Somewhat against the run of play, Queen now found themselves back on top after the difficult reception of *Jazz*. Two number-one singles in the United States meant a musical omnipresence they hadn't yet enjoyed in that territory, and the appeal naturally followed worldwide for the tour that followed *The Game*. The U.S. leg was huge, spanning three months and ending with three nights at Madison Square Garden. Their well-established central European fan base could be relied on to sell out arenas, and it would only be polite to include another stint at the Budokan in Tokyo, the scene of so many previous fevered triumphs.

But South America was a different prospect. For their short series of ambitious stadium concerts in March 1981 (dubbed "South America Bites the Dust"), they would play seven dates: five in Argentina and two in Brazil. The scale of the shows was unprecedented. Mercury told a newspaper, perhaps seeking to embolden the image of his own band, that he'd seen a recording of a typical Argentinian stadium rock show and compared it to "the sort of thing you might see in a small pub." Keeping the show on the road was estimated to have a daily expense of around £20,000 (approximately $101,000 in today's money).

On the first of two nights in Buenos Aires, the band played to 300,000 ticket-buying fans, easily making them the biggest concerts in the country's history. Footage of the band playing "Bohemian Rhapsody" at the Estadio José Amalfitano (enlarged and refurbished in 1978 to cope with the FIFA World Cup) shows the scale of the shows but also what it meant to a nation perhaps unaccustomed to having the world's biggest bands roll through town on a regular basis: it's possible to see, during the rock instrumental that closes the operatic section, a ghetto blaster raised triumphantly above a fan's head in an attempt to record the show. Maybe it was for personal use, maybe it was for bootlegging, but the sheer force of the performance and the crush of delirious fans bellowing along to Mercury's proclamations would surely have rendered any recording hilariously pointless.

The hysteria with which the band was met also necessitated their escape from the stadium in armored transport rather than the four comfortable saloons to which they were accustomed, but for once, there was no diva strop from Mercury, who considered careening through the streets of Buenos Aires with the sirens blaring the most exciting part of the whole experience.

"You Don't Know What It Means to Me . . ."

The concerts in South America also cemented one particular song in the band's catalog: "Love of My Life" was a favorite in set lists since it debuted on the *News of the World* tour in 1977 (though it was written for *A Night at the Opera* a couple of years earlier). Stripped back for live performance, the standard setup consisted of just May on twelve-string acoustic guitar and Mercury on vocals. Perhaps it was something to do with the language-defying power of a simple chorus, but the "Bring it back, bring it back" refrain was often sung only by the audience, leaving Mercury to merely direct them in their efforts like the proud conductor of a school orchestra.

For the shows in South America, performances of the song were especially warmly received, resulting in an opportunistic single release, specifically, the version from the 1979 live album *Live Killers* (which had received very little in the way of attention or positive notices). "Love of My Life" became an anthem in Argentina, and the single stayed on the charts for more than a year: there was no clearer demonstration of exactly what Queen meant to South America in 1981.

The Touring Finally Stops

As the scale of live shows continued to escalate, two final concerts in Montreal in November 1981 saw *The Game* tour finally come to a close after seventy-nine dates across sixteen months and three continents. These were filmed and subsequently released as a live album and concert film in 2007, providing a decent insight into the band's fatigued state. In much the same way as they had at the end of other mammoth world tours, their muscle memory in performance had become tight and responsive, but there it was again: the nagging sense that these moves had been done a thousand times, that it was time for something else.

Between continental legs of touring, Queen had indeed been working on whatever might be next. They had been flitting back to London periodically to add to what was becoming a logistically painful *Flash Gordon* sound track, but when they took some time to record in their new spiritual home at Mountain Studios in July 1981, they were joined by a collaborator by the name of David Bowie to write and record an iconic single that would shortly impact both of their careers in a seismic fashion. Bowie himself, owner of a small chalet on Lake Geneva, was just exiting his famed "Berlin" period and was no stranger to unexpected collaborations, having in 1977 crooned wholesomely alongside Bing Crosby on a rendition of "Little Drummer Boy." He had been experimenting with synthesizers, though to a much larger extent, the fruits of which had seen him become, once again, critically adored.

But the madness of Munich and the extracurricular frivolity with which the members Queen were constantly dabbling to varying degrees was to make an impact on the band's music. Deacon's time in New York with Chic, too, would make him an unlikely linchpin for what came next. All the ingredients were there, and with the benefit of hindsight, it is now completely logical that their next album would be a special kind of flop, but there is still a distinct weirdness to the encroaching post-imperial phase of Queen's career.

19

Another One Bites the Dust

John Deacon Saves Queen

Rarely in pop music do the stars align so perfectly as they did for Queen when John Deacon was inspired to write "Another One Bites the Dust." The band's best-selling single and their second U.S. number one, it guaranteed them musical immortality in a more insidious and far-reaching way than "Bohemian Rhapsody."

Deacon's assertion that he was the only member of the band who regularly listened to pop music from a nonwhite background placed him in a uniquely aware position, aware not only of the explosion of disco in the late 1970s but also of the resultant upswing in music expressly composed for the purposes of dancing. Of course, Deacon's assertion cannot have been completely true: Freddie Mercury would have had firsthand experience of the dawn and threatened death of disco in his offstage life as a familiar face in the gay districts of New York and Munich.

But Deacon was the one who'd been hanging out with Nile Rodgers and Chic and drove the song from its roots. It is his singular bass motif that still strikes the ear hardest today.

Why Was It a Hit?

Musically, "Another One Bites the Dust" is simple yet somehow alchemical. Reinhold Mack's production style and influence on the band during recording sessions certainly informed the sparseness of the song, which is limited to four core instruments of voice, guitar, bass, and drums, with minimal overdubbing. There is in Brian May's effected guitar noises something of a musique concrète influence (divorced from the song, it wouldn't be strange to hear the same noises in a Karlheinz Stockhausen composition), but, combined with the crispness and cleanliness of Mack's production, it remains accessible, uncluttered.

All manner of musicological arguments may be made to explain precisely why Deacon's bass line (and the bass line to Chic's "Good Times," from which it borrows) is so satisfying, but it's enough for our purposes to say that, again, it is the simplicity that marks it out in a career of complicated and sophisticated hits. The main figure of the riff contains just three notes, and at its most complex, you could only really say that Deacon's part consists of two complete melodic ideas. Basically, it pummels the listener with its messages until there is no option but to accept its charms.

Mercury's vocal is almost a schoolyard rap, a loosely relayed story of nefarious criminal dealings gone terribly wrong (would the "brim pulled way down low" of the main character's hat suggest a zoot-suited gangster? A cowboy perhaps?) that, despite its brevity, has an emotional core and a functional advantage of just sounding cool. By the second verse, after the bullets have ripped out of the doorway (to the sound of the beat, naturally), Mercury's character "Steve" pleads with his next victim before apparently dispatching them: "How do you think I'm going to get along without you when you're gone?" The world is one of violence and confused, messy retribution but is still one of the band's simplest narrative stories with almost no floridity or milked sentiment.

In keeping with the clean simplicity of the rest of the song, May's guitar is unrecognizable: with no histrionics aside from the aforementioned sound effects, the Red Special is utterly relegated, with May proving an able ape of the signature Nile Rodgers style, rhythmically effective but harmonically simple. Taylor, too, has to maintain only a certain feel for the duration of the song rather than anything elaborate, a partner piece to his work on "Dragon Attack."

All the musical elements that made "Another One Bites the Dust" a hit are governed by one thing: simplicity. That simplicity isn't the sole reason it topped the U.S. singles charts, but the "sore thumb" status of the song in the context of Queen's previous run of singles made it a complete surprise, almost as if the whole continent of North America suddenly realized that this band could be cool. Freshness, deployed at just the right time, can work beautifully for long-standing pop artists (again, David Bowie makes an excellent comparison point), and Queen's version of that also happened to align them with a cultural and racial community they had never even considered serving before.

Advice from the King of Pop

It's still surprising that the man responsible for writing "Thriller," "Off the Wall," and "Rock with You" for Michael Jackson, Rod Temperton, was originally from Cleethorpes, a distinctly indistinct and decidedly unfunky area of Lincolnshire, England. Perhaps there was a natural sympathy in Jackson for songwriters who assimilate and master musical styles wildly divorced from what might be expected from their background because he took to Deacon's composition in much the same way as he had to Temperton's.

Michael Jackson was a confirmed fan of Queen and eventually recorded a small suite of songs with Freddie Mercury, but his most lasting contribution to the Queen story was to advise the band to release "Another One Bites the Dust" as a single. The King of Pop met Queen while they were in Los Angeles to play a string of shows at the Forum in July 1980 and, having seen the show, was quick to impart his wisdom. According to Roger Taylor's recollections, Deacon's song was not on any personal short lists to be given a single release ("I remember saying, 'That will never be a hit.' How wrong can you be?" he told *Contact Music* in 2012), but it was Jackson who personally convinced them otherwise.

They took Jackson's advice, and the single was released, shooting straight to the top of the U.S. singles chart. It also hit number one in Canada, Spain, and Israel but only number seven in the United Kingdom. Despite that, the sheer size of these territories afforded the song a listener base that would cement it in pop history.

Did the Song Save Queen's Career?

It might be a stretch to say that the band was floundering for relevance as rock and pop music changed around them, but the huge commercial success and genuine cultural impact of "Another One Bites the Dust" undoubtedly gave them a longevity they may not otherwise have attained. Brian May later claimed that U.S. radio stations playing mostly nonwhite artists had mistakenly assumed that the band consisted of black musicians and had subsequently given them huge amounts of airplay. If that was indeed the case, then it would've been an important audience segment with whom Queen previously had no resonance. With a widened audience now established, it was perhaps understandable that Queen would decisively direct their next project toward a new, wider demographic: *Hot Space* was the result, an album that is almost the perfect definition of the maxim "Lightning doesn't strike twice."

But in 1980 and 1981, it was the song that defined Queen. One of the true marks of a cultural linchpin is the manner in which it is viewed by its contemporaries, and many would argue that there is no higher praise for a pop song than having it covered by "Weird Al" Yankovic, his generation's foremost parody songwriter. "Another One Rides the Bus" was a key track on Yankovic's first album, and Brian May was moved to deem it "an extremely funny record by a bloke called 'Mad Al' or something." Grandmaster Flash also sampled it in 1981 for his "The Adventures of Grandmaster Flash on the Wheels of Steel," a key text for the then burgeoning turntablist generation that featured "Another One Bites the Dust" alongside other influential tracks from the Sugarhill Gang, Blondie, Spoonie G, and, aptly, Chic's "Good Times."

Decades later, the song's influence persists. Busta Rhymes, Wyclef Jean, Gwen Stefani, and various Wu Tang Clan side projects have all either directly quoted, sampled, or covered the song or elements of it, confirming its life span beyond that of anything else the band recorded.

So if we're asking if the song and, indirectly, John Deacon really did save the band at a time when their cultural stock was in danger of becoming too reliant on heritage appeal, then the answer has to be yes. There's nothing to suggest that a form of cultural immortality wouldn't have arrived in some other form, but "Another One Bites the Dust" is a unique example of genre aping that went on to define aspects of many other genres itself. It is Deacon's lasting contribution to the band and, as a result, to pop music of the future.

20

Who Really Wrote the Music from *Flash Gordon*?

Flash Gordon Approaching . . .

When director Mike Hodges and producer Dino de Laurentiis made plans for the 1980 movie version of the *Flash Gordon* comic strip, few artists were better placed than Queen to compose a suitable sound track. The movie's deliberately heightened camp sensibility was the perfect bed for a series of instrumental tracks and two full Queen songs imbued with that same sympathy for the ridiculous. The resulting sound track has, in its way, become as notable as the movie itself.

Musically, it's a complete anomaly in the band's catalog by sheer dint of having next to no Mercury vocals (save for the album's bookend tracks, "Flash's Theme" and "The Hero") and the very heavy presence of synthesized sounds. Vangelis's sound track to Ridley Scott's visionary sci-fi noir *Blade Runner* wouldn't arrive until 1982, but a cursory listen to both might fancifully suggest a musical link between the two projects, though the subject matter and tone couldn't be more disparate.

Asked in 2009 about Queen's involvement in the sound track, Brian May confirmed that the sound track was indeed the first time the band had departed from traditional rock instrumentation: "This was the first time that we, as a band, recorded with synthesisers (previously we always had the declaration on our album sleeves 'No Synthesisers'). And I believe that this really is the first time that a proper score, to something other than a story about musicians, was ever applied to a film by a rock band."

May describes a scenario in which each individual member worked on his own musical themes for the movie. "All four of us made demos of our ideas in the first week of recording having seen the rushes. Dino [de Laurentiis, producer] began to be convinced, but he definitely did not like 'Flash' as a title song. It was the director Mike Hodges, knowing that the film was going to succeed on a camp level rather than a serious level, who persuaded him to let us develop the idea further."

Aside from Queen's rough contributions to the score, cellist and sometime musical arranger Paul Buckmaster was drafted in to write an orchestral sound track for the film with the intention of working in Queen's thematic ideas. However, as an untrained composer, Buckmaster's work was painfully slow. No cue sheet, a vital document detailing exactly when and where in the movie music would be required, was forthcoming from the production team, and Buckmaster was literally unable to articulate his ideas in a format that orchestral musicians could understand. The Royal Philharmonic Orchestra was booked for two weeks with fewer than two minutes of finished music to record. The expense of hiring such a prestigious ensemble was huge, and to have them effectively doing nothing for hours of prebooked sessions would have further implications on the movie's eventual financial success (or lack thereof).

By this point, the only tangible musical artifact provided by Queen themselves was fragments: for example, the short sequence of chords which would eventually form the foundation of "In the Space Capsule (Love Theme)." It was, in short, a logistical situation from which it would be difficult for an unschooled musician to escape.

"This Might Seem Like the End . . ."

Investigation into the circumstances around the music for *Flash Gordon* reveals the whole project to be one with two opposing interpretations. May's account highlights the compositional and editing role played by himself in particular, but there is a far murkier picture painted by one of the film's key contributors: the composer Howard Blake. By then an experienced composer of film sound tracks, Blake was drafted to complete the severely hamstrung musical score. His job was to compose an entire orchestral sound track for the movie under extreme time pressure and to weave it around whatever fragmentary ideas Queen had provided him with (supplied on demo cassettes). Blake's account of this process, supplied personally for this book, is relentlessly bleak and alleges that Queen's manager, Jim Beach, was the architect of a gross act of musical theft. He described the whole thing simply as "a very unpleasant episode in my life."

According to Blake, he was given ten days to complete the score, which would be written for orchestra and synthesizer. He wrote over an hour of music. During the last four days of this period, Blake was so sleep deprived that he suffered extreme exhaustion, bronchitis, and pneumonia, eventually requiring a doctor to administer Benzedrine to save his life. But the score was complete, and the National Philharmonic Orchestra (the Royal Philharmonic Orchestra presumably being unable to reschedule) would finally have something to play.

Having delivered the score and then having conducted and recorded it in three days at Denham Studios in Buckinghamshire (featuring Brian Gascoine, brother of popular U.K. quizmaster Bamber Gascoine, playing the solo synthesizer part), Blake was then excluded from the dubbing sessions. It was at this point that Blake began to suspect foul play. So limited was Queen's competency when it came to orchestral work that Blake alleges that the band effectively retooled his work, rerecording large portions of it on instruments more familiar to them and adding vignettes as they went along (Brian May's electric guitar version of the "The Wedding March," for example). Blake's summary of their skills beyond simply being in a rock band are damning: "They were at sea. They hadn't the faintest idea." It is these sessions that Brian May describes earlier, undertaken after Blake had introduced the band to the potential of writing music in this more mannered, atmospheric fashion as well as tutoring them in some of the writing and recording techniques necessary to achieve it. In his version of events, Blake saw the band soaking up his expertise and then deploying it without acknowledging his contribution.

It is Blake's belief that Jim Beach ("a very acquisitive lawyer") had his name removed from the credits of the sound track release to bolster the apparent contribution that the band had made to the film's music. Blake's view on the matter is simple: "He [Beach] couldn't give a fuck whether what I wrote was a work of genius or a complete load of shit.... What they didn't know about me is that I'm a fucking genius composer. It's actually one of my really great scores, and it got fucked up. I'm extremely angry about it."

What Did Queen Actually Record?

The production issues on the movie's sound track were obvious to all involved. If, as Blake states, there was indeed a period during which the band raised the drawbridge and worked internally, then it is described by May as being a feverish stretch. With the band scattered about Europe on vacation or generally on downtime between "main" Queen albums, May was the only member consistently near Anvil Studios and in a position to work on the material. The sheer amount of work needing to be done to get the sound track correctly recorded and synched to the movie itself was huge. "It was odd," said May in 2009. "I remember being in Anvil or De Lane Lea, with the film running on the screen, and all the production team sitting there watching me run about playing all the parts which I'd sketched in my head for the battle scene."

As May suggests, the sound track consists of compositions contributed by individual band members, with Mercury and May taking up most of the track list's real estate. Despite this and after the numerous production troubles, May had to act as a musical curator for the project (it's worth noting that Queen had also been working on *The Game* during the same period). It was a patchwork affair in which May would double himself on guitar, synthesizer, and bass, working his contributions around percussion outtakes that Roger Taylor had already provided in the early stages of the recording process.

The resulting miniatures as they appear on the sound track album display a markedly different character to what Queen enthusiasts may have been expecting at the time, a huge musical departure from the albums either side of its release. Nuggets of mood music and lowly pulsing percussion are interrupted regularly by the movie's set pieces, particularly a sequence in which Flash Gordon (played by an almost impossibly blonde Sam J. Jones) tackles a fleet of Ming the Merciless's henchmen by using his skill as a professional American football player and a climactic assault by Vultan's Hawkmen on the war rocket Ajax.

While the quieter, more atmospheric moments of the sound track sound convincingly ethereal and alien, it's the energetic interjections like the aforementioned battle scenes that show the limits of the conventional rock band format. In the context of the film, these sections are markedly less substantial than an orchestral sound track would have sounded in their place. The character of the film and its status as a cult camp classic go some way to legitimizing the rather more lightweight elements of Queen's score, something that could arguably have been muddied and confused by a more conventionally serious orchestral accompaniment.

What Happened to Howard Blake's Score?

Inevitably, YouTube currently houses many clips from *Flash Gordon* containing Howard Blake's original sound track cues in a reinstated version. An official release of Blake's sound track recording does exist but mostly in promotional CD format. It is an effortlessly lush suite, sophisticated and transportive, and hearing it alongside Queen's version of much of the same material makes for an uneasy comparison. During an interview for this book, Blake confirmed that his feelings toward the members of Queen were largely positive, describing Mercury as "a gifted musician" and adding that "if they [Queen] had collaborated with me, it would've been a lot better."

The sound track was nominated for a BAFTA in 1981, specifically the Anthony Asquith Award for Film Music, alongside John Williams's score for *The Empire Strikes Back*, Michael Gore for *Fame*, and Hazel O'Connor for *Breaking Glass*. According to Blake's recollection, the venerable British television host David Frost read out the nominations in full but mentioned Queen only when it came to *Flash Gordon*. The eventual release of the sound track album makes no mention of Howard Blake on the cover. Blake is listed on the back as having provided orchestral arrangements only. "The Kiss (Aura Resurrects Flash)" is the only track listed as having Blake as a cowriter. There emerges, then, two viewpoints: one that has Queen and particularly Brian May as the main composers of the sound track and a second in which Howard Blake's hour-long score was chopped up, assimilated, and rerecorded without so much as a cowriting credit given to him, a move encouraged by Jim Beach with the aim of making his clients appear to be at the height of their creative powers, perfectly able to write full-length sound tracks as well three-minute chart toppers.

When the credits roll on the movie itself, the first to appear is this: "Music composed, performed and produced by QUEEN available on Elektra Records and Tapes." No other names are listed as having contributed to the creative process of the sound track.

Blake sums up the whole painful episode like this: "I have nothing against the boys at all. They're nice little guys who played their guitars. But they were fucked up by their lawyer." After the recording sessions that May described were completed across various locations, Blake and May did in fact come together to evaluate the final piece. Some weeks after the final recording sessions for the album, May was in possession of the master cassette and sought Blake's approval: could they meet up at Blake's house in Barnes in southwest London to listen to it together? Blake, in the midst of a marital separation and with only one cassette player in the house, agreed. The cassette player in question was a Mickey Mouse–themed novelty contraption owned by Blake's

The musical motif that appears at the beginning of "The Kiss," originally conceived by Mercury but appearing here in Blake's score.   *Author's collection*

eighteen-month-old son and had only a very short electrical cable, meaning that the best way for May and Blake to listen to the whole score was to lie under the child's bed, each with a single earphone. It is a charming yet bizarre scene to imagine given all the hardship that had come before it.

The *Flash Gordon* episode is, apparently, something of a one-off in the Queen story. It is of course impossible to extrapolate one tale of industrial meanness and apply it to the rest of the band's career, but it does raise questions about the band's professional conduct when it came to songwriting credits. It is an issue about which the band was infamously prickly, ultimately solving the majority of such arguments by the time it came to 1989's *The Miracle* album, where all songs are credited to all members of the band.

How much of Blake's story is accurate is hard to ascertain without directly asking remaining members of the band and managerial figures (May and Taylor declined to be interviewed for this book), but there's enough tangible truth in his account to conclude that even if Queen and May in particular produced something interesting and worthy of their catalog, there was another, fuller, and more collaborative version of the sound track that never quite made it to record.

Queen's Two "Flash" Songs

Aside from the murk of confusion around Howard Blake's contribution to the *Flash Gordon* project, there are two songs on the final record that were undoubtedly led by Queen. Both the "Flash" single and the album's closing track, "The Hero," are in the same key and contain interchangeable musical elements (the famous thrumming, repeated bass note and the exclamations of "Flash!"). "Flash" is a notable single in the Queen catalog as another example of the band experimenting with the anthemic: in a way, rather than mythologizing themselves with songs like "We Are the Champions" and "We Will Rock You," using a fictional and fantastical character as inspiration allows them to indulge still more declamatory techniques. Although, having said that, it is perfectly possible to imagine the chorusing vocals singing "Queen!" instead of "Flash!" and the public at large would largely expect it of them.

A promotional video was knocked together to coincide with the film's eventual release, a mixture of constructed in-studio footage and clips from the film itself. The in-studio sections of the video show the band in resolute work mode, dressed down and serious as the movie plays on a large screen above them. John Deacon, whose bass guitar drives the early part of the song, has an expression of gentle reverence on his face, as if he understands that this is a job the band has been hired for rather than one on which they've had complete creative

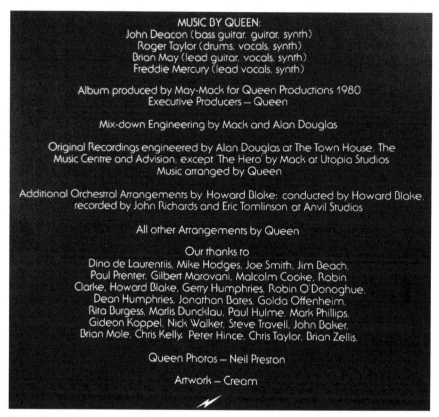

MUSIC BY QUEEN:
John Deacon (bass guitar, guitar, synth)
Roger Taylor (drums, vocals, synth)
Brian May (lead guitar, vocals, synth)
Freddie Mercury (lead vocals, synth)

Album produced by May-Mack for Queen Productions 1980
Executive Producers — Queen

Mix-down Engineering by Mack and Alan Douglas

Original Recordings engineered by Alan Douglas at The Town House, The
Music Centre and Advision, except 'The Hero' by Mack at Utopia Studios
Music arranged by Queen

Additional Orchestral Arrangements by Howard Blake: conducted by Howard Blake,
recorded by John Richards and Eric Tomlinson at Anvil Studios

All other Arrangements by Queen

Our thanks to
Dino de Laurentiis, Mike Hodges, Joe Smith, Jim Beach,
Paul Prenter, Gilbert Marovani, Malcolm Cooke, Robin
Clarke, Howard Blake, Gerry Humphries, Robin O'Donoghue,
Dean Humphries, Jonathan Bates, Golda Offenheim,
Rita Burgess, Marlis Duncklau, Paul Hulme, Mark Phillips,
Gideon Koppel, Nick Walker, Steve Travell, John Baker,
Brian Mole, Chris Kelly, Peter Hince, Chris Taylor, Brian Zellis.

Queen Photos — Neil Preston

Artwork — Cream

The credits as they appear on the reverse inner sleeve of the *Flash Gordon* LP. Howard Blake is thanked and credited as an arranger and conductor rather than composer. Also note the production credit for "May-Mack."   *Author's collection*

control. Of course, the irony of the video's in-studio setting is that such a scene almost certainly didn't take place during the recording of the sound track: the video implies that the rest of the score was laid down in this sober and studious environment, not the frantic scenes that Brian May described.

"The Hero" provided Mercury with a severe vocal challenge, according to May: "very high and demanding a lot of power in that top register. He said, 'Brian, you always write me these songs which fucking kill my beautiful voice!'" Both songs were often performed together live as a self-contained piece during live shows, omitting the clips of film audio and mirroring the pulsing bass with stage lighting at the audience's eye level. With Queen's live show often vaguely resembling a scene from *Close Encounters of the Third Kind*, it was a perfect addition to their set.

ORIGINAL SOUNDTRACK MUSIC BY QUEEN

The cover of the *Flash Gordon* LP, with a very conspicuous credit to Queen.   *Author's collection*

What Became of the Movie Itself?

After a relatively respectable showing at the domestic and international box office, the movie has become a cult classic. Its adherence to ideals of silliness and overacting flew in the face of science-fiction touchstones: the portentousness of Stanley Kubrick's *2001: A Space Odyssey* or the arch-atmospherics of Ridley Scott's *Alien*. In the veteran British actor Brian Blessed, the film managed to hire an iconic quote machine: his "Gordon's alive!" exclamation (which also features in the "Flash" single) is often quoted in many walks of popular culture. A second life on video and DVD was only natural.

The success of *Flash Gordon* impacted Queen in several ways, giving them in "Flash's Theme" another top-ten hit in the United Kingdom (and a number one in Austria) and a more general visual calling card, with Mercury sporting his "Flash" T-shirt at many live concerts and in the video for "Play the Game" (also from 1980). But more deeply than this, it was, regardless of the industrial upheaval necessary to get it written and recorded and the fallout with How-ard Blake, a sign that synthesizers could become a part of the wider Queen sound and that their ambitions shouldn't have to be confined simply to the rock album.

21

Hot Space

Is It Really That Bad?

Aperennial and tiresome pastime among the pop-critic intelligentsia is to highlight one execrable album by artists with an otherwise blemish-free back catalog, and a quick search returns dozens of published lists with titles like "10 awful albums by great bands" or "25 worst albums by legendary artists." Metallica and Lou Reed's *Lulu*, U2's *Pop*, David Bowie's ironically titled *Never Let Me Down*, and any of Prince's infamous "contractual obligation" albums usually have a strong showing, but on almost all of these lists, alongside some of those aforementioned, you will find Queen's *Hot Space*.

Considering that the critical reaction to Queen albums up until this point had at best been wildly varied, the frequent presence of *Hot Space* on such lists does seem incongruous at best, but the narrative has persisted. In truth, this most maligned of Queen albums captures the band in an especially difficult period of transition.

Musically, the unexpected success of "Another One Bites the Dust" had placed the Queen brand into a different audience demographic, one that Deacon and Mercury especially sought to exploit with, essentially, more of the same. This immediately set up a two-camp scenario in the band, with Deacon and Mercury on one side crowbarring funk and disco influences into the band's new material and May and Taylor on the other demonstrably trying to pen songs that would work in their traditionally rock-oriented live set. May told *Guitar Player* magazine in 1983 that he was constantly reacting to his guitar's reduced role in the band ("I used to listen to people plucking away on Motown records, and I really didn't like it"), immediately giving several key songs on the album an undercurrent of conflict.

Personally, things were no less complicated. The presence of Paul Prenter as Mercury's personal manager has long been thought to have irked other members of the band due to their sustained partying, but in truth, Taylor and May (Deacon by his own admission to a slightly lesser extent) were more than proficient at indulging themselves in similar ways. Given the one-dimensionally destructive depiction of Prenter in the biographical movie of Queen, *Bohemian Rhapsody* (for which both May and Taylor were consulting producers and key members of the creative team), it could be that this was as much a clash of lifestyles as it was a clash of artistry.

The nature of being a Queen fan means embracing the thought process behind *Hot Space* and accepting it. The artistry is there: their approach to songwriting was in flux anyway thanks to Reinhold Mack and a clutch of new influences, but the band's commitment to doing it properly cannot be faulted. More than any other album in the band's history, *Hot Space* was an attempt at a complete musical reinvention rather than a song-length genre experiment. That it was a kaleidoscopic semi-failure with one huge single tacked on the end ("Under Pressure") is symptomatic of the situation the band found themselves in. Let it be understood: *Hot Space* is not merely a bad album by a major artist— it's a Queen album in the deepest sense: complicated, flawed, and full-blooded.

Queen at the New York press conference for *Hot Space*. Note that John Deacon is the only one smiling.   *Walter Mcbride/Shutterstock*

Queen and the Duke: Under Pressure

Just as *The Game* contained a premade, tacked-on hit in "Crazy Little Thing Called Love," so *Hot Space* had "Under Pressure." Before full sessions for the album began in 1981, Queen had been working on a doodle of a Roger Taylor song named "Feel Like" at Mountain Studios. This work in progress was a jangling love song of honest but nondescript longing: very much unfinished but with a winning feel, the feel that this could develop into something if there was a better chorus wedged in somewhere.

In the same sessions, David Bowie, who was already acquainted with Mountain Studios after recording 1979's *Lodger* LP there, was drafted in to record backing vocals for another new song called "Cool Cat" (there's more to come on the results of that particular encounter), but Bowie was unhappy with his performance. Not wishing to waste time spent with influential and talented colleagues, both parties agreed to work on something else entirely, and Roger Taylor just so happened to have "Feel Like" kicking around his head, waiting to be punched up into a usable state. The ensuing creative battle to take control of the song and transform it was, according to more than one account, fueled by prodigious amounts of red wine at dinner and cocaine as evening turned into morning. Bowie's drug use was legendary despite attempts to refrain: one of the main reasons he moved to Switzerland in the late 1970s was to make his abstention as painless as it could be, but the temptation was too much. Reinhold Mack's account, as relayed in Mark Blake's book *Queen: The Untold Story*, suggests the entire session lasted nearly twenty-four hours in total and was adversarial yet somehow convivial.

Bowie, keen to assert himself against four already disparate musical personalities but with the distinct advantage of being critically adored for a decade, went on the offensive and improvised big lyrical and melodic ideas, butting them up against Mercury's contributions not in a spirit of collaboration but in one of combat. Mercury had the same approach as Bowie, and the resulting vocal mélange remains in the final version of the song for all to see. Harmonies are improvisatory and accidental, and a generous amount of finger clicking fills any textural holes in the song.

As a result of this unfocused approach, there's little definition in terms of traditional verses or choruses. Certain vocal hooks and phrases are repeated throughout, including the song's title, and Mercury's scatting (a series of "oom-ba-da"s) renders the song a breeze for karaoke novices. The guitar line, on the other hand, survives the transition from "Feel Like" essentially unchanged.

Despite these unfocused and singular fragments, the one musical element that passed most effortlessly into pop culture history was the song's simple bass line. There are differing accounts of who was truly responsible for this iconic nugget of music history that would eventually go on to be sampled by Vanilla

Ice: John Deacon originally attributed it to Bowie, but Bowie claimed it was already being worked on by the time he arrived. What does appear to be true is that, during a break in the session, Deacon quite spectacularly forgot how to play the famous bass motif completely and had to rely on Taylor's recollection to make sure it made it onto the tape.

Call it a miracle of alchemy or the innate genius of two major recording artists trying to outdo one another, but despite the utterly chaotic circumstances of its creation, the final piece was an immediate hit. "Under Pressure" went straight to number one on the U.K. singles charts in October 1981 (their first since "Bohemian Rhapsody" six years earlier).

How's Your Staying Power?

After the success of "Under Pressure," Queen went back to the very important business of capitalizing on the worldwide hit that was "Another One Bites the Dust." They returned to Giorgio Moroder's Musicland Studios with Mack in early 1982 and remained there until March, throughout which time the distinctly divided band gradually cobbled together an album of quite spectacular musical confusion. Deacon barely played his bass guitar, which was mostly thrown out in favor of synthesized bass, and Taylor's booming percussion is particularly notable by its frequent absence.

Perhaps most surprisingly, reed and brass arranger extraordinaire Arif Marden (the man responsible for encouraging Barry Gibb to sing in high falsetto) was drafted to give some pep to the album's opening track, Mercury's "Staying Power," a rare example of Queen engaging a collaborator to give a musical color or character they were unable to reproduce themselves. Marden's arrangement is grafted hermetically to the song's inherent groove: it's only Mercury's voice and the merest hint of Brian May's Red Special that would remind a listener at the time that this was indeed the same Queen who began previous albums with swampy squalls of guitar feedback.

"Staying Power" is a highlight, certainly, but there are other songs on *Hot Space* that display the confusion in the band with perfect eloquence. Brian May's "Dancer" is a good-natured attempt at the kind of genre tourism that the guitarist previously found so effortless, almost as if he was agreeing to experiment with funk and rhythm and blues but drew the line at wasting his best riffs on the chorus. Deacon's only solo composition on an album that is still full of his influence, "Back Chat" is more successful but limped only to number forty on the U.K. singles chart. It also features a spectacularly bad-tempered guitar solo from May in the most aggressively tinny tone he ever employed.

It's tempting to imagine the more rock-oriented songs on *Hot Space* arising as part of a bargaining process: Taylor and May had given the new sound a fair shake, but now it was time to beef up the rest of the album with something dependable, something traditional. That duality is part of what makes *Hot Space* such a revealing listen, and songs like Taylor's "Calling All Girls" and May's "Las Palabras de Amor" would ordinarily have fit on albums either side of *Hot Space* without any fanfare. "Calling All Girls" is an especially strange curio, a partially acoustic song of nondescript longing that was released as a single only in North America and Poland and that also inspired a deeply unexpected music video, a parody of George Lucas's pre–*Star Wars*, pre–*American Graffiti* sci-fi head-scratcher *THX-1138*.

The tussle continues as singles like "Body Language," which features almost no electric guitar at all, provide the counterpoint to May's "Put Out the Fire," the guitar solo of which he repeatedly fluffed, eventually nailing it while drunk. Taylor's "Action This Day" displays a fondness for the B-52s and Talking Heads, while Mercury's "Life Is Real (Song for Lennon)" is a Beatles pastiche right down to the plinking piano and gently echoed vocals. In short, there are too many stylistic elements at play here to term *Hot Space* simply a funky misstep.

Did David Bowie Actually Rap on "Cool Cat"?

Incongruous as it may seem, David Bowie did in fact perform a short rap on *Hot Space*, specifically during "Cool Cat," the song he'd originally intended to collaborate on when he recorded "Under Pressure" at Mountain Studios. He also provided some backing vocals for the song, specifically some hushed "bum-bum"-ing, but Bowie eventually decided that his contribution to the track was below his usual standards and demanded it be left off the final version of the album. However, he made his displeasure clear only at the last minute after the record had already been for test pressing, which is how, possibly to Bowie's chagrin, canny bootleggers were able to confirm the existence of the Bowie rap.

The rap itself is perhaps not as notable as the reputation built up around it over the years, but it is yet another anomalous element on *Hot Space*. Bowie raps quietly in an exaggerated, almost Dickensian-underclass version of his existing London accent, which gives his flow an immediate novelty value, if not any real clout with the hip-hop community. It's easy to imagine a reticence on Bowie's part: despite successful collaborations across his career with Brian Eno and others, this was perhaps a generic step too far into the esoteric. In terms of pop lore, Bowie's rap verse has taken on a life of its own as a "did that really happen?" moment, its status as something that Bowie expressly wanted striking from his own record only adding to the mystique around it. As with so many of these supposedly bizarre moments in pop culture, the truth is far more understandable than the attractive story.

Was *Hot Space* Just a Forgotten *Thriller*?

The critical response to *Hot Space* in 1982 was one not of outright hostility across the board but rather more of confusion (even *Rolling Stone* gave it a tepid yet carefully qualified three-star rating). But one vote of confidence could have come from the King of Pop himself, Michael Jackson, who was another visitor to Queen's studio in 1981 and worked with the band on three compositions that would surface only much later (more on this in chapter 37). It's difficult to find any actual verification, but several accounts claimed that Jackson saw *Hot Space* as an important touchstone when he was writing material for *Thriller*. Brian May recognized in a 1989 interview that there were similarities between the two albums, but *Hot Space* was, in his opinion, a victim of bad timing.

We know Jackson was fond of the band in general, so it does seem highly plausible that *Hot Space* would've been on his mind when he was assembling the ingredients for *Thriller*, which went on to become one of the biggest-selling albums in pop history and a cultural touchstone for an entire generation. *Hot Space* didn't fare quite so well in critical terms, but in the United Kingdom, it sold initially just as well as *The Game*. In the United States, however, *Hot Space* shifted approximately a million units, a quarter of the number *The Game* managed (due in no small part to the success of "Another One Bites the Dust").

Hot Space on Tour

Just as the album itself ushered in a period of substantial change to the band's sound, so the world tour that followed required a complete rethinking, including the first-ever regular auxiliary musicians joining them onstage. In the end, the right man for the job was a figure from the band's past: Mott the Hoople's ex-keyboardist Morgan Fisher, who joined them for the European dates. Fisher also had a connection to Queen through Tim Staffel, with whom Fisher had formed the band Morgan in the early 1970s. His main duties were to fill in the keyboard and synthesizer sounds now required to effectively re-create the material from *Hot Space*. His counterpart for the North American and Japanese legs of the tour was Fred Mandel, who went on to become a key creative figure in the band's mid- to late 1980s albums. Some material from *Hot Space* was tweaked for the tour to fit into a style more befitting the band's natural strengths in the live arena, notably an amped-up and guitar-heavy version of "Staying Power."

Aside from the musical changes, though, it was effectively business as usual on tour: the same venues, the same routes, and the same cars from airport to hotel to arena and back again. Beneath the surface of this huge and self-perpetuating live concert machine, there was a deeper confusion within Queen. *Hot Space* had damaged them and frustrated them. Roger Taylor had found time to release a solo album of New Wave–inspired electro-rock songs in 1981 titled *Fun in Space*, recorded at Mountain Studios (where else?) and eventually reaching a fairly respectable number eighteen on the U.K. album charts, but was keen to work on the follow-up. Freddie Mercury was keen to take the disco experiments of *Hot Space* and mold them into something more personal and after returning from tour had begun assembling material for a solo album.

The need to break from each other had become impossible to ignore, and it was decided that Queen would have a year off from their usual album cycle so that individual members could work on other projects. It was to be the first major break the band had taken in almost a decade, and it couldn't come soon enough.

The official program for the U.K. leg of the *Hot Space* tour.

Martin Skala, QueenConcerts.com

22

"I'll Pay the Bill, You Taste the Wine"

Queen at Leisure

Queen's reputation as rock's foremost bacchanalian and Dionysian practitioners of their generation is well-founded, but perhaps a more suitable Greek god to characterize their collective attitude toward revelry would be Comus, the god of festivity. In the mythology, Comus was famed for his nocturnal exploits in particular, always intoxicated, and wearing a floral wreath on his head. Attendees at his gatherings would swap clothes no matter their gender. In a painting titled *Reign of Comus* by Lorenzo Costa, one of Comus's legendary shindigs is well under way, and the debauchery is clear to see: guests

Lorenzo Costa's "Reign of Comus," which resides in the Louvre in Paris.
Wikimedia Commons / Public Domain

in various states of undress gambol in and out of a lake, their limbs and actions presumably loosened by copious amounts of wine. A lyre player is visible in the foreground, surrounded by adoring revelers.

Many bands in the supposed golden age of rock 'n' roll of the 1960s and 1970s would lay claim to being the most extreme when it came to partying and more still in the 1980s by the time hair metal had made it onto MTV. The stories that came out of this culture of sexual and substance abuse, exacerbated by the extreme on-the-road boredom suffered by touring (always male) musicians, are spectacularly varied in their methodology but united by a strongly depressing and pernicious undertone of grubbiness and victimization. Led Zeppelin sexually assaulting a groupie with a mud shark, Steven Tyler legally adopting and impregnating a sixteen-year-old female fan, David Lee Roth paying roadies to convince audience members to come backstage and have sex with him in specially designated camping tents: all of these oft-repeated stories have definite victims.

It would be missing the point to claim that Queen had any kind of moral high ground over and above these examples, but their distinctly Comusian methods of partying certainly seemed to result in a more wholly positive and uplifting brand of debauchery. It would also be tempting to conclude that the most outwardly peacockish member of the band, Freddie Mercury, was the main instigator of the band's legendary soirees, but they were too collaborative a group to allow Mercury to take the reins every time they needed to cut loose. Queen's sustained and prodigious program of excessive celebration was borne not just from a desire to transgress but equally from a need to publicly flaunt their spending power and fine taste. A Queen party, at least when the doors opened, was not a grubby occasion but rather more an exquisitely planned disaster with impeccably gauche styling.

What Were Queen's Wildest Parties Like?

Without a doubt, the most notorious party the band ever threw was to celebrate the release of *Jazz* in 1978, a night that would later come to be known as "Saturday night in Sodom." With an album to promote and a U.S. tour to kick off, the band took over the Fairmont Hotel in New Orleans for Halloween night with the intention not of terrifying their party guests (somewhere between four hundred and five hundred of them) but of bowing to their every salacious whim. There was a budget of £200,000 earmarked for the evening's entertainment and catering, but some accounts suggest that even this may have been a conservative assessment given the lavish display of opulence.

After the band played a winning show at the city's Municipal Auditorium, invited guests were escorted to the Fairmont and led into the building by a full marching band. Once settled, they could explore any number of redecorated ballrooms made to resemble teeming swamplands and help themselves to as much Cristal wine, caviar, and cocaine as they could ingest while still conscious.

Mercury masterminded this particular event (though the others in the band were more than willing attendees) and tasked the U.S. publicist with sourcing as many street performers as possible and bringing them to the party. But these were not your average tip-seeking performers and jugglers; instead, guests would sip their drinks in the company of a heavy-set nude woman smoking cigarettes in her vagina. Contortionists and snake swallowers would vie for attention with nude hermaphrodites serving drinks and demanding their tips be slid into the nearest bodily orifice. Prostitutes of various genders and persuasions lingered in the bathrooms waiting for anyone who required what Mercury termed "lip service" rather than room service. Video screens played the music video for "Fat Bottomed Girls" on repeat, while nude (again, always nude) women wrestled in a slick pool of chopped meat. Serious accusations of political and social ignorance were leveled at Queen throughout their career, from playing concerts in apartheid-era South Africa to impelling crowds of Thatcher-bludgeoned working-class concertgoers to "drink champagne for breakfast," but it's spiriting to note that their cast of sex workers and drug providers was a celebration of equal opportunity.

What's most surprising about this event is just how normal the band itself seemed to find it. To them, it was little more than a lark, a necessary part of the promotional business of launching an album and a tour. And if that meant nude women wrestling in chopped meat, then, well, the budget would have to come from somewhere. Pictures from the Fairmont Halloween party show John Deacon wearing a distinctly unglamorous woolen tank top, standing between a nun and a black-and-white minstrel, and a white-blazered and lightly buffed Roger Taylor surrounded by laughing women. Mercury signed any body part held under his marker pen but looking more like an amused frat boy than the ringleader of an orgiastic circus of sex and drugs.

Almost matching the Fairmont party in notoriety and its tales of excess is Freddie Mercury's thirty-ninth birthday party in September 1985, for which the singer hired out Old Mrs. Henderson's, Munich's famous club that celebrated cross-dressing in all its permutations. The rules, as outlined on the party invitations, were that all guests would dress in black and white only, and they had to cross-dress. There was a heavy camera presence at the party itself (capturing footage that would end up in the music video for Mercury's solo single "Living on My Own"), so it's possible to survey the crush of bodies, the fake zebra heads, the monochromatic candlesticks wedged into the ginormous birthday cake, and a harlequin-suited Mercury at the center of it all, epaulets on the shoulders of his specially made military jacket. It's also possible to clock Paul Prenter and Mercury's eventual long-term partner, Jim Hutton, the latter wearing little other than a black bow tie.

There are snatches of footage that capture Mercury alone in the sea of faces, confusedly or absentmindedly looking upward, away from the morass in the way that any worried party host might. No matter the scale of great celebration, there's always a host who cares about the well-being of his or her guests, and perhaps this is what separated Queen from their peers when it came to partying in style: would the parties have been quite so legendary if they hadn't organized them with such care?

Were There Really Dwarves Carrying Bowls of Cocaine on Their Heads at Queen Parties?

The presence of diminutive carriers of Colombian marching powder at some undisclosed party or other has, thanks to the pithy nature of its retelling, become one of the most folkloric Queen stories. It's nearly impossible to find actual confirmation or photographic evidence of dwarves with bowls of cocaine strapped to their heads, but, given the accounts of goings-on that we do have, to single out this one detail is a little like singling out one cowboy in the posse when they're all guilty of horse rustling.

Given that many more transgressive things went down at countless Queen celebrations, this focus on one of the more tepid and mythical happenings is perhaps just symptomatic of our collective desire to turn pop culture events into nuggets. Whether it did or didn't happen is now immaterial: to the public, Queen is the band who employed dwarves to carry bowls of cocaine on their heads at parties, just as Brian Wilson is the guy who wrote songs in a sandpit or Keith Richards is the guy who snorted his father's ashes.

Did Freddie Mercury Actually Take Princess Diana to a Gay Club?

One of the most persistent stories to follow Mercury's name around is reported by the entertainer and actress Cleo Rocos in great detail, telling of the night Freddie Mercury, his close friend Kenny Everett, and Rocos (who was a costar on Everett's television show) took Diana Spencer, otherwise known as the Princess of Wales, to a gay club in South London. According to Rocos's account in her 1999 book *The Power of Positive Drinking*, the quartet had been lounging at Mercury's Garden Lodge home in Kensington, watching reruns of *The Golden Girls* with the sound on the television turned down so they could improvise their own dialogue over the top.

Not wishing the festivities to end, it was mooted that the quartet should head out to the Royal Vauxhall Tavern, London's oldest and more venerated gay venue, which had previously played host to the likes of Diana Dors and was a favorite haunt of Mercury's. Spencer was keen to tag along despite being quite literally one of the most famous and recognizable people in the entire world. To smuggle her in undetected (it was a shade more usual for Rocos, Everett, and Mercury to be seen there), Spencer was dressed in military jacket and sunglasses. The attention on the other three was sufficient that no one noticed that a member of the royal family was accompanying them, and Spencer enjoyed a fairy-tale night as a member of the public instead, ordering drinks and dancing with her friends.

Which Queen Songs Were Written about Their Partying Habits?

There's a distinction to be made between Queen songs about their partying and Freddie Mercury songs about his promiscuity. So, while it wouldn't be incorrect to say that "Don't Stop Me Now" is about having a good time and, indeed, having a ball, this is confined specifically to Mercury's personal assault on the late 1970s gay scene rather than encompassing the rest of the band. And even though Queen's enthusiasm for debauched celebration began early in their career, it took a number of years for them to actually start singing about it explicitly.

References to their harder party lifestyle seep in around 1978, with songs like "Let Me Entertain You" ("If you need a fix, if you need a high") and "Fun It" ("Everybody in the night time should have a good time all night.... Don't shun it, fun it!"), but this really reached a peak with the songs from *Hot Space*. It's interesting to note that, even in these good-time songs about sex and partying, there is an element of contrition, of loneliness. May's "Dancer" opens with the line "I'm not invited to the party, been sitting here all night," immediately casting Mercury as the outsider rather than the instigator (although obviously he does eventually attend the party with aplomb).

The music video for "It's a Hard Life" from 1984, too, conveys the melancholy of the entertainer who can't entertain himself, the terminally morose man surrounded by every decadence imaginable. Costumes scream of the very excesses that Queen was famous for displaying, but Mercury sulks and huffs in his peacock-influenced red outfit as the party goes on around him. This was in 1984, when much of the band's partying had already been done (though there was still plenty to come), so there is perhaps reason to believe that the band was showing a certain degree of self-awareness and that celebrations of this magnitude may not entertain the soul so much as the senses.

Later songs show a more circumspect and melancholy attitude to the business of partying. In the aptly titled "Party" from 1989's *The Miracle* album, the focus is on the aftermath of some typically legendary revelry: "But in the cold light of day next morning, party was over. . . . Everybody's gone away, why don't you come back and play?" It closes with a repeated "goodbye, the party is over," which quite sharply displays the band's collective fatigue with the decadent and sociable lifestyle with which they'd become inextricably entangled. By 1989, Mercury's battle with AIDS and the resultant health complications had quite dramatically ended that chapter of the band's career, and the resultant musical material perhaps displayed an unconscious disdain for the lives they previously led.

It might not be too trite to conclude that this evolution of songwriting mirrors the evolution of a great party: the boundless enthusiasm and material means to celebrate in style give way to regret at having overindulged, the partygoers left picking over the details of the previous night's triumphs, tragedies, and traumas. This is perhaps the only way in which Queen's partying ways didn't align with those of Comus: perhaps they were just too human to achieve his levels of unending festivity.

Freddie Mercury with his thirty-eighth birthday cake in September 1985, the knife already plunged in.   *Alan Davidson/Shutterstock*

23

Let's Give 'Em the Works!

Four Men on the Prowl

Queen ended the *Hot Space* tour as colleagues. Critically, they were in no-man's-land after the damp squib that was their funk and disco odyssey, and while the live shows had been typically successful, there had been little to distinguish them from previous rounds of the same old venues. The moustache and the Munich lifestyle were still confusing Queen fans who read about the band's exploits in the tabloids. The best course of action, it was decided, was to rest the band for a short time. Rumors of a full split had dogged the band regularly for several years and had always been quashed, but this time around, it was harder to convince the public that all was well, as outside influences began to pull individual members in different directions.

Paul Prenter's influence on Freddie Mercury as his personal manager had massaged the singer's desires to record a solo album, and although the results wouldn't surface until the release of 1985's *Mr. Bad Guy*, the impetus and, crucially, the belief that there was a life outside of Queen was there. Roger Taylor had already begun to write and release solo material, and Brian May's natural conviviality and established place in the pantheon of legendary rock guitarists allowed him to collaborate with Eddie Van Halen on *Star Fleet Project*, a tie-in EP to accompany a Japanese children's TV show that transferred to British television in 1983.

John Deacon's whereabouts during this period are tricky to ascertain, but earlier features suggested that the majority of his time away from the band was spent in relative seclusion with his family, and any aspirations to write solo material were generally done in by his own admission that he couldn't sing.

Asked on British television show *Nationwide* in 1982 about rumors of the band's imminent splitting up and what drove them to stay together, Taylor suggested that it had nothing to do with money and everything to do with achievement, that every chart-topping single or album was reason enough to carry on. There is a strong careerist aspect to Queen throughout their history, and this slightly hollow aim of simply continuing to attain accolades (biggest, first, fastest, and so on) certainly offers one explanation for their ability to overcome any personal difficulties and continue working together. All this press speculation, combined with the desire among individual members to explore other creative avenues, had, it seems, ultimately little to do with the band's continuation. When they did eventually return to the studio in August 1983, it was still only nine months after they'd finished the *Hot Space* tour: clearly, the lure of more achievements was too strong to resist.

This time, they would convene for the first time in Los Angeles, with Reinhold Mack taking his now usual position behind the desk. Sessions for what would become *The Works* took on Mack's natural streamlined work ethic, and the resultant songs had more in common with the honed precision of those from *The Game*, complete with still more chart-assailing singles. Production moved to more familiar climes in the winter of 1983, back to Giorgio Moroder's Musicland Studios in Munich (much of Mercury's life, both personal and creative, was now based in that city).

Even the album's eventual cover art holds significance. Showing the band seated in casual dress and lit so that their shadows cast dark silhouettes on the white wall behind them, it is the band saying, "This is Queen, and we are now an uncomplicated band." The reason behind the album's existence was simple: to remind the world that, after a substantial wobble, Queen could still deliver. Taylor's proclamation in the studio once the band had reconvened was simply, "Let's give 'em the works!"

What Was "Radio Ga Ga" Really About?

If we view *Hot Space* as the point where the songwriting pendulum swung toward Freddie Mercury and John Deacon's sensibilities, then Queen's eleventh album, *The Works*, sees it begin its journey back toward Roger Taylor and Brian May. Certain elements trialed on *Hot Space* survived the creative process, most significantly Taylor's growing enthusiasm for electronics and motorik rhythms. The first single from the album, Taylor's "Radio Ga Ga," occupies a logical and satisfying middle ground between the more noodling aspects of albums like *Hot Space* and *Flash Gordon* and baldly anthemic songs like "We Are the Champions." Taylor took inspiration from his three-year-old son's assessment of a song he heard on the radio while they were in Los Angeles, that whichever unfortunate track happened to be playing was merely "radio caca," and constructed around this profanity a song ostensibly about the increasing importance of the music video over radio airplay but one equally dominated by self-reference.

When Mercury sings, "We hardly need to use our ears, our music changes through the years," it is a wistful recognition of the band's chameleonic musical evolution. Across a decade of experiments of wildly varying success, Taylor's lyrics quite blithely explain the band's creative philosophy in one single line.

References to landmark radio events like Orson Welles's dramatized documentary version of H. G. Wells's *The War of the Worlds* are made, while director David Mallet's music video for the song steeps it further in science-fiction history, borrowing images from Fritz Lang's *Metropolis* and featuring a rather bored-looking Queen lounging in a *Blade Runner*-indebted flying car. *Rolling Stone* magazine's earlier claim that Queen was the world's first fascist rock band may have found some traction in the video's closing section, which depicts a futuristic rally: whether the crowd's rhythmic clapping and fist raising is designed to be utopian or dystopian remains unclear.

The song is deservedly one of the band's most perennially popular works and went on to achieve pop immortality the following summer when it was

The program for the European leg of *The Works* tour, showing the band in their rallying poses from the "Radio Ga Ga" video.

Martin Skala, QueenConcerts.com

performed at Live Aid (see chapter 25). And while it is most definitely Taylor's composition (perhaps his greatest), it was Mercury who arranged its constituent musical elements into a pop structure and, more important, touring keyboardist Fred Mandel who helped program the ever-complexifying synthesizer parts.

Banned in America

The Works spawned four singles in total, but only one of them could claim to have upset middle America to the point where it was banned by MTV. The music video for "I Want to Break Free" is a landmark in the history of the medium not simply because it was banned but also because of the way it balances a promotional stunt with an artistic statement. This wasn't quite on the scale of, say, Michael Jackson and John Landis's "Thriller" video, but with a production budget of £100,000 and the involvement of no less hallowed an institution than the Royal Ballet, it was not an insignificant undertaking. Juxtaposing a parody of the British soap opera *Coronation Street* with an extended ballet sequence inspired by Vaslav Nijinksy's performance as the faun in Debussy's symphonic tone poem *Prélude à l'après-midi d'un faune* is an attempt to synthesize everything that Queen saw themselves as being capable of: silliness and seriousness, frivolity and fantasy, domesticity and the divine.

Despite this lofty aim, it was the *Coronation Street* parody that caused the controversy. The band appeared in drag, specifically to mimic female characters in the soap, but with Mercury still sporting his trademark moustache, prompting accusations of the normalization of transvestism and the potential corruption of any youths watching. As with so many controversial pop culture artifacts, their prohibition only enhances their notoriety and influence, and so it was with "I Want to Break Free." The band stalled its progress on the U.S. singles charts, but it hit number one in South Africa, Belgium, the Netherlands, and Austria and number three back home in the United Kingdom.

Musically and poetically, it's weighted with an existential weariness for which the song's writer, John Deacon, had previous form. It's a cry for freedom from drudgery, the same premise he explored on "Spread Your Wings," but on this occasion, the themes of the song married perfectly to the accompanying video. There's an instrumental interlude (featuring a synthesizer solo played once again by *The Works'* secret weapon Fred Mandel) that coincides with Mercury's ballet section before the song's final verse thuds the viewer in a melancholy heel turn straight back to *Coronation Street* and, therefore, normal life.

The Machines Take Over

Elsewhere on *The Works*, the influence of electronic music is in strong evidence throughout. With the exception of songs like the rockabilly ditty "Man on the Prowl" and the closing acoustic number "Is This the World We Created?" having made their peace with synthesizers some years ago, *The Works* sees Queen in full sandbox mode, playing and experimenting with the fervor of unschooled savants.

"Machines (Or Back to Humans)" is the most egregiously uncool example because of its clear debt to Kraftwerk and the rest of the German school of straight-laced electronic music, but the commitment to its own central premise, that humanity is being threatened by an unnamed technological threat (basically evil robots with evil robot voices), is admirable. A heavily vocoded and partially incomprehensible Roger Taylor duets with Mercury, who delivers tech-paranoia lyrics like "Its midwife's a disk drive, its sex life is quantized" with complete conviction, and a similar tussle takes place between the clanging synthesizer breakdowns (programmed by Mack) and the "human" members of the band represented by crashing cymbals and power chords in unison.

"Keep Passing the Open Windows," on the other hand, sees that fusion between organic and electronic sounds more artfully achieved, any synthesizer lines acting as decoration to an existing song rather than the basis for its creation. That song also holds a strange place in the Queen catalog, originally written with the intention of being included on the sound track to the movie adaptation of John Irving's novel *The Hotel New Hampshire*, of which Jim Beach was a producer.

Queen Goes Full Spinal Tap

The tour that followed the release of *The Works* was, the band freely admitted, more of the same. The same cities, the same countries, the same continents: just with a few more set-list options than before. The ever-more-elaborate stage shows reached a new height of technical ambition, with a multileveled set based on Fritz Lang's *Metropolis* that gave ample ledges and staircases from which to leap and strike declamatory poses. During one such declamatory performance of "Hammer to Fall" in Hanover's Europahall, Mercury fell down one of the stage's many staircases, causing the show to be halted while he was escorted from the stage. In bootleg recordings, it's possible to hear the crowd chanting "Freddie!" repeatedly before Mercury was helped back to the piano for the final few songs.

There is something decidedly ridiculous about the scale of Queen's stage show by this point. The set had ballooned in spectacle to the point where band members risked falling off it at any moment, a dedication to stagecraft memorably lampooned in Rob Reiner and Christopher Guest's rock mockumentary *This Is Spinal Tap*, which also arrived in 1984. Although the Hanover incident was predated by the movie, the scene in which mustached bassist Derek Smalls (Harry Shearer) is incapacitated by a fiberglass cocoon is only a short leap of the imagination from Queen's *Metropolis* set.

Fred Mandel didn't join the band for the live shows this time around, his role being filled by another soon-to-be-stalwart side musician, Spike Edney. Although the tour was larger in physical scale and took in the major arenas of Europe, Japan, Australia, and New Zealand, there was no North American leg, and the band wouldn't return there until after the death of Freddie Mercury and the retirement of John Deacon. But still, that feeling of having played the same territories over and over again for nearly a decade lingered. And it was to have one dire consequence.

Why Did Queen Perform in Apartheid South Africa?

It's important not to leaven the possible interpretations of Queen's decision to play at South Africa's Sun City complex in October 1984 with any undue retrospective leniency. It was the single most self-damaging move the band made

Ticket stub for one of Queen's controversial concerts in apartheid-era South Africa.
Martin Skala, QueenConcerts.com

in its entire career, if not in financial respects, then most definitely in terms of their moral standing. At this time, South Africa was still deep into its period of institutional racial segregation, otherwise known as apartheid. The possibility of playing in South Africa in 1984 was open to all major recording artists, but there was a very clear mandate from the Musicians' Union in the United Kingdom stating that to do so would result in fines and blacklisting, such was the moral stance on the issue. As such, to play live in apartheid-era South Africa was to be complicit in one of the most heinous acts of racial segregation in modern history.

Playing a string of nine concerts at the Sun City resort's Super Bowl venue (an enclave legally immune to South Africa's stringent rules on live entertainment) was in direct contravention of the Musicians' Union's guidelines but was explained away in a characteristically simplistic way by the band. These shows were not political in any way, according to interviews given around the time. As they saw it, concerts were for fans, no matter the political situation in the country they called home, and the band had a duty to play concerts for their fans wherever the demand was present.

In another display of Queen's at-times-spectacular lack of self-awareness, the incident didn't trouble them any further or seemingly ellicit any response or apology. The United Nations placed them on a blacklist and, according to a 1985 *New York Times* article, they were rendered illegible for any major charity performances affiliated with the international organization. Alongside artists including the Beach Boys, Dolly Parton, Frank Sinatra, Glen Campbell, and Liberace, they remained blacklisted until the collapse of apartheid in 1994. (Tina Turner and George Benson managed to get themselves off the list by writing to the United Nations promising never to play in South Africa again.)

Such moral issues seemed to wash over the band, who would always take the broad-strokes defensive position that, when it came down to it, it was music that mattered. It casts a new light on songs like "Is This the World We Created?" a response to the encroaching famine across Africa that would eventually inspire the Live Aid concert. The hypocrisy is plain but apparently did not register with Queen.

What Was Queen's Only Christmas Song?

At the close of November 1984, Queen released "Thank God It's Christmas," their only specifically festive song. The tradition and potential commercial power of releasing a Christmas single was not lost on the band, but, despite ambitions of recording a perennial seasonal hit to be counted alongside Slade's glam-rock classic "Merry Xmas Everybody," Taylor and May's rather sedate Yuletide effort was swamped by Band Aid's "Do They Know It's Christmas Time" and reached only number twenty-one. It has enjoyed something of a seasonal resurgence on U.K. radio in recent years, but Brian May suggested in a 2018 interview that the real reason for its poor showing on the charts was its lack of an official music video.

Either way, it was not quite the tonic required to rescue the band's 1984. It was a year of change and adaptation as new creative avenues were explored but also one of failures and frustrations. The beginning of 1985 saw them take on the Rock in Rio festival twice, playing to more than a quarter of a million people, and the fulfillment of their touring obligations in Asia and the Antipodes. Mercury's first solo record, *Mr. Bad Guy*, was imminent, and plans for the next Queen album were effectively nonexistent. For perhaps the first time in the band's history, there was a credible threat of a substantial hiatus.

24

Video Ga Ga

Queen's Greatest and Strangest Music Videos

So much of what we perceive about Queen is controlled by their music videos. As a band, they were naturally inclined toward image control, but in their music videos, they were able to precisely convey, with the close collaboration of directors, their intentions in what became a veritable buffet of visual flamboyance. There were, as with so many aspects of the band's career, triumphs and missteps, controversies and excesses. Their most obviously arresting and groundbreaking videos became landmarks in the medium and have been discussed in this book (and many, many others), so this chapter features some lesser-known highlights and overlooked gems from the catalog. Inevitably due to the widespread emergence of music videos, they lean toward the middle and later periods of the band's first incarnation.

"We Are the Champions"

A testament to the power of crowdsourcing, the video for "We Are the Champions" was the result of the official Queen fan club being invited to the New London Theatre to play the role of an adoring crowd while Queen performed the song. It is also a video that perfectly understands the song it accompanies and, as such, shows Freddie Mercury as part of the communal experience, accessible, close enough for fans to reach out and snap his leotard. The grainy nature of the footage gives a curious and warming homespun feel to the video, most evident during the second chorus when the camera whips around to floor level just as Mercury turns, arm outstretched, to sing the song's title to the throng.

The video also sells the idea of Queen as a live band more clearly than ever before. For example, the staged concert section of the "Bohemian Rhapsody" video is clearly in an empty room, whereas here we see Queen as they were meant to be experienced in 1977: live, at close quarters, and together with a fervent and obsessive crowd, self-proclaimed champions leading a room full of followers. A similar tactic was used much later in the video for "Friends Will Be Friends" although with a much larger budget and crowd.

"Back Chat"

Freddie Mercury's entrée into the gay clubbing scenes of Munich and New York was the inspiration for this video, which positively drips with gay iconography. We see Mercury thrusting his groin repeatedly into a giant piston and swinging from metal poles and cages while all around him fists grasp oversized wrenches. His dancing is also consciously far more suited to the clubbing scene than any previous, more theatrical prancing displayed onstage or in their music videos. This is dancing not just for the stage but also more for close quarters, preferably with company.

John Deacon looks impossibly young and quite joyful, perhaps because the song and its musical direction were his. The shift in power in the band even extends to Brian May's use of a Fender Telecaster rather than his usual Red Special, a more utilitarian and workmanlike instrument than his signature flamboyant ax. Toward the end of the video, during the "Don't talk back" refrain, there's a glimpse of May seemingly cursing his instrument, claw-handed with frustration.

The "Back Chat" video makes for an interesting counterpoint to the video for "Body Language" (also from *Hot Space*), a much more suggestive piece that depicts Mercury as an arch-observer of sexual excess rather than a participant in the culture surrounding it.

"One Vision"

"One Vision" was constructed for the purpose of announcing Queen's return— and not just their return but also their very positive, loud, and jovial return. Rumors of the band's disintegrating personal relationships and all-around boredom with the project that was Queen in the mid-1980s had been all but silenced by their performance at Live Aid in 1985, so this first music video since that momentous gig sought to recapture the magic by showing them in their crucible: at work in the studio. Wherever possible, the band shares microphones and recording booths. They wear vests, they laugh and mug for the camera, they lounge around smoking and reading magazines between takes. It's a mix of actual footage from the "One Vision" sessions and more choreographed casual scenes, but the effect is plainly arresting. Without spending any serious money on sets and costumes, they successfully recast themselves as a band of friends.

Queen's reliance on the power of self-reference, too, is in evidence in the video's opening, which sees the band in their iconic Marlene Dietrich "diamond" formation from the *Queen II* album cover and "Bohemian Rhapsody" music video morph into their contemporary selves before Deacon and Taylor turn to look enigmatically at each other as if to say, "Is this what we are now?"

"One Vision" would form something of a template for Queen videos going forward, namely, showing the band in scenes of constructed creativity. They'd already done this in the video for "Someone to Love," but the technique became much more dominant after "One Vision": both "Headlong" and "No-One but You (Only the Good Die Young)" strive to show that in-studio kinship, the bond between a group of musicians that fans have known for decades. It is a visual comfort blanket, a warm welcome to an area behind the façade of an elaborate stage show or an expensive and cinematic music video.

"Princes of the Universe"

As an official tie-in with the movie release of *Highlander* in 1986, "Princes of the Universe" holds an interesting place among Queen's music videos as simultaneously their most obviously cinematic and one of their more performatively raw and bracing. As was the fashion of the time with major tie-in songs, the video is littered with clips from the movie in question, but more unusual is lead actor Christopher Lambert's in-character appearance as Connor Macleod. Although he's in the video for only a matter of seconds, he is seen crossing his sword with Mercury's microphone stand as the band perform on top of New York's Silvercup building (re-created in Elstree Studios for the movie).

The performance itself is notable for its gusto and darker-edged styling, with the band dressed in muted attire: macs for everyone apart from Mercury, who sports a utility waistcoat and jeans. Huge crane shots swoop across their performance area, and the wind machines are well and truly engaged, but the technical prowess is matched by the band's commitment. Deacon and May thwack at their guitar bodies, while Mercury is in a seemingly constant state of iconic posing, arch-backed and close-eyed, with his mouth open as wide as it can go. Again in a Queen music video, May is seen without his trademark Red Special, this time replacing it with a most uncharacteristic Japanese Washburn RR11V (similar in shape and styling to the Gibson Flying V). "Princes of the Universe" wasn't released as a single in the United Kingdom and didn't deliver huge sales in the territories where it was, and as a result, it holds the status of an overlooked Queen classic, much beloved by die-hard fans who were overjoyed they could produce such heavy material this late in their career. It's also one of the most kinetically potent clips of the band in their vast videography, which is perhaps ironic given the huge contrivance of its premise. Production footage of the shoot itself is an exercise in the tedium of shooting music videos and features Christopher Lambert hungrily puffing on cigarettes between rehearsal sword fights with Mercury, who bounces on his toes in an effort to stay fresh and engaged. Taylor and May spend most of their time side of stage, laughing at this mock duel in slow motion.

"The Miracle"

In what is perhaps the most overtly self-referential statement in all of Queen's music videos, the 1989 promo for "The Miracle" stars four child doppelgängers as individual band members. The likenesses and mannerisms as the quartet mime the song is impressively detailed, from Brian May's habit of pulling his guitar neck vertical and close to his face during solos to John Deacon's baggy T-shirt and tiny shorts combo. The young Freddie Mercury, played by Ross McCall, is seen careening through different aesthetic periods of his performing life: black and white leotard with shaggy hair, leather cop outfit, Live Aid vest and jeans combo, and Wembley Stadium yellow military jacket.

After several clanging visual hints are dropped, the climax of the video sees the real members of Queen emerge from a cloud of smoke (in a manner not dissimilar from the popular U.K. TV show *Stars in Their Eyes*, of which the band would almost certainly be aware) and perform with their tiny counterparts. As conceptual ideas in Queen videos go, it's one of the simpler efforts from a time when budgets were plentiful, and they could've afforded something flashier (the video for "Breakthru," for example, reportedly cost £300,000). Tonally, it is characteristic of a band that, by this point in its career, was happy to indulge in reminiscence, confident that their huge audience would understand their visual language.

It's pertinent to consider Mercury's appearance in particular in this video, sporting the yellow military jacket made iconic by the band's Wembley Stadium concert in 1986. Three years later and deep into a battle with the illness that would eventually kill him, the singer's appearance is beginning to publicly change. Later videos would see him become increasingly sallow, but "The Miracle" is one of the earliest public acknowledgments that things were changing: to see him in the same jacket used at the height of the band's stadium-conquering powers, now visibly deteriorating, suggests a decision made by someone with a remarkable sense of duty.

"The Invisible Man"

Queen took a certain delight in reflecting contemporary and future society through their music videos, and in "The Invisible Man," they achieve this by lampooning the emergent home video game market (both Sega's Mega Drive and Nintendo's Game Boy were launched in the same year). Simultaneously, they also referred back to the domestic drudgery they wistfully mocked five years previously in the video for "I Want to Break Free" by depicting the young son in a bickering suburban family suddenly terrorized by video game characters (the band). The domesticity owes a debt to scenes of the humdrum life of the McFly family from *Back to the Future* but also predates a much more American style of music video that reached its zenith with John Landis's video for Michael Jackson's "Black or White." The Landis video famously featured Macaulay Culkin and George Wendt in comedic roles, with Culkin's role in particular bearing a strong resemblance to the child role in "The Invisible Man."

Queen's video is full of visual tics and details that both enrich the domestic setting and show the band's visual sensibility at its most self-satisfied. The kid's T-shirt, for example, is emblazoned with "The Beach Blobs," which isn't an especially funny joke or a convincing name for a parent-baiting band along the lines of the Beastie Boys. Again, the self-reference in Queen's music videos is in evidence in the deliberate placing of a Queen poster in the kid's bedroom (specifically the album cover for *The Miracle*) and the intentionally egregious and gauche Brian May guitar solo, which is accompanied by multiple superimposed Brian Mays, each with lasers spouting from the end of his guitar.

Also present is some digital wizardry that looks painfully dated to contemporary eyes but would, at the time of release, have been relatively competent. The band sports generically futuristic outfits and moves in a robotic judder to suit the video game aesthetic (save for John Deacon, who bobs agitatedly throughout and wears a Stetson). If there is a general statement or ideological thrust in the video, it reaches a denouement when the kid replaces his own cap with Deacon's Stetson, thereby becoming trapped in the video game itself, presumably so we conclude that video games are a tempting evil in which it is all too easy to become imprisoned. This makes for a typically broad-strokes message in line with other Queen videos of the period ("Scandal" = "newspapers are bad," "Breakthru" = "here's a train literally breaking through a brick wall in pursuit of romance") but one delivered with a visual verve quite independent of anything they'd done before.

25

Live Aid

Was It the Greatest Rock Performance of All Time?

One of the great ironies in Queen's history as a band is that in a career defined by ever-complexifying live concerts designed to be as immersive and advanced as contemporary technology would allow, the performance that sealed their immortality in pop culture was one of their very simplest. It took place during daylight hours with no sign of modified staging, no canopy of customized lights, no stunt costumes, and no flash-bangs. They were onstage for twenty-one minutes, not the usual two hours, during which they would normally have time to create, manipulate, and maintain an atmosphere all their own.

Queen was halfway down the bill. They were not even close to being the most important thing about Live Aid.

Freddie Mercury on stage with John Deacon at Live Aid.   *Alan Davidson/Shutterstock*

How Did Queen End Up Playing Live Aid?

It's safe to say Queen was not at the peak of their powers in the first half of 1985. Their appearances at Sun City in South Africa had given them a cultural tarring that most of the rock establishment felt was wholly deserving. And while *The Works* was undoubtedly a popular album that spawned big singles, there was a wider feeling that the band was irrelevant, overtaken: a feeling also present within the band itself. Treadmilling their way between albums and tours and playing to the same crowds in the same cavernous and impersonal venues had rendered them bored of their lot and, thanks to their colossal South African misstep, very much out of favor with the prevailing climate.

On paper, there would've been a considerable list of artists who would be more deserving of and appropriate for a slot at Live Aid, which had aims to be the single greatest pop music event the world had ever seen. The brainchild of

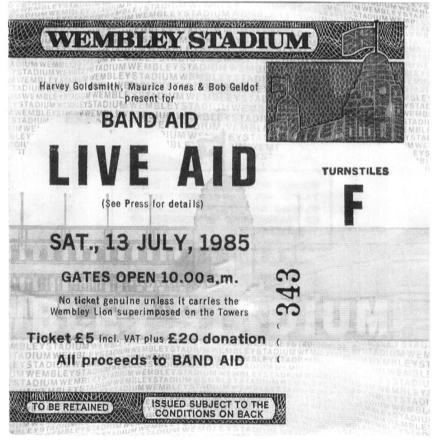

Ticket stub for Live Aid.   *Martin Skala, QueenConcerts.com*

Bob Geldof, singer of the Boomtown Rats and the man who called Brian May to secure the band's appearance, and Midge Ure of Ultravox, the concert was a televised, dual-venue, multi-artist stadium concert staged to raise money for the worsening famine in Ethiopia: in short, the modern zenith of celebrity fund-raising. Confirmed for the July 13 Wembley Stadium show was a veritable roll call of rock royalty current and emerging: U2, the Who, Paul McCartney, Elton John, David Bowie, Sting, and more. Queen would follow Dire Straits in the late afternoon, quite a distance from the headlining slots to be taken by the likes of McCartney and the Who.

Out of place, out of favor, very possibly out of practice: Queen was very, very nervous. And they were about to play for a television audience of 1.9 billion people, at that time the largest in history.

Why Was Queen's Performance So Acclaimed?

Footage of Queen in rehearsal for their Live Aid set (discussed in the introduction to this book) captures what is for some the absolute essence of the band's strengths: a collegiate and professional approach to conjuring magic. The alchemical fusion of nerves and adrenaline can account for only so much of what eventually happened in those mere minutes onstage. The rest was accumulated across a decade of huge shows, of accrued reflexes that could control an audience with the bend of a finger on a steel-wound string. Their rehearsal time was to exercise those muscles, to remind the limbs of the band that this was how to do it.

When British comedy duo Smith and Jones (who had almost no worldwide profile and seemed still more incongruous dressed as policemen) invited Queen to take the Wembley Stadium stage, the band that jogged into position was the product of this combined preparation. Mercury's heels touched his backside, such was the spring in his step. Standing around the halfway line at Wembley Stadium, it must have been difficult to pick out which of the figures onstage were the artists and which were the technical staff, of which there seemed to be dozens. When it came to the first notes played, it was not the muted, atmospheric tape recording they might have used on tour. A few customary plinks of the piano from Mercury and some taps of the snare from Taylor to check sound levels to assure themselves everything was switched on, and "Bohemian Rhapsody" begins. It's the behavior of a band still in rehearsal mode, cracking on with the work that needs to be completed. Even their clothing, utterly casual without a hint of costumery apart from Mercury's vest and studded armband, was that of jobbing musicians, not stadium-filling millionaires.

But far from being clinical as a result, it shows Queen to be essentially composed not of spectacle and bluster but of hits and confidence. As "Bohemian

Rhapsody" segues into "Radio Ga Ga," it's clear the band had settled, with Mercury running backward and forward with his mouth open in awe of the occasion, of the sounds his bandmates were making. At this point, Live Aid became fun for Mercury, and the song is where much of the set's reputation as an exemplar rock performance comes from. "Radio Ga Ga" had been a hit in the United Kingdom, but the Roger Taylor–penned live favorite had never been put to the test like this before. It wasn't even that the audience needed to be cajoled or encouraged to participate with the clap-clap-praise chorus; their reaction was instantaneous.

The Wembley Stadium concert's simultaneous equivalent in the United States took place at John F. Kennedy Stadium in Philadelphia, Pennsylvania, and when Queen began to play in London, the footage was relayed on giant screens to the assembled crowd (Queen's set began at 6:41 p.m. Greenwich Mean Time, five hours ahead of Eastern Daylight Time in Philadelphia). Even across the continents and without the band actually being there, 90,000 people clapped along too. This was a communal musical experience the likes of which the band hadn't dared anticipate, and it was only to become more potent.

The Note Heard round the World

A regular feature of Queen's live shows was a call-and-response–style series of wordless, improvised snippets sung by Mercury. Typically, these would be short phrases, like "Ay-oh," beginning simply so that the audience could mimic them competently but soon increasing in complexity so that Mercury might confuse them. This began several years before Live Aid and would often end with the audience "beating" Mercury by managing to keep up with his vocals. He would sometimes retort with a "You bastards can sing higher than I can!" or a simple "Fuck you," but at Live Aid, it was a far less adversarial exchange. The climax of his "Ay-oh" routine, one five-second held note (a high A, in full chest voice) and its response, became known as "the note heard round the world," an emblem of what Live Aid hoped to achieve. And rather than signing off with a clipped insult, Mercury simply tells the crowd, "Alright!," his encouragement more in keeping with the tone of the day.

This continued as Mercury pirouetted with camera operators during "Hammer to Fall," mimicked Brian May's guitar poses with his microphone stand, and continually sprinted around the stage when he wasn't at the piano. He was every inch the entertainer, sweating with the joy and effort. But mingled within all the good-natured stage work from Mercury are several delightfully inappropriate reminders that this was a man with a reputation as a serial sex adventurer, most unsuited to a teatime television audience. Mercury can be seen performing a cunnilingus mime between the climactic notes of "Radio Ga Ga" before relaxing into a come-hither legs-akimbo pose on the floor, then later masturbating the microphone stand and bending to present his behind to the audience during "Hammer to Fall." Even if the band's surprisingly relaxed appearance and the overarching do-good nature of the event had taken the more extreme edges off Mercury's persona, he was still keen to express his brazen sexuality on the biggest stage in the world.

Champions Once More

"Crazy Little Thing Called Love" breezes past with a pleasingly raucous final verse and chorus (but is essentially unchanged from its usual live incarnation), as does "We Will Rock You," but it's the closing "We Are the Champions" that brings the set back to its world-dominating best. Viewed with contemporary eyes, again, the hypocrisy of Queen's appearance at Live Aid is only exacerbated by this most self-aggrandizing of songs, but the band's invincibility to such accusations was now complete. By this point in the running order, there had been genuine stars on the bill, but performances had arguably been lacking in something truly spectacular. Tonally, the occasion begged for an artist to take control and assure the 72,000 ticket holders that this was indeed an A-list event, ticket holders who had so far enjoyed the rather less bombastic tones of Spandau Ballet, Nik Kershaw, and Sade.

The performance of "We Are the Champions" wasn't technically flawless. Mercury slides into the notes at the limits of his register (he would customarily leave some of these to Roger Taylor in the live scenario), but the sweat on his shoulders twinkling under the stage lights as the mid-July evening descended is more important. Even this band, one so preoccupied with perfection and precision in their performances, could see that the nuances of the occasion mattered more than simply hitting their cues. Just look at John Deacon's clear and unassailable glee, his eager bowing to the crowd.

Closing with a signature song (they could've chosen several) was, indirectly, an ingenious maneuver, and the resulting spike in sales of both *The Works* and their first greatest-hits volume was only one example of the evidence required to conclude that this was a landmark performance. In an infamous televised outburst, Geldof told the nation when BBC presenter David Hepworth started giving out an address for postal donations, "Fuck the address, let's get the numbers," a mixture of sore disappointment with the current fund-raising total of £1.2 million and also having watched Queen's set and being suitably galvanized into action.

Mercury and May returned to the stage later in the evening to perform an acoustic version of "Is This the World We Created?," a song they admitted appeared to be custom written for the occasion. It's a footnote to the day as a whole, but this nugget of quiet toward the climax of the day is a far more exposed and polished affair than the band's main set.

Their early evening performance, though, was an undiluted triumph, perhaps the biggest in Queen's history. They had, against the odds, succeeded in turning the public back toward them, reminding their lapsed audience that there really was no other band like this. But the longer-lasting effects of Live Aid were still to be seen. This twenty-one-minute performance was inarguably key to the band's second life and eventual cultural immortality. Whether or not it really was the greatest rock performance in history is arguable and ultimately immaterial: all that really mattered was that it was the *right* rock performance for that moment.

26

Queen Reenergized

A Kind of Magic

There's nothing like a television audience of 1.9 billion people to remind you that you've got a salable product and a back catalog of indestructible hits. That's what Queen discovered after Live Aid, and it was a realization that took them to their widest concert audience yet.

Gimme Fried Chicken

With this great reemergence of the band into the public arena came a new ease of being around one another, a desire to be working hard toward a singular musical goal. Nowhere is this more clearly expressed than in the video for "One Vision," the band's first new single after Live Aid. Recorded at Musicland rather than Mountain Studios, it still captures the band in the throes of this new comfortably collaborative character and is one of the few songs by this point attributed to all four composers. Corralled by Mercury, the band began recording sessions in September 1985, just two months after their twenty-one immortal minutes onstage at Wembley Stadium, and the mood was invigorating. (A cynical interpretation would conclude that the band collectively noticed there was money to be made on the back of this recaptured relevance, but a juggernaut brand of this size doesn't get to where Queen did without noticing these things.)

Ideologically as much as musically, the song is everything the band had worked toward. It's not overstating its importance in the songbook to label it as one of their most significant works, thanks to the remarkable discipline it displays. Synthesizers are, by now, an expected part of the Queen sound, but their use here is not overbearing or a novelty: they are integral to the song's sound, not just a decorative addition to it. The original idea for the song's lyrics was Taylor's, inspired in part by no loftier source than Martin Luther King Jr.'s "I Have a Dream" speech, but eventually the words were pulled around by Mercury and the rest of the band in a fit of workshopping.

When the King-inspired midsection arrives ("I had a dream when I was young, a dream of sweet illusion"), it is quite summarily stamped on by one of Mercury's wildest screams, a seemingly unguarded studio moment that nonetheless conveys the rock abandon that runs through the whole album. And finally, as if to ram home the point that the band was now so effortlessly creating music again after more than a decade of prima-donna-ish battles for authorship, "One Vision" concludes with another in-studio elaboration: rather than finishing on a chorus of "one vision" as expected, we instead hear a multi-layered vocal of "fried chicken," the result of endless fiddling with the lyrics to make them scan correctly with the melody. Studio outtakes show Mercury, limp and with folded lyric sheet in hand, singing variations on the chorus, such as "one dump, one turd, two tits, John Deacon."

Was *A Kind of Magic* Actually Just the *Highlander* Sound Track Album?

Never a band to shy away from a promotional opportunity, the album also acted as a companion piece to the fantasy movie *Highlander*. Its status not as an official sound track but as a themed album that lends its songs to the movie was a mite confusing to audiences who were worried about another album of *Flash Gordon* soundscape burbling and pastiche, but that didn't stop the album from becoming one of the band's biggest sellers in the United Kingdom. It landed immediately at number one and remained on the album chart for sixty-three weeks throughout the second half of 1986 and deep into 1987, the kind of lingering hit the band had perhaps thought was now behind them.

In the event, the songs inspired by themes from *Highlander* were "Princes of the Universe," "Who Wants to Live Forever," "Don't Lose Your Head," "Gimme the Prize (Kurgan's Theme)," "One Year of Love," and "A Kind of Magic": six out of a total of nine.

"A Kind of Magic" represents the absolute maturation of Roger Taylor's songwriting for Queen, proving him to be the band's latest bloomer but also one of its more effective. A restrained pop boogie, the song is also notable for its cinematic video in which a caped Mercury enters a dilapidated theater and charms the remaining three band members into life with a mix of animated characters (who appear on the album's cover) and pyrotechnics. This high-end, shiny production was in keeping with a new visual dimension to the band. Although Queen's videos had often been ambitious, there was now a curated feel to them, one fully conversant with and chameleonic among several cinematic styles.

Both Mercury's "Princes of the Universe" and May's "Gimme the Prize" feature the same pulsing guitar riffs, which act as a binding across the album and the ferocity of which caused the director of *Highlander*, Russell Mulcahy, to describe the latter as his least favorite of the band's songs for the movie. Both songs are remarkable for their unpretentious use of volume and distortion, an almost anti-radio series of guitar sirens accompanying some of Mercury's most rasping vocals. This was not so much a return to early metal influences (see chapter 9) as it was an exploration of the current vogue pop metal, a sound that had been brought into the mainstream by Poison and Van Halen, albeit with a markedly operatically dark edge.

"Who Wants to Live Forever" can be counted as one of May's crowning achievements in sophistication, but he achieved it with some help from conductor and composer Michael Kamen (who went on to write scores for the *Die Hard* movies and *Robin Hood: Prince of Thieves*). Despite being seen playing their instruments in the song's music video, there's no role for Taylor or Deacon in the song. May and Mercury share the vocals across verses with no clear beat or tempo in a style that borrows heavily from operatic recitative, made all the more explicit by Mercury's appearance in the video, itself an impression of classical sophistication (suit, bow tie, and pocket square). With its reliance on these tropes associated with operatic and classical traditions, it's a song that diversifies Queen's core sound in a way the band would revisit on their *Innuendo* album.

A Kind of Magic is perhaps the most consistent album from the second half of their main recording activity, more cohesive than *The Works* and more comfortable than *Hot Space*. But it also marks a transition into their later period, one that would see their studio experiments continue to flourish with an inimitably variable success rate. But first, there was the matter of the band's biggest concerts yet.

Queen's Last-Ever Tour

For reasons that were to become painfully plain in the following year, the concert tour that supported the release of *A Kind of Magic* would be Queen's last. Indeed, the final concert of the tour would be the band's final performance in its classic configuration, making their Knebworth show momentous in ways more important than sheer scale and spectacle. Mercury's health concerns as the HIV he contracted developed into an incurable AIDS diagnosis would go on to define the final years of the band, but for this album, anything less than the biggest possible concert expression of their new material would've been considered a failure. The *Magic* tour, as it became known, was the pinnacle of Queen's work as a live band. Promoter Harvey Goldsmith noted that ticket sales for the two Wembley shows and further concerts at Newcastle's St. James' Park and Manchester's Maine Road stadium sold out in a matter of hours, the fastest he'd ever seen.

Mercury raises his crown aloft in salute to the crowd at Wembley Stadium in July 1986.
Alan Davidson/Shutterstock

With Spike Edney in tow to facilitate the band's reliance on synthesizers, the shows rolled through only the biggest and most cavernous arenas in Europe (there were no legs outside of the band's home continent this time). Set lists nodded to all eras of the band's history, even to the point where the band would reintroduce the rock 'n' roll covers section toward the end of each show, meaning songs like "Tutti Frutti" were suddenly back in the repertoire. But in the main, the material was picked to represent Queen as they were at that moment. Each show began with "One Vision," the perfect depiction of the band as welcome returnees, and concluded with an almost song-by-song re-creation of their Live Aid set: "Bohemian Rhapsody," "Hammer to Fall," and "Crazy Little Thing Called Love" and then encores of "Radio Ga Ga," "We Will Rock You," and "We Are the Champions."

Mercury in front of the Wembley Stadium crowd in his iconic yellow military jacket.
Alan Davidson/Shutterstock

Knebworth: The Last Real Queen Show?

By 1986, Knebworth House had played host to a litany of legendary acts for one-off large-scale concerts, earning it a reputation as the pinnacle of U.K. live arenas. Pink Floyd in 1975, the Rolling Stones in 1976, the Beach Boys in 1980: all of them had audiences of more than 100,000 people, but Queen managed to pack in a record-equaling 120,000 on August 9, 1986. Billed as "A Night of Summer Magic," the lineup also featured fellow Live Aid performers Status Quo, along with Big Country and Belouis Some. The capacity wasn't quite as big as some of Queen's international shows in previous years, but as far as the band was concerned, live dates didn't get much bigger than this.

Footage taken to document the momentous show for a future video release shows queues of coaches lining the roads around the venue, sun-drenched revelers bellowing along to Status Quo's "Rocking All Over the World," and truckloads of equipment being ferried across the site by quad bike. Naturally, the band didn't concern themselves too much with the preparations and arrived in a personalized helicopter that took off from a helipad on the Thames in

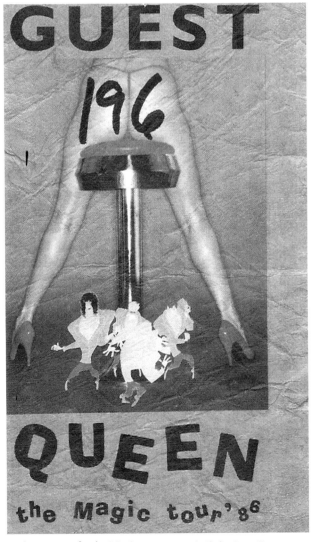

Backstage pass for the *Magic* tour.   *Martin Skala, QueenConcerts.com*

central London, then swirled over the Knebworth crowd before depositing the musicians backstage. Mercury emerges in a loud, oversize shirt. Deacon ducks the spinning rotor blades with completely unnecessary caution. Taylor trades warm-up vocal exercises with Mercury. During the show, May's mid-set guitar solo lasted for nine minutes. When it came to Mercury's a cappella call-and-response with the crowd, he brought the section to a close and congratulated his vocal sparring partners: "You fuckers are good, I tell you." Crown held aloft during May's closing arrangement of "God Save the Queen," Mercury utters his last words onstage with the band he'd invaded, shaped, misguided, and rescued on countless occasions: "Good night, sweet dreams, we love you." It was another in a long line of huge Queen shows, at this point seemingly unlikely to be their swan song in the live arena.

The show itself had a tragic coda when a Queen fan, twenty-one-year-old Thomas McGuigan, was stabbed in an altercation near the front of the stage and subsequently died. The emergency services were quick to level blame at the event organizers and the sheer density of the capacity crowd, but a spokesperson for the band at the time described the event's organization in glowing terms, adding that the band members (all of whom had immediately departed the show for various vacation locations) were "horrified" by the incident.

Not Burning Out but Fading Away . . .

As we see in the coming chapters, it would be wrong to call the Knebworth show the last concert Queen ever played. May and Taylor would perform for crowds of this size again, very much under the Queen banner, but Knebworth was still a turning point in the life of the band.

After the success of A Kind of Magic and the accompanying frenzied period of activity had passed came the longest gap between albums that Queen had yet experienced. Before the band herded itself back together again, there would be extended spells of musical dabbling for each member.

27

Queen Becomes Equals

"Do I Look Like I'm Dying?"

In October 1986 as he was strolling through Heathrow Airport, the very same place he'd thrown baggage from plane to carousel when he was a teenager, Freddie Mercury was accosted by a journalist from the *Sun* newspaper. Mercury had been on a shopping trip to Japan to buy furnishings for his Kensington home and was in no mood to be questioned. The journalist, Hugh Whittow, asked Mercury about rumors that his sexual promiscuity had resulted in a major health issue, namely, an AIDS diagnosis. Whittow was met with a frosty response from Mercury, who asked, "Do I look like I'm dying?" But by this time, news of Mercury's visit to a Harley Street clinic to be screened for the debilitating disease had already been the talk of the national papers.

"I've had a wonderful time in Japan," Whittow quoted Mercury as saying before he climbed into his chauffeur-driven car, "and now I've got to put up with this rubbish. Now go away and leave me alone."

This exchange is a fair barometer of how the British tabloid press was treating Mercury at the time. The perceived luridity of his private life was manna for journalists with inches to fill and no doubt fueled Queen's already dismissive collective attitude toward such publications. But it's also notable for Mercury's reaction: worry, indignance, a plea for solitude. The division between Mercury the performer and Mercury the shy retirer had long been in evidence, but now it was being paraded more publicly than ever.

The truth, of course, is that Freddie Mercury *was* dying. According to his partner, Jim Hutton, his diagnosis was eventually confirmed in April 1987. It was supposed to be a secret, but given the increasing scrutiny and attention from the tabloids, that seemed an impossibly naive dream.

What Did Queen Do between Albums?

Four men of means and creative energy to spare couldn't be silent for long, so the intervening period between Queen's Knebworth show in 1986 and their eventual regrouping in the studio in January 1988 was a typically fruitful one.

Mercury achieved a long-held ambition and released his second solo album, a collaboration with operatic soprano Montserrat Caballé titled *Barcelona* (see chapter 37), while Roger Taylor formed an entirely new band called the Cross. After writing and recording an album of new songs (titled, with typical subtlety, *Shove It*), he took out a newspaper advertisement scouting for musicians who could take the material on tour. Queen regular Spike Edney joined Taylor and three hired hands for an extensive tour of the United Kingdom and Germany, with Taylor relishing his opportunity to stand at the front of the stage on a project he could call his own. *Shove It* featured all the other members of Queen in various auxiliary roles, most notably Mercury singing backing vocals on "Heaven for Everyone," which would go on to be reworked for Queen's final album featuring Mercury, 1995's *Made in Heaven*.

May loaned his guitar skills to Genesis guitarist Steve Hackett's solo album *Fastback 86* and produced a hit single sung by his second wife, actress Anita Dobson. The song, titled "Anyone Can Fall in Love," was a version of the theme music from *EastEnders* with added lyrics, the hugely popular British soap opera of which Dobson was a major star in the role of Angie Watts. Musically, it had very little synonymity with anything connected to May or Queen and, seemingly, was a purely affectionate gesture.

John Deacon, not usually one to take on more extracurricular musical work when privacy was an option, worked on some small projects between Queen albums. Deacon cowrote the song "No Turning Back" with the Immortals for inclusion on the sound track to *Biggles*, a distinctly British children's literary character given a quite spectacularly underperforming cinematic treatment, released in 1986. He also appeared in the music video for "Stutter Rap (No Sleep til Bedtime)," a novelty hit by Morris Minor and the Majors that parodied the Beastie Boys' then omnipresent "No Sleep till Brooklyn" and made it to number four on the U.K. singles chart. Deacon can be seen in the video playing electric guitar and wearing a blue wig.

It Ain't Much I'm Asking: Queen Becomes Equals

In the history of rock 'n' roll, one depressingly dry and ego-driven aspect of the music publishing process has been the downfall of countless ensembles: credit, specifically, songwriting credit and the apportioning of revenue based on that credit. From the Beatles on, the thorny issue of claiming certain musical ideas within songs has traditionally been one that leads to arguments, breakups, and legal disputes. To give a more contemporary example, the Kings of Leon has admitted in interviews that there would be interpersonal fights in the recording studio because someone happened to pick up a tambourine during the recording of songs that went on to become huge commercial hits.

As a band made up of stylistically diverse composers who would freely noodle with each other's songs, Queen was about as prone to this pitfall as it was possible to be. When the extent of the collective noodling on "One Vision" became so mingled as to obscure Roger Taylor's original impetus for the song, the credit went to all four band members. Although the rest of *A Kind of Magic* was a mix of solo songwriting credits, it was still a watershed moment: as such, with their thirteenth album, *The Miracle*, Queen joined the likes of the Doors, the Sex Pistols, and Black Sabbath by crediting all songs to all writers. Musical elements are still traceable to individual members, but the ideology of the decision represents the creative fulfillment of what was becoming increasingly inevitable: to carry on, Queen had to put the collective in front of the individual.

Even the album's cover stays true to their new united front: a photo composite of all four band members' faces, using the now forgotten Quantel Paintbox, much loved by television networks creating graphics and logos for their news programming. Although mildly unsettling to look at and dated in hindsight, the morphed super-face has an almost Mount Rushmore quality to it, an endlessly examinable piece.

What Happened to the Moustache?

One of the most notable elements of the cover is the absence of Mercury's moustache, which had now been purged. The erasure meant much more than the simple removal of some facial hair: one of the band's most iconic features was now missing, an emblem of the band's heyday lost. It would be convenient to conclude that Mercury's decision to lose the moustache was due to the mounting tabloid pressure and retrograde coverage of what was quite openly described as the "gay plague," an attempt to distance himself from any outré references to his sexual activities (some newspapers had by now settled on "bisexual" as a comfortable catchall label for Mercury's persuasion).

But the truth is more likely a simple desire to change characters, as was Mercury's wont every few years. His new look on the album cover is almost automaton, blankly clean and perfect. Not for the first time, there's a possibly unknowing nod to Kraftwerk, specifically *Trans-Europe Express*, with the pristine appearance of all four faces and the blank stares on them.

Due to an overlap with the recording and promotion of Mercury's *Barcelona* project, the cover from *The Miracle* doesn't represent Mercury's look from the associated music videos, in which he often appears businesslike and lightly bearded. The beard's presence and thickness would fluctuate not with stylistic demand but rather with the severity of Mercury's AIDS-related symptoms (facial blemishes and gauntness were common as ailments took hold).

Miracle Workers

Queen eventually entered the studio to begin sessions for *The Miracle* in January 1988, the first time they'd done so since late 1985. The gap was so uncustomarily large that the album originally went under the working title of *The Invisible Men* until it was amended shortly before release. Recording took place across multiple locations as usual, mainly at Olympic and Townhouse Studios in London and their own Mountain Studios complex. However, the protracted recording process lasted an entire year, with a total of around thirty song ideas bandied about for possible inclusion. The process of whittling down these ideas was exhaustive but efficient: song nuggets were not seen through to their completion, and only those deemed the cream of the crop were developed. Regular producer Reinhold Mack yielded control to David Richards (who eventually went on to buy Mountain Studios from Queen in 1995) and took work elsewhere, seeing albums like Extreme's self-titled debut through to completion.

The first evidence that Queen had, in fact, returned after a lengthier gap than fans were accustomed to was the album's first single, "I Want It All," which arrived on May 2, 1989. Written by May (though credited, like all the songs on the album, to Queen), it displays an aggressive lyrical streak the band hadn't foregrounded as much since songs like "Death on Two Legs." The lyrics see Mercury's take on a Rocky-esque character ("A young fighter screaming, with no time for doubt, with the pain and anger can't see a way out"), something it would've been easy to see in himself given his circumstances. The song's video bears out this new seriousness, showing the band in performance surrounded by industrial flight cases, lit in stark monochrome and without a hint of humor that the band would so often display even with their more wrought material (e.g., "It's a Hard Life").

The album itself begins with "Party," a peculiarly downbeat experiment that separates Queen's musical elements from one another, Mercury's stacked vocal harmonies accompanied only by percussion for vast portions of the song and May's Jeff Wayne–esque guitar broken down into nugget-like solos. But it's the lyrics here that are the most interesting: although the party itself is very much part of the song, it's the aftermath and specifically the hangover that Mercury dwells on, a far cry from the abandon of "Don't Stop Me Now," where the thought of a difficult morning after couldn't have been further from his mind.

Many songs on *The Miracle* display a curious mix of wonder and anger, even introspection, making it one of the band's most emotionally raw expressions. The manner in which those emotions are expressed is distinctly void of subtlety, affirmation again that the tone really had changed inside the band. The album's title track, also released as the final single from the album in November 1989, dabbles in such lofty themes as world peace, the enormity of Mother Nature, intercontinental war, and in vitro fertilization and concludes with a singsong plea for the time "when we can all be friends." It's a remarkable composition in terms of its musical complexity and sharp tonal shifts, but it's the broad strokes of the lyrics that say more about the fruits of their more collaborative songwriting approach.

On a less successful note, May's "Scandal" is a rather elementary stab at the press (see chapter 17), ostensibly about the guitarist's new relationship with Anita Dobson and the invasion of his privacy as his previous marriage broke down. But given the arguably more invasive tactics used against Mercury in tabloid discussion of his health, it's impossible not to associate Mercury's plight with the song's content over May's.

Coming to Terms with the End

There's a heartbreaking moment during a BBC Radio 1 interview from May 1989, just a week after the release of *The Miracle*, with all four members of the band when host Mike Read asks if there's any chance of Queen touring the album. After Roger Taylor politely passes the buck, it falls to Mercury, who by this time was only too aware of the limits to his physical abilities, to answer the question. Stumbling, he eventually, simply and quietly, says, "Oh dear," and improvises a response, citing a desire to break the cycle of recording and touring relentlessly. It's a rare unguarded moment toward the end of a career that saw Mercury fight hard to retain composure at all times. Such a raw example of his human honesty, electing not to perform for an interviewer, sticks out like an upturned nail in a carpet. Mercury is, however, clear that he is the main reason the band won't tour.

The constant struggle to keep any hint of Mercury's condition under wraps was often too much to bear. In one 1986 interview in Hungary, before the recording of what became Queen's *Live in Budapest* live video, Mercury told his interviewer about the possibility of coming back to play another show in years to come: "If I'm still alive, I'll come back."

Interviews with the other members of the band after Mercury's death state that the exact nature of his diagnosis remained a mystery until later on, specifically before they went into the studio to record what would become *Innuendo*, but it's clear that the general feeling was that *something* wasn't right, even though Mercury himself certainly knew. Whether it was the AIDS diagnosis of which the newspapers seemed so certain or some unknown issue that would break the band apart, it was enough to bring these four individuals, who had spent so much of the past decade finding reasons to stick together and not pursue other projects, closer together, united in the knowledge that the clock, whatever it might represent, was ticking.

28

Heading Out to Sea

Innuendo

Rushing Headlong on Borrowed Time

Public and press speculation about Freddie Mercury's health was becoming almost unbearably fierce. But in a manner really achievable only by those with a certain level of fame and notoriety, the Michael Jacksons of this world, there was no official word on why Mercury appeared so terribly thin onstage in February 1990 at the BRIT Awards, dwarfed by his baby-blue suit as Brian May accepted the band's lifetime achievement award. Before the four of them shuffle off quietly to the polite applause of the British music industry, Mercury leans into the microphone and utters his last words in public: "Thank you, good night."

The next day, the front page of the *Sun* newspaper featured a picture of a wide-eyed Mercury in the back of a car as he left London's Groucho Club under the headline "Are You OK Fred?" The accompanying story, written by Piers Morgan long before his rise to notoriety, quotes "close friends" who attribute his weight loss and "gaunt" appearance to Mercury's desire to shed a few pounds and his lack of stage makeup.

By now, Mercury knew his fate. He had contracted the HIV virus, but it had now developed into AIDS, the second and final phase of a process that had become common. Mercury and the rest of the band, indeed anyone in the entertainment industry, would be all too aware of what this most recent diagnosis would mean. The band's renewed work ethic, a seed planted during the recording of *The Miracle*, was about to become all the more frenzied as Mercury made it clear that this would likely be the last time they worked together. To escape the constant attention of newspaper journalists, the band returned to Mountain Studios and the calmer climes of Lake Geneva, where they could focus their efforts. Any press inquiries were met with answers stating that Mercury was simply well and working, an economic half-truth at best.

Mercury told his bandmates he would work on the album "until I fucking drop." For his part, he almost did.

Don't Take Offense at My Innuendo

Queen's fourteenth album—and their final album recorded with all four members present—is aptly one of their most musically shocking. *Innuendo*, from its coy title on, contains the band's most purely experimental work in years. By now, they had become such sophisticated dabblers with multiple musical palettes that the added pressure of Mercury's declining health turned the album into a splurge of barely regulated ideas, again with joint songwriting credit going simply to Queen.

This scattergun approach is audible from the first notes of the album. The title track is one of the darkest and strangest songs the band ever recorded, not simply or self-consciously strange in any wacky sense but strange for its sharp turns, its ornate lyrics, and its appointment of Yes guitarist Steve Howe for an extended instrumental interlude. It bears comparison with Maurice Ravel's visionary 1928 orchestral piece *Boléro* thanks to its use of a snare drum *ostinato* (a musical term for any repetitive musical phrase, literally "obstinate" in Italian), a piece that had a working title of, appropriately enough, *Fandango*.

The song is, like "Bohemian Rhapsody" and "The Prophet's Song" before it, divided loosely into three parts. After the deliberately sluggish rock opening, Steve Howe's flamenco-inspired midsection is a complete stylistic about-face, the result of Howe simply passing through Montreux toward the end of the album's recording sessions and being cajoled by his old friend Brian May into an intense afternoon of noodling. Howe remains the only non–Queen member to have played guitar on a Queen record. Howe's flamenco-inspired composition is then given over to a synthesized orchestral section, leading many to label the song as a spiritual sequel to "Bohemian Rhapsody."

While it's tempting to note the similarities to the band's most feted song, "Innuendo" is a different beast that captures the band in its darkest mood, from the furious Brian May guitar solo that takes up Howe's material to the return of the snare ostinato of the opening, a sinister bookending of the whole six-and-a-half-minute experience. There is a swirling, circular inevitability to the song that simply isn't present in any other work from their back catalog.

In the past when Queen lyrics have tackled issues of humanitarian upheaval (war, firearms, a general lack of fellowship among humans), it's commonly conveyed in broad strokes, an urge for the listener to take action against these societal ills. But with "Innuendo," there is a more nihilistic and vague acknowledgment that these ills are so pervasive as to be unstoppable: "Our lives dictated by tradition, superstition, false religion, through the eons and on and on. . . . Yes, we'll keep on trying." Even in the song's video, created for the single release a month before the album arrived in February 1991, there is an unsettling abandon in the technologically bizarre mix of stop-motion animation, archive footage of the Nuremberg Rally, and highly stylized rotoscoped imagery of the band in performance (each member's style apes a particular artist: da Vinci, Picasso, Pollock, and so on).

Titling the song "Innuendo"—and indeed the album itself—acts as a comment on the band's sudden seriousness. Although songs on *The Miracle* had been more existential and worldly in theme, Mercury's deteriorating health throws all previous frivolity into sharp relief. His delivery of the line "Don't take offence at my innuendo" is dolefully plain, almost as if to address the long-term Queen fan: "I'll still laugh, but it's just not that funny any more."

I'm Coming Down with a Fever

Following the nihilism of "Innuendo" is an equally dark piece of lyrical desolation albeit dressed up in Mercury's still-sharp sense of humor. Written partly in collaboration with his close friend, actor and singer Peter Straker (Mercury had produced his 1977 album *This One's on Me* with Roy Thomas Baker), the lyrics can be read on the surface as simply a list of absurdities but also as a direct comment on Mercury's illness. Mental symptoms of the complications arising from AIDS can include discombobulation and confusion, and being aware of this, Mercury decided to capture in song the symptoms he worried he would encounter: "I'm coming down with a fever, I'm really out to sea. . . . This kettle is boiling over, I think I'm a banana tree."

According to Jim Hutton's memoirs, Mercury and Straker stayed up late into the night perfecting the madcap couplets, dissolving into fits of laughter as they became more and more outlandish. While it is heartening to imagine the stricken artist tackling his demons in such a way, the pressure of the circumstances was not lost on the rest of the band. When it came to making the music video for the song, the main issue was protecting Mercury from further speculation around his health despite the song obliquely addressing exactly that issue. Shot entirely in monochrome and starring a ghostly-looking Mercury in a thick wig; extra layers of clothing; and heavy makeup, it is the very essence of hiding in plain sight, retaining and even harnessing his flamboyance to disguise his illness. The visual cues in the video occupy the same tone as the song itself, rendering the whole experience simultaneously whimsical and nightmarish.

The cover art for the album and singles, all of it either by or inspired by the French artist and caricaturist Jean-Jacques Grandville, further intensifies the air of chaos. Grandville's drawing titled "Juggler of Universes" contains the same level of darkly gleeful disorder as the album it accompanies, its use as a major iconographic element of the *Innuendo* campaign an indicator of the tone within the songs.

Jean-Jacques Grandville's "Juggler of Universes," taken from his 1844 series of lithographs entitled *Un Autre Monde*.   *Wikimedia Commons / Public Domain*

Freddie's Farewell

In common with *The Miracle* before it, there is also a quiet sense of nostalgia and reflection running through *Innuendo*, exemplified nowhere better than on what would come to be known as Freddie Mercury's unofficial good-bye gesture to the world. But even divorced from this context, "These Are the Days of Our Lives" is very possibly the most sentimental song the band ever recorded. It's also interesting to note that the bulk of its musical composition was handled by Roger Taylor, by this late stage in the band's career a fully formed composer: how different his role seems at this point than the one occupied as simply the drummer who wrote the occasional track about girls or cars (or both together, of course).

Lyrically, it is entirely fixated on nostalgia and the notion that the best days are well and truly behind us. But more complicated than that, when Mercury claims that the rest of his life since those halcyon days of childhood elapsed has been "just a show," it is an elaborate and theatrical dismissal of a career that was inarguably spectacular and influential. It could sound haughty and ungrateful, even over-privileged in the wrong hands, but Mercury's gift of humanizing the lyrics of others works to his favor. Indelible context is, again, the poetic means by which a Queen song transcends the usual capabilities of a pop song.

It could be argued that the musical content of the song is inconsequential, that lyrics that apply so snugly to the singer delivering them could accompany any composition. And wouldn't it have been an apogee in Queen lore for those lyrics to be delivered over the top of a strident three-act progressive metal genre experiment? But to have these lyrics accompanied by one of Queen's softest musical works is a sign of the band's gradual slide into comfort. Although *Innuendo* as a whole contains some of their most shocking artistic statements, it's as if "These Are the Days of Our Lives" was never going to be anything other than wholly tasteful, perhaps even predictable.

The video, again shot in black and white to hide facial blotches and the ever-degrading pallor of Mercury's face, uses this tastefulness as a springboard for a few wilder touches. Nothing as wild as nude models riding bicycles or an orgiastic tribute to Nijinsky, but Mercury's sudden and knowing smile after he sings that life is "just a show" and his cat-plastered waistcoat are acknowledgments of that decadence and flamboyance. When it comes to the final line, that now iconic "I still love you," it is first delivered in song and then spoken again straight after, with a laugh and with a jazzy guitar run from Brian May just behind it, bringing levity to a statement that would be, for many people, Mercury's last.

The Final Curtain

In a video interview on the set of the music video for "These Are the Days of Our Lives," Roger Taylor describes Freddie Mercury as being able to get the best work out of his bandmates through his sheer drive and enthusiasm alone. This had been true for the band at various times throughout its life span with caveats: arguments over authorship, over musical ideas muffled by an overplayed guitar solo, over which songs would make suitable A-sides or even B-sides. For the *Innuendo* sessions, though, it seems the arguments were less about individual musical ideas and more about what could realistically be completed in the time afforded to the band.

Mercury's stamina was waning, and intense recording sessions would require periods of convalescence before resuming. Songs like "Don't Try So Hard" show Mercury's voice at the breaking point, veering from high falsetto into sharp screams. But the knowledge that there would be no tour to accompany this album also swayed its creative direction and made it more internal and inward-looking, allowing for stranger interludes, for example, "Bijou," with its inverted song structure placing a vocal solo at the middle of a guitar instrumental and "All God's People" with its hysterical preacher-man vibe. That song in particular was a hangover from Mercury's sessions for his collaborative *Barcelona* album with Montserrat Caballé, retooled for *Innuendo* as a confusing dream in which Mercury's exhortation to "Love, love and be free" comes with a dark caveat.

Even stranger is Mercury's parting ode to his pet cat Delilah in the song of the same name. One can only imagine Brian May's face when told by Mercury that he should use the Red Special, the instrument that defined rock guitar solos for more than a decade, to convincingly mimic the sound of a cosseted calico. "Delilah" has become a byword for Mercury's impishness and his dedication to traditionally camp notions of excess, placing all his artistic efforts in a song that could never be understood by its dedicatee.

The most poetically charged song from these sessions is "The Show Must Go On," specifically written about Mercury's declining abilities as a performer and delivered as he was experiencing the very thing he details in the lyrics. It wasn't the final vocal he recorded, but it was by some accounts one of the hardest to complete, the most physically draining. Written in close collaboration with Brian May in particular (Deacon and Taylor worked on the circular grind of the main chord sequence), the concerned guitarist was dubious about Mercury's ability to deliver what was turning into a grandstanding piece, a song that demanded a vocal intensity he would have found elementary just a few years earlier.

Armed and very likely numbed with shots of Stolichnaya vodka, Mercury was miraculously able to deliver enough takes to complete the song. It is littered with iconic lines that embody not only Mercury's performative spirit but also the cruel pressure under which it was placed: it is this tension that drives the song and makes it capable of breaking a heart. Mercury is messianic in his delivery of the song's midsection, convinced his life will not end but simply change (a belief that has no place in Zoroastrianism): "My soul is painted like the wings of butterflies, fairy tales of yesterday will grow but never die, I can fly my friends!"

It is of course tempting to retroactively interpret many of the band's lyrics with a sense of import or foretelling. But with the songs that make up *Innuendo*, it is a rare case in which pieces written shortly before the death of their composer can be said to comment directly on it, occupying the same almost mystical plane as David Bowie's *Blackstar* album some twenty-five years later. There is plenty more to the story of Mercury's final recordings on *Made in Heaven* that would follow posthumously, but as a farewell gesture, *Innuendo* is almost cosmically apposite.

29

Too Much Love Will Kill You

The Death of Freddie Mercury

In June 1991, during final sessions for *Innuendo*, Freddie Mercury announced that he was leaving the sanctuary of Montreux and Mountain Studios, where the band had been working as cheerfully as they could under the circumstances, and returning to his home in Kensington, West London. He didn't mention any plans to return, but neither did he mention any plans to stay there once he'd arrived.

Just two months earlier, a grainy photograph of Mercury covered the front page of the *Sun* newspaper under the headline "Tragic Face of Freddie Mercury." He's bundled up in a scarf and serious-faced, but he doesn't look as ill as he does, say, in the video for "Headlong" or "These Are the Days of Our Lives." Reading the newspapers in those months, it seemed that Mercury's end was expected, that it could happen at any moment. The truth was, as usual, more complicated, and his health and abilities had been fluctuating through recording sessions in Montreux. But this move back to Kensington was for a reason: Mercury was heading home for the last time, and he knew it.

In this final period of illness, he was tended to by friends and staff, notably his partner Jim Hutton, who would work in shifts with Mercury's chef Joe Fanelli and his personal assistant Peter Freestone. Also present were his longtime confidante Mary Austin, Dave Clark of the Dave Clark Five, Peter Straker, and his Queen bandmates. He remained positive in outlook, but the physical effects of Mercury's gradual degeneration were undeniably shocking. He lost his vision, and a persistent wound on his foot led to severe damage. Revealing the extent of the trauma to his foot during dinner with friends, Brian May recalled in 2017 that he was not disgusted, only upset at the pain through which Mercury was evidently going.

Peter Freestone recalls in a blog Mercury asking to see items in his art collection for the last time on November 20, 1991. They duly carried him to his favorite pieces, but he was still able to walk around the room and lucid enough to talk about them. He ate and drank less and less. Some accounts suggest his bones became brittle, breakable. Eventually, the strain of bronchial pneumonia he'd contracted became too much for his ailing immune system to cope with. On November 22, Jim Beach issued a statement to the press on behalf of Mercury, publicly confirming for the first time that he was suffering from AIDS. It read,

> Following the enormous conjecture in the press over the last two weeks, I wish to confirm that I have been tested HIV positive and have AIDS. I felt it correct to keep this information private to date to protect the privacy of those around me. However, the time has come now for my friends and fans around the world to know the truth and I hope that everyone will join with me, my doctors and all those worldwide in the fight against this terrible disease. My privacy has always been very special to me and I am famous for my lack of interviews. Please understand this policy will continue.

By 7 p.m. on November 24, he was dead. His parents were called to his bedside when it became clear that the end was suddenly imminent, but they didn't make it in time. Outside Garden Lodge, the floral tributes piled up in a fashion that prefigured the intense show of public grief after the death of Diana, Princess of Wales.

How Did the Press React?

The decision to maintain absolute silence in terms of an official acknowledgment that Mercury even had AIDS until barely a day before he died is testament to his fierce sense of privacy. The newspapers, of course, had been preparing their coverage in anticipation of the announcement. It was inevitably the tabloid press that featured Mercury's death most prominently and with the widest mix of angles. The *Sun* led with a picture of Mercury, arms outstretched and draped in a Union Jack flag, underneath the headline "Freddie Is Dead." The *Daily Star* opted for a picture of Mercury with fists clenched around his microphone stand, his face twisted in what could conveniently be either performative emotion or genuine anguish. The *Daily Record* displayed a simple headline of "Freddie Mercury Dead" and beneath that a subheading of "Now Mary [Austin] Gets His Cash."

In the United Kingdom, Health Minister Virginia Bottomley was moved to comment on Mercury's death and frame it as a catalyst for greater awareness, mentioning also the retirement of Magic Johnson from professional basketball due to his recent HIV diagnosis.

Just a week after Mercury's death, Brian May and Roger Taylor appeared on the breakfast television show *TVAM* to draw attention to the single rerelease of "Bohemian Rhapsody" (backed with "These Are the Days of Our Lives"), launched to raise money for the Terrence Higgins Trust. They also mooted the possibility of a large-scale tribute show, what would become the Freddie Mercury Tribute Concert. The interview is notable also for the bizarre appearance of TV magician Paul Daniels on the sofa next to May, presumably waiting his turn to be interviewed on breakfast television. Daniels is asked if he was a fan of Queen, and in a strangely admirable show of honesty, he admits that he had no interest in them whatsoever and that within a week psychic mediums will be claiming to be able to reach the late singer for comment. Taylor stares at fingernails, picking them occasionally.

The media reaction to the death of Freddie Mercury focused on his status as a non-heteronormative figure in the entertainment business, the first high-profile victim of what many of the papers had historically called in all seriousness the "gay plague." There were, in television news profiles and interviews with commentators, reminiscences and considerations of his huge impact on the music world, but the balance tipped more often toward discussion of his outwardly prolific sexual appetite and the symptoms of his medical condition.

Discussion and analysis of Mercury's death and the fallout for those around him continued to fill column inches and television screens for years beyond the event itself. Alleged bitter relations between Jim Hutton and Mary Austin became a national talking point in late 1994 when Hutton's memoir, *Mercury & Me*, was published, in which Hutton claims Austin evicted him from Mercury's Kensington mansion immediately after his death. Hutton himself died in 2010, also from AIDS. In a manner that now seems common, Mercury's death continued to reverberate. The deaths of both Michael Jackson and Prince in the decades that followed would conform to a similar pattern of press activity: initial lip service was paid to their musical influence, but the real meat of the coverage was in the medical, sexual, and social details. For Mercury, it still occurs with every significant Queen-related press event. Interviews with May and Taylor for their own projects, musical or otherwise, are more often than not headlined with a reference to Mercury. The media currency of his death remains stable.

What Happened to Freddie Mercury's Ashes?

In keeping with his Zoroastrian religious upbringing, Mercury's funeral was conducted almost entirely in Avestan, a language derived from Zoroastrian texts. It was a small affair in a small chapel and with a small guest list of around forty people. Among the attendees were his Queen bandmates, close personal friends like Mary Austin, as well as Elton John, pictured on the day ashen-faced in a tiny black cap and thick spectacles, almost as if it were a bespoke Elton John funeral outfit.

After the service, Mercury was cremated at Kensal Green Cemetery. It was Mercury's wish that his ashes be left in the care of Mary Austin, to be disposed of at a later date. Austin was also left Mercury's Garden Lodge mansion in Kensington, and according to some accounts, the ashes spent the next two years in Mercury's old bedroom before being scattered in a secret location. In a slightly ghoulish quirk of Queen fandom, the whereabouts of Mercury's ashes once they were scattered have been the topic of much discussion. Speculative locations include the foot of the cherry tree outside Garden Lodge (this was Jim Hutton's preferred theory); on the island of Zanzibar, where Mercury spent his first years; and on the shores of Lake Geneva, the place that had figured so heavily in his adult professional life.

In 2013, the *Daily Mail* reported on the discovery of a plaque at Kensal Green Cemetery that had presumably been there unnoticed for many years. On the plaque, below the name of Farrokh Bulsara and the dates of his birth and death, is a message in French: "Pour etre toujours pres de toi avec tout mon amour," which translates as "To always be near you with all my love." It is accompanied by one initial, "M," which could indicate that the plaque's organizer was Mary Austin. The plaque's very existence also deepens the mystery, as plaques are available to commemorate those whose ashes now lie in the cemetery's "scattering garden," indicating that Mercury's final resting place wasn't quite as romantic as some of the mooted possibilities. It does, however, put Mercury in the company of fellow scattered stars like Ingrid Bergman, Alan Rickman, and Christine Keeler. Among those buried (rather than cremated) in the same location are William Makepeace Thackeray, Wilkie Collins, and Harold Pinter. Wherever Mercury's remains did eventually settle, it's perfectly in keeping with his character that it be somewhere private, illustrious, and potentially unknown: a delicious mystery that continues beyond his demise.

What Next for Queen?

For Taylor, May, and Deacon, the arrival of the inevitable was no less painful for their having known it was coming. Famously, it would take several years before any kind of recorded musical activity would take place. Aside from the raw glare of the events around Mercury's death, the media scrutiny, and public outpouring of grief, this was still the loss of a beloved friend and companion who had built with them a cultural and industrial empire. There was a period of emotional turmoil to follow as the three remaining members struggled in various ways to get past the death of their friend, but first there was an army of Queen fans to help through a shared tragedy. They responded in the most natural way they could: they played together.

30

The Freddie Mercury Tribute Concert

Who Played?

With a public figure so watched and beloved as Freddie Mercury now gone, dead in almost romantically tragic circumstances, the expectation for some kind of public outpouring of grief and celebration of his life was high. As it happened, the idea of a tribute concert had been mooted by the remaining members of Queen the very night that Mercury died. It could only be at Wembley Stadium, the venue that had become synonymous with the band's reign as the biggest live act in Britain, if not the world.

May, Taylor, and Deacon would all anchor the concert, playing a greatest hits set with a gaggle of note-perfect backing singers, heartfelt acoustic tributes, and a revolving cast of guest musicians that saw Liza Minelli sharing a stage with James Hetfield of Metallica. These elements provided a similar chaos to proceedings that had pervaded the very same stadium at Live Aid back in 1985.

But before the main headlining Queen set, there would be a Live Aid–style series of mini-sets from the various guest performers, turning the whole concert into a three-hour extravaganza that took up the evening of Monday, April 20, 1992.

Who Played?

The complete list of guests and their contributions was as follows:

Opening Sets

- Metallica
- Extreme
- Def Leppard (also performed "Now I'm Here" with Brian May)
- Bob Geldof

- Spinal Tap
- U2 (performed in California via satellite link)
- Guns N' Roses
- Mango Groove (performed in Johannesburg via satellite link)
- Elizabeth Taylor (delivered a speech on HIV and AIDS)

"Queen +" Set

- Joe Elliott and Slash—"Tie Your Mother Down"
- Roger Daltrey and Tony Iommi—"I Want It All"
- Zucchero—"Las Palabras de Amor"
- Gary Cherone and Tony Iommi—"Hammer to Fall"
- James Hetfield and Tony Iommi—"Stone Cold Crazy"
- Robert Plant—"Innuendo," "Crazy Little Thing Called Love"
- Brian May accompanied by Spike Edney—"Too Much Love Will Kill You"
- Paul Young—"Radio Ga Ga"
- Seal—"Who Wants to Live Forever"
- Lisa Stansfield—"I Want to Break Free"
- David Bowie and Annie Lennox—"Under Pressure"
- Ian Hunter, David Bowie, Mick Ronson, Joe Elliott, and Phil Collen—"All the Young Dudes"
- David Bowie and Mick Ronson—"Heroes"
- David Bowie—a reading of the Lord's Prayer
- George Michael—"39"
- George Michael and Lisa Stansfield—"These Are the Days of Our Lives"
- George Michael—"Somebody to Love"
- Elton John and Axl Rose—"Bohemian Rhapsody"
- Elton John and Tony Iommi—"The Show Must Go On"
- Axl Rose—"We Will Rock You"
- Liza Minnelli (leading all performers except for Elton John)—"We Are the Champions"

Rehearsals for the show had a supportive atmosphere, a long way from the competitiveness of Live Aid. Footage exists of George Michael, at the time only twenty-nine years old, running through "Somebody to Love" with May, Taylor, and Deacon, as well as a coterie of backing musicians and a gospel choir. Lurking around the edges of the nondescript rehearsal room, it's possible to see Seal and David Bowie standing next to one another in quiet admiration, Bowie huffing on a cigarette and smiling. Michael's virtuosic performance purposefully omits the climactic a cappella vocal cascade that Mercury made so famous, clearly intending for the audience to fill that particular gap on the night. When the song finishes, there is warm applause.

Interviewed before the show itself, Elton John told a television reporter that he expected the remaining members of Queen to feel "strange" and that it was "the closing of a chapter of a book."

Inevitably, the simple absence of Freddie Mercury was going to leave a musical hole in the evening. The song that opened the main Queen set—and therefore the first song the band performed since the departure of their singer—was "Tie Your Mother Down." Wanting the concert to be a celebration of Mercury's life, an early, bluesy number fit the bill perfectly, a reminder of the effervescence of the band at its strongest. But inevitably, as the stage pyrotechnics pump dry ice into billowing clouds around the stage and May, Taylor, and Deacon attack the song's introduction, there is an incredible and impossible expectation: the ear naturally expects Mercury's voice to take the lead vocal. When Brian May does the honors for the first verse instead, it is like a quashed sneeze. The effect is immaterial, the delivery just not what we wanted. It is undeniably poignant and strange.

Joe Elliott of Def Leppard handles the second verse on, and from this point, large portions of the concert inevitably have the feel of a revue show as guests parade across the stage in quick succession. The atmosphere is broadly celebratory but understandably does not avoid mawkishness. Brian May's solo performance of his own song "Too Much Love Will Kill You" (not, as is sometimes thought, a tribute to Mercury) is at the very limits of his vocal range, and the emotion of the occasion clearly causes him to wobble uncomfortably, while David Bowie's surprising and apparently spontaneous decision to recite the Lord's Prayer in its entirety after performing "Heroes" elicits a gamely positive reaction from the audience when it could very easily have resulted in a chorus of jeering.

May takes on a de facto spokesman role, introducing most of the acts and handling between-song banter, while Roger Taylor seems uncharacteristically reverential throughout. John Deacon seems the most outwardly subdued, however, perhaps even confused by the pageantry on display. He appears utterly unmoved by Zucchero, for example, and actively baffled by Gary Cherone of Extreme pointing at him in an effort to induce some kind of reaction from the quiet bassist. Eventually, he gamely boogies a little with Cherone, but it is the boogie of someone forced by the pressures of public visibility into appeasement.

A Parade of Legends

The success of the Freddie Mercury Tribute Concert is ultimately measured by the caliber of guest artists willing to abandon their tour schedules, drag themselves out of the studio, or board an intercontinental flight to perform for a few minutes. That the concert itself was built so clearly on the same model as Live Aid certainly helped, as did the 72,000-strong audience and the estimated television audience of more than 1 billion people worldwide, but the sheer density of pop music legends on display confirms Mercury's status among them.

Among the more interesting performances are those by artists not traditionally associated with rock idioms of Queen's songs, the likes of Seal and Lisa Stansfield, both an early indicator that the material would have life beyond the man who originally sang it. Similarly, Queen's influence on speed metal is truly confirmed when one of the genre's great proponents, James Hetfield of Metallica, actually turns up to perform "Stone Cold Crazy." When Annie Lennox emerges with thick black eye makeup alongside a mint-suited David Bowie to give an extremely serious rendition of "Under Pressure," it's an assurance that those songs had passed into the canon not just of great rock songs but of popular culture itself.

Bowie becomes a linchpin of the second half of the concert, introducing Mott the Hoople and playing alto saxophone on "All the Young Dudes" and rattling off "Heroes" with Mick Ronson, guitarist from his Spiders from Mars group. There's a segue away from rock heraldry, though, and George Michael and Lisa Stansfield's duet of "These Are the Days of Our Lives" shows just how malleable Roger Taylor's songwriting had become. It would be hard to imagine a larger musical distance between that song and, say, "I'm in Love with My Car."

The strongest measure of Mercury's influence on popular culture on display at the tribute concert, however, was not the sheer star power of the musical guests. Mercury's pulling power in Hollywood, a world intangibly far removed from Feltham in Middlesex and the Parsi enclaves of Zanzibar, was evidenced by Elizabeth Taylor's perfunctory speech on the AIDS crisis and also by Liza Minnelli's closing performance of "We Are the Champions." Had Marlene Dietrich been well enough (she died of renal failure in May 1992), one gets the impression that she too would've been in attendance. As Brian May pointed out before announcing her to the stage, Minnelli's status as a link to the true golden period of Hollywood is the endorsement (not that it was needed; that would have most tickled Mercury). "We Are the Champions," with its status as Mercury's "My Way," could have no stronger affirmation.

As Minnelli leads the final chorus of the song backed by the rest of the night's guest performers, it's interesting to note their eclecticism: Zucchero arm in arm with Seal, Lisa Stansfield singing harmonies with Def Leppard and Axl Rose, and George Michael cradling Minnelli herself. The act of these artists being united is the very definition of "one night only" and a neat encapsulation of just how deeply the Queen songbook was now embedded on the global stage.

But at its heart, the concert was a farewell and inevitably a distressing one. Reminiscing in *Classic Rock* magazine years later, Black Sabbath guitarist and performer on the night Tony Iommi described the scene: "Immediately after the show was over, in private, it hit Brian very hard. Hit them all. It was so, so sad. John was just in bits. It was a case of: 'Right, that's it, over, final.'"

Liza Minelli stands between Roger Taylor and Brian May at the Freddie Mercury Tribute Concert.   *Andre Csillag/Shutterstock*

The Mercury Phoenix Trust

Far from a celebration of Mercury's life alone, the tribute concert had another aim: to raise awareness of the worldwide AIDS crisis and raise money for a then undecided good cause to combat its spread. To that end, proceeds from the concert were used to establish a new charity, the Mercury Phoenix Trust. According to the charity's official website, it was launched by May, Taylor, and longtime Queen manager Jim Beach. There is no mention of any involvement on the part of John Deacon, who, around this time, effectively retired from Queen and the wider music business.

Alongside fund-raising and work to increase awareness of AIDS and related issues, part of the charity's activity today also includes operating what was the original Mountain Studios in the Montreux Casino as a tourist attraction, featuring the preserved studio facilities and an exhibition of memorabilia.

31

Made in Heaven

How Did Queen Record an Album without Their Singer?

F reddie Mercury's final musical works were not the sessions he battled through for *Innuendo*. After that album's release, knowing full well that he was nearing a point where he wouldn't be able to contribute anything to Queen any more, in the first months of 1991, Mercury used what strength he had to produce polished vocal takes in Mountain Studios with the rest of the band in attendance and with David Richards on production duties. These sessions had an inevitable desperation about them, the unenviable sense that they could end at any moment. The band noodled on arrangements and song ideas without making anything too permanent, borrowing Mercury when he felt well enough to contribute a few hours of work. But alongside that desperation, there was also an urgency, a feeling among the band that these were the most important recordings they had made to date. Mercury's resolute wish was that whatever takes were left should be turned into Queen songs (there's no real confirmation that Mercury then wanted them commercially released, but it's an easy assumption to make).

The effect of the singer's death on his bandmates was emotionally catastrophic. May and Taylor threw themselves into solo projects, while Deacon shut down almost completely and shunned any media interactions whatsoever. It wasn't until the following year that Taylor and Deacon began to tinker with the recordings Mercury left behind with the vague notion of finishing them off for an as-yet-unofficial project. May, who was on tour promoting his debut solo album *Back to the Light*, joined his bandmates in 1993 and declared the material they'd assembled so far to be inadequate. The natural tinkerer in May, the man who single-handedly reworked the entire *Flash Gordon* sound track, decreed that this would be a hybrid Queen album, an album of Mercury vocals and existing improvisations reworked into songs the band would have released anyway.

Of course, this was to be a technical challenge the likes of which the band had not yet faced. The sheer painstaking effort required in arranging every other musical element around just the vocals sounds like the punch line to an elaborate musicians' joke, but it was anything but. It shows in the album's execution: although Brian May has claimed in the past that it is in fact Queen's strongest album, the truth of the matter is that *Made in Heaven* is an album that, despite its noble intentions, is fundamentally hamstrung by the circumstances of its own creation.

Is It a Proper Queen Album?

The results of Mercury's frenzied vocal offloading in Montreux, what we might tentatively call his own personal *Made in Heaven* sessions, simply didn't produce enough material for a full album. So May, Taylor, and Deacon looked to Mercury's solo albums for precious extra musical tidbits that they might rework as Queen songs. Resourceful though it was as a tactic, it means that *Made in Heaven* is part odyssey-esque romp through soundscapes with Mercury vocals on top and part covers album. But to answer the above question: it has the appearance of a full Queen album, and had Mercury not passed away prior to its recording, there would be no reason to assume that *Made in Heaven* was anything other than a traditionally recorded entry in the discography.

The album's opening track, "It's a Beautiful Day," is a simple Mercury improvisation, a snatched few lines of melody and piano—certainly the beginnings of a larger piece, but, because of the ineffable impact of Mercury's absence, that's all it could remain. No compositional continuation could occur at the song's most basic level. No bridges or choruses could be added, even if they did exist on paper, because there was no one to take the lead vocal. Queen's answer to a situation like this was to build an elaborate synthesized orchestral arrangement around it, one tangential possibility for a song that could've gone anywhere. This example characterizes so much of the album, each track nothing more than a guess at the definitive version.

Delving back further still into the vaults, "Let Me Live" actually has its origins in the 1983 sessions for *The Works*. In its original form, Rod Stewart was on hand to record a guest vocal, something that for reasons unknown didn't make it to the finished album. Mercury's verses remain, obviously, but May and Taylor each take lead vocals where Stewart's would've occurred, turning it into a patchwork song bolstered by gospel backing vocals, a close musical relative of "Las Palabras de Amor." Incidentally, those backing vocals were at one point musically similar to those of Erma Franklin's soul classic "Piece of My Heart" (Queen's song in fact opens with the line "Why don't you take another little piece of my heart?"), necessitating some last-minute reediting to avoid possible legal action.

The Last Song Freddie Mercury Ever Recorded

If *Made in Heaven* has a centerpiece, then surely it is "Mother Love," which contains the final recorded vocal performance Mercury ever gave. Written by Mercury with May, it's a doom-laden piece with an appropriately portentous story behind its recording. During Mercury's last recording sessions, he and May worked together to capture the song verse by verse. Prior to recording the final verse, Mercury told his friend and cowriter that he was tired and that he needed to go and rest. "I'll finish it later," he told May, though he never did. Taking Mercury's promise to finish the song later as a challenge, it was May who eventually sang the final verse four years later.

The lyrics of "Mother Love" sprinkle still more of the same poignancy that affected so many moments of *Innuendo*, foretelling and depicting with excoriating rawness what was to become of Freddie Mercury: "I can't take it if you see me cry, I long for peace before I die." It's difficult to imagine the atmosphere in the studio for such a recording. Coming four years after comparable lines from songs like "The Show Must Go On," the intensity of these pivotal lyrical moments is afforded some distance, but it's important to note that the basics of many of these songs emerged when Mercury was close to death.

The composition of "Mother Love," which took place aside from Mercury and May's initial work together in 1991, however, gives the song that centerpiece status. Continuing their long tradition of studio experimentation, there is an audio montage section at the song's climax that mixes together audience sounds, the fudgy synthesized vocal sounds from the introduction to "One Vision," a snippet of Mercury's "Ay-oh" call-and-response routine, and even a few seconds of the Larry Lurex version of Goffin and King's "Goin' Back" (see chapter 5 for more on this recording). Just before the Larry Lurex section of this self-sampling smorgasbord, there is an almost incomprehensible sound that, if various online sources are to be believed, contains a sonic moment from every Queen song recorded up to that point, pasted together into one connected piece of tape and run through a player at high speed. The obvious objective in so doing was to enhance that feeling of reflection, of legacy.

While "Mother Love" may have been the last vocal Freddie Mercury ever recorded, the last song he ever wrote, "A Winter's Tale," comes later on the album. A Christmas song of sorts (the single release was wrapped in green paper), it details the objects Mercury could see as he stared out at Lake Geneva, capturing him in a reflective mood. In these words of a dying man, the wonders of the natural world, the swans, the mountains, and the reddening skies, are what matter now.

"Fab!": How "13" Waved Mercury Off

The overlaps with other areas of extracurricular Queen activity continue across *Made in Heaven*. The Mercury singles "Made in Heaven" and "I Was Born to Love You" are given major instrumental reworkings, while Taylor's "Heaven for Everyone," which originally appeared on the first album by the Cross, is reinstated with a full Mercury lead vocal recorded years earlier. John Deacon's little-known B-side "My Life Has Been Saved" from 1989 was resurrected, and Brian May's "Too Much Love Will Kill You," which premiered at the Freddie Mercury Tribute Concert and was included on his own solo album, is given maximum reverence and sentimentality (though it is actually unchanged from a version recorded by the band in 1989 for inclusion on *The Miracle*).

And then for all this apparent shoehorning of existing content, there is a remarkable stretch of work at the album's climax, some of the most adventurous and bizarre recordings the band ever made: a reprise of "It's a Beautiful Day" with an extended rock coda; then a four-second track titled "Yeah," which is simply a dropped-in Mercury "Yeah" from "Action This Day"; and, finally, a twenty-two-minute soundscape odyssey named "13." That last track, partially the result of longtime Mountain Studios producer David Richard noodling with an Ensoniq AR10 sampler, is responsible for tipping the entire album's length to more than seventy minutes, making it easily Queen's longest and most exhausting. Originally, "13" was available only on the CD edition of the album (though it did make it onto some promotional cassettes). The standard cassette left it out completely, and the vinyl edition contained only the first few seconds. It wasn't until a vinyl reissue in 2015 that the song was included in full, taking up the entirety of the fourth and final side.

Taken out of the context of the album, "13" serves as a stand-alone farewell from Taylor, May, and Deacon: a farewell both to Mercury and from themselves. In a manner arguably pioneered and popularized by Brian Eno, the gentle synthesizer washes evolve at a glacial pace with only a few sampled and looped interjections of Mercury speaking ("Are you running?") and laughing to complete the collage. Although of course this would never have happened, it's easy to imagine the Mercury of "A Winter's Tale" staring out of his Montreux window as the piece winds to its conclusion.

There is a popular and tempting fan theory that views "13" as a musical depiction of Mercury's ascension to heaven. Certainly, the contemplative nature of the piece and its celestial climax put the listener in mind of parting clouds and sunshine, but even at their most sentimental, Queen can still pop the balloon at any moment: Mercury's final utterance of "Fab!" after silence has finally descended snaps the atmosphere as if to gently mock it, to suggest that we shouldn't think too hard about these serious matters of life and death.

How Was the Album Received?

Due to the uniquely poignant circumstances of its recording, critical reception of *Made in Heaven* tended to tiptoe around the fact that it is overlong and indulgent and the clear struggle to stretch Mercury's scant vocals across the whole piece. Broadly positive notices commended the band on the meticulous nature of the work and the studio wizardry required to achieve a seamless effect, the appearance of an album recorded in the traditional manner.

Somewhat expectedly, the album went straight onto the U.K. album charts at number one. It repeated the feat in many countries across Europe, reflecting the ongoing fondness for the band throughout the continent. Mercury was, after all, frequently both a resident and a visitor. It's the band's best-selling album in Germany (behind the first two greatest-hits volumes), having shifted more than 1.5 million copies.

If one can judge an album with such extenuating emotional circumstances as a success, then *Made in Heaven* certainly was one. But the effect of the album's recording and release on the band was different. With no knowledge of the myriad offshoots that were to bring the Queen brand into the twenty-first century, there was an air of finality to the band's statements afterward. John Deacon, for example, told *Bassist* magazine in 1996, "There is no point carrying on. It is impossible to replace Freddie." It seems inconceivable now, but in 1995, it would be quite natural to conclude that Queen's final musical statement had been made.

32

Queen In-Between

What Did the Band Do from 1995 to 2005?

T he simple answer to the question at the top of this chapter is, together, not a lot. The more complex version of events could be considered the beginning of a great expansion of Queen as a brand, moving into the role of a company licensing its iconography for use in countless other media and situations, and the strangely subdued exit of one key creative component in John Deacon.

What Was the Original Lineup's Last Recording?

After the completion of *Made in Heaven*, there was no immediate pressure to release any other material, no desire to raid the vaults more than they had been already. May, Taylor, and Deacon entered a short period of stasis that was alleviated only by two short bursts of Queen-related activity. The first of these was a tribute to Mercury, a single in 1997 titled "No-One but You (Only the Good Die Young)," which also appeared on a new compilation of their harder-edged guitar-driven songs: *Queen Rocks*.

It is the final recording released under the name of Queen alone and the last featuring John Deacon. Written mostly by Brian May, the song has tonal similarities to a number of eulogistic songs written after tragic events, sharing a musical bloodline with works such as Eric Clapton's "Tears in Heaven," written after the death of his son Connor, and Elton John's reworked tribute to the late Diana, Princess of Wales, "Candle in the Wind." In fact, Brian May claimed that inspiration for the song came as much from the death of public figures like Princess Diana and Gianni Versace as it did from Freddie Mercury, but the association with his lost bandleader is indelible.

The music video for the single release is in line with the developing aesthetic of the latter part of the Mercury years: humor removed, replaced with tasteful reflection. A fizzing flute of champagne sits on the grand piano played by May as he takes the lead vocal (shared with Taylor), the flute that Mercury would have raised to the audience as he toasted them and wished they might all drink bubbly for breakfast like he did.

It arrived at number thirteen on the U.K. singles chart in January 1998 after it was released before Christmas in the rest of the world (perhaps to avoid getting caught up in the inevitable chart battle for the coveted Christmas number one in the United Kingdom).

Deacy's Last Stand

John Deacon's final live appearance with the band he'd joined nearly a quarter of a century before was to be, of all things, at the ballet. It seems not completely incongruous for the remaining members of Queen to return to the stage in an accompanying role at one of Freddie Mercury's most beloved and admired disciplines.

The Béjart Ballet, founded by Maurice Béjart and renowned in their native Switzerland and beyond, paid tribute to Mercury in Paris with the commission of a work called *A Ballet for Life*. It's unclear whose suggestion it was to reunite the band to mark the occasion, but it's likely that Elton John had something to do with it (John had by this point become something of a benevolent unpaid counselor to pop musicians), who took vocal duties for a performance of "The Show Must Go On" as part of *A Ballet for Life*. According to Taylor, John likened the band to a racing car with no driver, simply waiting to be taken for a spin. The show itself took other songs from the Queen catalog and matched them with Béjart's visionary ballet choreography, inspired by Mercury's legacy and the theme of those who departed too soon (Béjart was deeply concerned by the AIDS crisis).

Little seen (even though it's widely available to view online), the performance is a curiously affecting mix of bombast and restraint. Elton John rushes around the stage in declamatory style while the band offers sober accompaniment, situated on a blank, synthetically white stage. It's not until the first chorus that veiled dancers gradually emerge from the floor, at which point the piece begins to resemble performance art, a good deal more serious than the knowing Nijinsky pastiche that Mercury had incorporated into the video for "I Want to Break Free."

Deacon's decision to retire completely from public life had already been made by this point, so his final public appearance and performance with the band was a seismic moment. But since then, Deacon has become something of a mythical figure, a constantly Googled "where are they now?" contactable only remotely even by his bandmates. Newspaper articles would talk of his quiet life, his enthusiasm for golf and his six children, and, for a short time, his dalliances in a central London strip club, but he was essentially invisible by choice.

Elton John performing with Queen at the opening night of *A Ballet for Life* in 1997, John Deacon's last live performance with Brian May and Roger Taylor. *Richard Young/Shutterstock*

One YouTube video of Deacon from around 2016 shows him harried by Queen fans mobbing him for autographs as he covers his face with his hand in apparent exasperation. In another from 2017, the wielder of a phone camera approaches Deacon while he sits in his car and proceeds to hand him a marker pen and no fewer than seven guitar pick guards to sign. Glum-faced, Deacon acquiesces.

The Rise of Queen +

As of 1997, Queen was, as far as public appearances went, essentially a two-piece band. After reuniting with Zucchero in 1998 for a set of three songs at a benefit concert held by the operatic tenor Luciano Pavarotti in Modena, as well as dueting with Pavarotti himself on May's "Too Much Love Will Kill You," May and Taylor gradually increased their number of collaborations with a range of musical suitors under the name of Queen +.

Founding member of the Fugees and hip-hop wunderkind Wyclef Jean remixed and rapped over a new version of "Another One Bites the Dust" in 1998 to tie in with the release of the movie *Small Soldiers* (it also appeared on the third volume of Queen's *Greatest Hits* the following year). The artist billing for this version was Queen + Wyclef Jean, although there's no evidence of direct collaboration between the two parties. There is, however, an entertainingly bizarre music video directed by Michel Gondry in which Wyclef plays a sleepy security guard who must recover a stolen mannequin of Freddie Mercury, made all the more surreal by Wyclef's continual refrain of "Freddie Mercury, where you at?"

Closer to home, Taylor and May took Queen into the new millennium in a collaboration with the now forgotten British boy band 5ive, who reworked "We Will Rock You" for single release and a performance at the annual BRIT Awards. The BRIT Awards performance opened the ceremony, introducing Taylor and May to a new and younger audience, while the single release itself sent the song to the top of the charts, unhindered by lines like "As long as 5ive bring the funk, Queen bring the rock!"

May and Taylor's next major collaboration was one that apparently vexed John Deacon sufficiently to make him comment on it in the press. The anachronistic adventure film *A Knight's Tale* from 2001 (which starred Heath Ledger in the lead role) featured a sound track of rock staples, including Queen's "We Will Rock You" and a version of "We Are the Champions" as performed by British singer and former Take That member Robbie Williams. The singer's profile as a rebel in reverse, having left a fairly clean-cut boy band to forge a solo career with a harder musical edge and some widely publicized substance dependencies, grated so much on Deacon that he was supposedly moved to tell a reporter from the *Sun* newspaper that "it is one of the greatest songs ever written but I think they've ruined it. I don't want to be nasty but let's just say Robbie Williams is no Freddie Mercury. Freddie can never be replaced, and certainly not by him."

Despite the undeniable success of some of these collaborations in keeping Queen's music in the public consciousness, a more pervasive feeling of the band becoming ever more in thrall to commercialization lingers over this period. It would be naive, however, to characterize this as a new development: it's impossible to ignore the rampant lust for cash on display throughout the band's career ever since they escaped their deal with Trident and took their business affairs in-house. Financially prudent moves litter the golden periods of the band's career, and their constant displays of material excess and willingness to accept commercial opportunities were seen only as a positive, a means to making an ever more outlandish creative product.

However, the perception of this attitude is undeniably less palatable in the wake of Freddie Mercury's death and John Deacon's retirement. With only half the band's classic lineup representing its public image, that commercial thrust has been construed by many as being in poor taste. May and Taylor's refrain of "Freddie would've loved it" is regularly applied to newer projects (e.g., the *We Will Rock You* musical and the *Bohemian Rhapsody* movie) as a method of alleviating any fan discomfort, but the perception remains: for some, the legacy is in constant danger of being mishandled.

When Queen was inducted into the Rock and Roll Hall of Fame in 2001, Taylor and May's brief but gracious acceptance speeches were followed by the appearance of Freddie Mercury's mother, Jer Bulsara, who collected his statuette on behalf of her late son to a standing ovation. Again, despite the grandeur of the occasion, Deacon was nowhere to be seen, true to his retired status. May and Taylor played a short televised set, including a curiously inert performance of "We Will Rock You" in which the two original members took a lead vocal verse each and were joined by Taylor Hawkins and Dave Grohl of Foo Fighters for a more spirited take on "Tie Your Mother Down."

Arguably the most visible appearance of Queen in the public eye during this period was largely due to Brian May. In 2002, to celebrate the Silver Jubilee of Queen Elizabeth II, May and Taylor were due to perform a short set of Queen hits with the London cast of *We Will Rock You*. The duo was accustomed to performing with the cast of the musical thanks to several special appearances at the show's home of the Dominion Theatre in London, but the very opening of the entire concert, which was televised for a viewing audience of 200 million, saw Brian May standing precariously on the roof of Buckingham Palace playing his arrangement of "God Save the Queen." Taylor was situated on the stage below, supported on percussion by the Royal Academy of Music Symphony Orchestra and Michael Kamen (who had, coincidentally, arranged and conducted parts of Queen's "Who Wants to Live Forever"). While this performance, especially Brian May's role, undoubtedly contained all the requisite "rock god" hallmarks (among them the danger of a large fall, an overlong and raucous guitar solo, and an outlandish jacket), this was an event completely synonymous with the establishment. Whereas Live Aid had been at least partially imbued with a rebellious spirit, the Party at the Palace couldn't have been more mainstream: a clear indication of where May and Taylor were taking the brand. Later in the same show, Taylor stepped in on drums to accompany Phil Collins on "You Can't Hurry Love," while May played guitar for a bizarre collaboration between Cliff Richard and the lightweight pop ensemble S Club 7 for Richard's song "Move It," proving that their capacity as sidemen was nothing if not inclusive.

As the 1990s disappeared and a new century arrived, Queen + seemingly became just as busy as Queen had ever been. Now established as a two-piece open to collaboration with a huge range of artists, the Queen live experience became more malleable and adaptable than it had ever been as an unmoving four-piece. As such, there are countless examples of blockbuster guest artists joining the band for the odd number here and there, the sheer volume of which makes it difficult to catalog here. There was, however, one highlight among the performances that gave the world new Queen material and new political caché.

Making Amends in South Africa

Due to their ill-judged decision to play several huge concerts in apartheid South Africa in the early 1980s, Queen's public history with the nation was checkered at best. But in the wake of Freddie Mercury's death from AIDS and the burgeoning epidemic in South Africa, a sudden commonality became clear. In 2003, former President Nelson Mandela's 46664 initiative (so called to reflect his Robben Island prisoner identification number) was launched with a series of concerts to raise awareness of HIV and AIDS, the first of which took place in Cape Town and featured the likes of Anastacia and Beyoncé alongside heritage acts like Robert Plant, Bob Geldof, the Who, Bono and the Edge from U2, Ladysmith Black Mambazo, and Zucchero: all artists comfortably within Queen's circle.

Taylor and May performed a set containing two new pieces. The first was titled "Invincible Hope" and featured a recording of a Mandela speech, whereas the second used the dialing tones of the numbers "46664" as a musical foundation for a May-led protest song that takes up a thread he began with compositions like "White Man" and "Put Out the Fire." It features a bravura Bob Dylan–esque gabbled delivery of a powerful and heartfelt manifesto (or platitudinous ramble, depending on your tolerance for millionaire rock stars pontificating on societal ills). They also performed staples of the back catalog with guest vocalists, notably the Soweto Gospel Choir gamely attempting the operatic section of "Bohemian Rhapsody."

Whether or not the band's complicated set was credible as a display of humanitarian influence, the political upshot was that May and Taylor ended up working closely with Nelson Mandela himself, going some way to cleansing their reputation in relation to South Africa.

33

We Will Rock You

The Queen Musical

As the Queen brand and its associated musical products became more infused into the marketplace through advertising and various collaborations with May and Taylor, one particular project has proven its lasting effect more than most: the Queen musical *We Will Rock You*. Discussions among Jim Beach and the remaining active members of the band around the possibility of a stage musical based on the Queen songbook had begun as early as the

The gold statue that stood above the entrance to the Dominion Theatre during the West End run of *We Will Rock You*.   TMP_An_Instant_of_Time/Shutterstock.com

mid-1990s, but even with interest from Robert De Niro's production company Tribeca, an appropriate narrative angle just couldn't be decided on.

The unlikely deadlock buster was Ben Elton, the British comedian, writer, and novelist famous for his sitcom successes, including the *Blackadder* series (written with Richard Curtis) and *The Young Ones*. Elton had worked with musical impresario and wunderkind Andrew Lloyd Webber on his 2000 show *The Beautiful Game* with limited commercial success but still convinced May and Taylor that a bold new direction was the key to getting the Queen musical to finally work.

Elton's vision for the show placed it not in the open-air sports arenas of Europe or even in a psychedelic Kensington in the early 1970s. Elton had been watching the Keanu Reeves sci-fi-philosophy adventure movie *The Matrix* and paying close attention. As such, the action of *We Will Rock You* was to take place in the last place anyone could've predicted.

What Is the Plot?

In the twenty-fourth century, all musical instruments have been banned. Earth has been renamed the iPlanet and is populated by Ga Ga Kids, who experience only synthetic entertainment, adapting Roger Taylor's lyrics to read, "Radio ga ga, video goo goo, internet ga ga," and, later, "Marketing blah blah." In this world, rock 'n' roll has been forgotten. It's into this techno-futurist landscape that characters with names like Galileo Figaro, the Killer Queen, Scaramouche, and Khashoggi and a band of rebels calling themselves Bohemians deliver Queen's greatest hits at regular intervals, the main narrative thrust seemingly driven by the song titles themselves (e.g., the Seven Seas of Rhye is an actual location, and one character is lobotomized to the sound of "Another One Bites the Dust").

As with so many fanciful narratives, *We Will Rock You* is dominated by a prophecy, namely, that musical instruments, now banned on the iPlanet, are actually kept in the ruins of Wembley Stadium. In the second act of the show when this prophecy is explained, it becomes clear that John Deacon, Roger Taylor, and Brian May are in fact integral characters: the prophecy was apparently dictated by them before they were sentenced to death (even though he is mentioned in the show and several of his songs appear, Deacon's retirement plans were unchanged by the prospect of a Queen musical). The lead character, Galileo, journeys to Wembley Stadium, the place of champions, where the musical's title song reinvigorates the planet. At one point, the power of rock music is e-mailed to every inhabitant in this terrifying new society, beginning a new cultural revolution. The show ends on the traditional closing pairing of "We Will Rock You" and "We Are the Champions" and an encore of "Bohemian Rhapsody" sung by the whole cast.

Why Did the Critics Hate *We Will Rock You* So Much?

One of the main problems critics found with *We Will Rock You* was its supposed lack of coherent plot, seeing it as an excuse to merely shoehorn in as
many Queen song titles as possible, thereby springboarding the musical content of the show. In a career that wasn't exactly festooned with critical praise,
the reviews for *We Will Rock You* were among the very harshest the band ever
received. "Lots of shows boast books that are little more than pretexts for the
numbers, but few connect the song-and-dance dots as baldly as *We Will Rock
You*," wrote Matt Wolf in *Variety*. The *Guardian*'s Brian Logan described Elton's
premise for the show as being "as sixth form as it sounds," while Charles Spencer of the *Telegraph* called it "a pathetic, adolescent piece of work."

But aside from these practical concerns around craft and traditional musical
construction, there was a bias at work. In 2002, it had been a long time since
Queen was considered a current concern let alone a worthy one. Critically, there
was a perception of Taylor and May as moneygrubbers, apparently willing to
dilute the brand of Queen and its legacy with whatever promotional opportunity might drop into their in-boxes. Deacon's staunch decision to reject any
further involvement had him labeled as "the one who got out." As such, a project
like *We Will Rock You* stood no chance of winning the critics over and only
fueled the ongoing and increasingly bitter attitude of Taylor and May toward
them and the press in general.

Elton's book for the show, however, contains some serious bias of its own. At
the time of his writing it, television shows like *Pop Idol* in the United Kingdom
were becoming all-encompassing. The perceived inauthenticity of manufactured
pop music artists that sprung forth from these reality TV talent contests were,
in Elton's book, the beginning of the end of popular culture as a rebellious act.
Of course, that Elton chose to air these opinions on the commodification of
pop music in a hugely expensive West End production honed to make as much
commercial revenue as possible is an irony in itself, but nevertheless, the anti-
pop bias of *We Will Rock You* served only to make Queen appear increasingly
culturally irrelevant and insincere and the Queen brand ever more compromised.

How Successful Was It?

Despite the excoriating reviews, Tribeca's involvement remained solid throughout the production, and De Niro was an occasional onstage guest at press events
and participant in promotional activities. The success of so-called jukebox musicals like *Mamma Mia!* encouraged spectators to believe that this show would,
too, defy the critics and become a viable hit, and, of course, it did exactly that.

We Will Rock You opened on May 12, 2002, at the 2,000-seat Dominion The-atre on London's Tottenham Court Road: not quite the heart of Theatreland, but only a stone's throw from legendary rock venues the 100 Club and the Astoria. The cast was largely unknown, save for Nigel Planer as the wizened rebel char-acter of Pop (a noted comic actor, Planer had appeared as Neil the gentle hippy in Elton's sitcom *The Young Ones*). Among the cast was Kerry Ellis, with whom Brian May would go on to have a fruitful musical relationship. The commercial impact and audience satisfaction were immediately visible: standing ovations followed nightly sellouts, and a huge statue of Freddie Mercury was erected on the theater's façade, soon becoming a focal point for London itself.

International versions of the show began to receive similar audience reac-tions, with productions operating in Australia, Japan, and Spain and a special one-act version for Las Vegas. In 2005, the show overtook *Grease* to become the longest-running show in the Dominion Theatre's history. Touring productions of the United Kingdom continued and still do at the time of this writing, with a steadily increasing number of amateur productions now emerging, curiously aligning the songwriters of Queen with the likes of Gilbert and Sullivan.

As the original London production wore on, another irony working against Elton's book arose as the role of Killer Queen was taken over in 2010 by Brenda Edwards, at that point most notable for having competed in the ITV talent show *The X Factor*. Despite this, the show's juggernaut status continued until May 31, 2014, when the curtain finally came down on *We Will Rock You*'s stunningly long run, eventually totaling 4,600 performances in the same theater. The final performance of the musical at the theater in which it had opened saw May and Taylor rise through the stage to play along with the cast for the closing encore of "Bohemian Rhapsody" and "The Show Must Go On."

The Legacy of *We Will Rock You*

The musical is, in a way, both the first and the last thing one would expect the remaining creative forces of Queen to curate. Roger Taylor professed in several interviews early in the show's West End run that he hated musicals as a genre and had walked out of a screening of *The Sound of Music* as a child because he found it sickening. May, too, showed no signs in his musical career of wanting to extend a narrative project for longer than a single song or, if pushed, a single side of an LP.

Freddie Mercury, on the other hand, had grandiose ambitions to unite high culture and pop music: and while the musical as a medium is rarely considered one of the high art forms, it does have its stylistic roots in opera and oratorio. Mercury's enthusiasm for the genre extended to his involvement in 1986 in the musical *Time*, for which he provided vocals for a single release of the title song.

Mercury did not feature in the musical itself in any performative capacity other than this, with the cozy British pop icon Cliff Richard (of "Devil Woman" fame) taking the lead role until David Cassidy relieved him later in the musical's two-year run. Mercury's single was taken from a concept album of songs from the musical, masterminded by Dave Clark of the Dave Clark Five, and featuring guest vocalists Stevie Wonder, Dionne Warwick, and Julian Lennon as well as Laurence Olivier in a speaking role (Olivier was "in" the musical itself as a projected talking head named Akash). Curiously, the video for "Time" was shot between performances of the musical at the Dominion Theatre, where *We Will Rock You* would remain resident for so long. The two musicals also shared a choreographer in Arlene Phillips, and both productions necessitated overhauls of the theater's technical capabilities, most notably a new public address system for *We Will Rock You*.

In an interview with the *New Zealand Herald*, Roger Taylor recounted a tale of Mercury attending a performance of *Time* and being so drunk by the interval that he insisted on selling ice cream, causing a near riot as the audience gradually registered who was handing over the tiny tubs of mint chocolate chip. In the same interview, Taylor also says that Mercury would've loved *We Will Rock You*. It's undeniable that Mercury's love for the theatrically absurd might easily have extended to the Queen musical. It is, of course, conjecture: but this is the same Freddie Mercury who walked out of recording sessions with Michael Jackson, who prized the rich and varied tones of an operatic soprano as the height of musical sophistication. Looking back dispassionately, there's a chance he would have been confused and outraged by what could be viewed as a loosely hung-together series of Queen cover versions by perky young singers with stage school voices.

As a cultural artifact, the continuing longevity of *We Will Rock You* is in part predicated on the continuing success of Queen's songs in the public consciousness. The same is true of *Mamma Mia!* and the songs of ABBA. While the songs are loved, so too will the musicals sell tickets all over the world. There are many differing views on May and Taylor's handling of Queen's musical legacy, and the musical offers for many an argument that it is not being handled with care and respect. But at the peak of their commercial powers, Queen was accustomed to huge successes. Any venture into musical theater would be subject to the same approach, the same intolerance for anything less than a decent return. In this way, *We Will Rock You* is simply another element of the band's creative portfolio: bizarre and unique, wildly polarizing, critically reviled, but enormously popular and lucrative.

34

How Do You Replace Freddie Mercury?

The Birth of Queen +

During a television interview, Mercury once described the work ethic of Queen as being relentless, an ongoing entity that would continue regardless of personnel, even himself: "If I suddenly left, they'd just replace me." He couldn't help but add, "Not easy to replace me, huh."

If a line was drawn under the classic Queen lineup at the point of Freddie Mercury's death, then officially it was thirteen years before the band regrouped in a meaningfully permanent fashion, making Mercury's statement into an undeniable truth. As we've seen, collaborations between individual band members and guest stars were plentiful in this period, going under the banner of Queen + whenever it involved both Roger Taylor and Brian May (John Deacon officially retired from any public-facing Queen business in 1997). The question asked in the title of this chapter is a little misleading, as both remaining active members of the band made it clear that any new collaborations would not be an act of replacement or in any way a suggestion that Mercury's voice was replaceable. Inevitably, though, comparisons were always going to be drawn: any potential permanent guest vocalist would have to sing songs indelibly marked with Mercury's voice, and creative decisions would have to be made regarding which elements of his recorded performances were sacrosanct and which were ripe for personal adaptation.

"Our Hero and Our Friend"

Ultimately, one collaboration among the many that May and Taylor worked on in the 1990s stuck a little more than others. With the commercial power of the Queen brand at a particularly potent apogee after the success of *We Will Rock You*, the band (essentially Taylor and May) was inducted into the U.K. Music

Paul Rodgers with Queen, performing at London's O2 Arena, October 2008.
Fabio Diena / Shutterstock.com

Hall of Fame, a now defunct televised awards ceremony that followed the model of its U.S. counterpart. Queen was inducted after a public vote that saw them triumph over their counterparts in the "1970s" category, including the Sex Pistols, Elton John, David Bowie, and ABBA.

For the live performance from London's Hackney Empire that followed their induction, Taylor, May, and a backing band were joined by Free and Bad Company vocalist Paul Rodgers. Rodgers was introduced to the stage by May as "our hero and our friend," and it is true that their relationship spanned the decades: Smile was on the same bill as Free (erroneously billed as "The Free" in some advertisements) back in 1969. The bands' histories weren't exactly entwined, but May in particular had found himself playing Free's "All Right Now" with Rodgers on numerous occasions, and Free's drummer Simon Kirke worked with John Deacon for their Man Friday & Junior Jive project. In short, Rodgers was on paper a logical choice for a vocalist to take this one single TV gig.

But what started as a single show condensed for television (they performed "We Will Rock You," "We Are the Champions," and Free's "All Right Now") soon ballooned into something much more significant and, indeed, the next major iteration of the Queen brand. Watching that three-song performance, Taylor in particular seems reenergized, with a dedicated flamboyance to his drumming. May and Rodgers share the stage more equally than May and Mercury ever did, and Rodgers for his part is effortless, reinterpreting rather than redecorating Mercury's existing vocals on "We Will Rock You."

It was with that spirit of renewed interpretation that Rodgers, Taylor, and May eventually regrouped officially in 2005. Their first official Queen + Paul Rodgers show was in South Africa, another appearance for Taylor and May at Nelson Mandela's 46664 series of concerts to raise worldwide awareness of the ongoing AIDS crisis. It's immediately clear from recordings of that first official show that the ensemble is not yet simpatico. Rodgers attempts Mercury-esque vocal sparring with the crowd, which, at least on film, doesn't elicit much reaction. Similarly, when he asks the crowd to sing along with the chorus of Bad Company's "Can't Get Enough," he notes the lack of participation by saying into the microphone, "We'll try that one next time." Rodgers also tries to quiet the ensemble ("Easy boys…") so that the crowd has a better chance of singing along, but the collective reflexes that build between musicians aren't quite there yet.

The inevitable settling of a "new" vocalist singing songs so strongly synonymous with a departed colleague is too jarring, too confusing. The Queen + Paul Rodgers live experience, in its first iteration, fell somewhere between a greatest-hits set and a clamor for enforced audience participation, mingled with occasional well-placed Bad Company cover versions. Just as with the classic lineup of Queen, it took time for the band to coalesce. The cruel difference here was that developing a comfortable dynamic took place in front of an international television audience rather than at a community center in Truro in the early 1970s.

Queen Officially Returns

Traditionally, there is no better way for a band to find its feet than to keep playing live—and that's exactly what Queen + Paul Rodgers did. Much of the first part of 2005 was spent touring the United Kingdom, Europe, Japan, and the United States, a familiar route to all three core members of what was now the working version of Queen (augmented by a band of hired hands, among them Spike Edney). The first official show on this tour took place at the Brixton Academy in South London, a legendary venue but not a huge one: the perfect size for an audience made up of Queen fan club members. It was reported in the media as Queen's first official concert since the end of the band back in the 1990s (despite the South Africa show and ignoring that May and Taylor were hardly inactive during this period), and anticipation was understandably at a peak.

With the lights in the auditorium dimmed, the song that introduces the band is not, as fans may have expected, a recorded version of "Procession" or the opening synthesizer strains of "One Vision." Eminem's "Lose Yourself," with its tinkling piano and thudding, trebly guitar sample, is the song that brings Queen back to the fans: it's not until well after the chorus that Paul Rodgers slips onto the stage, lit by a single spotlight, to deliver a hushed snatch of a song named "Reaching Out." This song was originally the product of a project named Rock

Therapy, a charity single on which Rodgers and May appeared (along with Lulu and Charlie Watts from the Rolling Stones) back in 1996. So far, these artistic choices were, to say the least, left of center. Once Rodgers has delivered the introduction, Brian May also slides through the curtain to play the opening riff of "Tie Your Mother Down," at which point the curtain falls to the stage to reveal the rest of the band, and something approaching business as usual is resumed.

In a Reuters report before the Brixton concert, Taylor answered the more cynical commentators in the press who had questioned May and Taylor's motivation for reactivating the Queen brand for the upcoming tour: "We're not doing it for the money." But he also couldn't help admitting, "Although it helps, it's very nice." And looking at the Brixton show in particular, it does appear that there is a genuine sense of enjoyment coming from the stage. Whether or not critics have a point when they accuse Taylor and May of exploiting the band's legacy to fund their retirement (which, even now, doesn't appear to be imminent), it's difficult to ignore both the emotional and the commercial power of Brian May strumming the chords from "Love of My Life" as the audience sings the song back to him, word perfect and pregnant with thirty years of nostalgia.

Set lists from this tour are, like the band's South Africa show, a mix of reliable Queen bangers and token Free and Bad Company songs. For "Bohemian Rhapsody," a video projection and live audio recording of Freddie Mercury would play while Taylor and May played along. After the operatic section (simply the studio recording as per classic Queen concerts), Paul Rodgers would return to the stage to sing the rock section and portions on the outro. In the Hyde Park concert, Rodgers's natural lean toward the blues leads him to improvise extensively over the closing passage of the song, one of many examples of two musically opposing forces gradually easing into one another's orbits.

It is an undeniably strange sight to behold: someone who isn't Freddie Mercury strumming the acoustic guitar introduction to "Crazy Little Thing Called Love" or Taylor and May bending their tempo to accommodate a particularly melismatic vocal improvisation from Rodgers. Even with the ongoing tweaks and improvements to the live shows, even at this early stage, it was tricky to imagine that Paul Rodgers could bring something to songs like "I Want to Break Free" that hadn't already been defined for rock history. A cultural behemoth the size of Queen simply couldn't please everyone with Paul Rodgers no matter the intentions behind their genesis.

Live reviews from 2005 were perhaps predictably mixed. The *Independent* claimed that "in a world of lumpenproletariat mundanity, Queen remain a right royal treat," but the *Evening Standard* was harsher: "The truth of the matter is that that great show-off Freddie Mercury will be spinning in his grave." None other than the venerable Robert Christgau reviewed the ensemble's 2005 live recording of their show at Sheffield's Hallam Arena with typical pithiness: "Where Freddie Mercury was a true queen, Paul Rodgers is a big disgrace." But despite the mixed reception, the kinship among this new core trio of Queen musicians was now established, and there was only one place left to go: the studio.

The Cosmos Rocks

On the back of their world tour and a second U.S. tour that saw them selling out venues until May 2006, Queen + Paul Rodgers sought to capture their new dynamic on a new album: the first Queen album since 1995's *Made in Heaven* and the first to be recorded and assembled in a traditional fashion since 1991's *Innuendo*. Roger Taylor's home studio, the Priory, gave the band privacy and freedom to work and experiment across much of 2007 before *The Cosmos Rocks* was released in September 2008.

In a question-and-answer session filmed for the Queen YouTube channel around the time of the album's release, Rodgers sits between May and Taylor like a child at a school parents' evening as the trio discusses the genesis of certain songs and the excitement they all feel at having discovered a new dynamic. In these conversations, the emphasis is on the immediacy of the recording sessions. Unlike the traditionally painstaking Queen approach of multiple locations, numerous takes, and exhausting months of working on mere minutes of recorded material, Queen + Paul Rodgers appeared to adopt an approach more suited to Rodgers himself: loose sessions, improvisation, and quick takes once each band member knew his part well enough to play through it. Of course, there is a certain amount of polish to *The Cosmos Rocks* that would undoubtedly have come during its mastering phase, but the essence of it is performative: these are songs designed for the live arena rather than for headphone dissection.

Even after all the band's time spent together playing live and preparing new material in the studio, the compositional version of Queen + Paul Rodgers suffers from the same "between-two-stools" mentality, which critics immediately pointed out when they made their official live debut—that this was, in some ways, the Queen that fans knew and loved but mingled with something new and confusing, something that would inevitably suffer in comparison to their nostalgia.

On one hand, the album's opening song, "Cosmos Rockin'," begins with haunted guitar feedback and a synthetically altered voice asking, "What planet is this?", a pure example of Roger Taylor's love of the carnivalesque nature of early science fiction, the lingering influence of which can be traced back through Queen songs like "Machines (Or Back to Humans)" and indeed to his solo albums. Acting as a counterpoint, though, Rodgers's contributions to *The Cosmos Rocks* are traditional in the extreme. They include blues harmonica on "Surf's Up . . . School's Out!" and a gospel-tinged, southern-fried rock shuffle in

"Call Me." His "Time to Shine" borrows hugely from the Who's "Pinball Wizard," which, to be fair, would place it in the original Queen canon alongside swathes of their 1970s material.

But Rodgers also shows signs of a deep understanding of his colleagues' work. "Warboys" actually sounds like something Roger Taylor would've composed: a simplistic portrayal of the imbalance of political honchos sending lower-class grunts to die on the contemporary battlefield (the anti–Iraq War movement found much liberal traction around this time). Aside from his own compositions, his vocals sound most comfortable during the numbers on which he is allowed to pull and play with the phrasing, such as on May's "Some Things That Glitter," and it is revealing to hear how May and Taylor cope with the billowing and swelling around him.

The reviews for The Cosmos Rocks weren't all unkind, but many did bemoan a certain irrelevance and, inevitably, drew comparisons between Rodgers and Freddie Mercury. Rolling Stone was barely tepid: "Under Rodgers' command, [The] Cosmos Rocks evokes an unmemorable stretch of drive-time radio." Uncut took outright issue with this "ill-fitting rebirth, fronted by the defiantly ungay, unIndian and uneccentric Paul Rodgers." Commercially, the album was by no means a disaster, landing in the top ten across many traditionally Queen-sympathetic European countries (Germany, the Czech Republic, and Switzerland) and at number five in the United Kingdom.

Whether or not those involved feel that it is worthwhile to compare Rodgers and Mercury, the accumulated goodwill for the latter means that it is unavoidable. On a technical level, the starkest difference could be characterized like this: with Freddie Mercury (and, lest we forget, John Deacon), Queen was a hermetic ensemble, collectively pointed toward the same goal of the best possible recording or performance of the song in question. With Paul Rodgers, his natural looseness as a singer means that any other musicians can ever really be only accompanists attempting to follow and contain him. This isn't to favor either of those approaches over the other, but one reason for the general uneasiness around this particular iteration of Queen could simply be that the dynamics were off. It's not that Paul Rodgers isn't Freddie Mercury: it's that Queen + isn't Queen.

Public appetite for the band didn't seem to be waning, and the requests kept on coming in. For example, May and Taylor's relationship with Nelson Mandela's 46664 campaign for AIDS awareness had continued throughout this period, and the band was invited to perform at a special concert in Hyde Park to celebrate the South African former president's ninetieth birthday in June 2008.

Away from the live stage, one of the stranger results of the Queen + Paul Rodgers period has a neat symmetry to it. For their first run of live shows, the group would begin each concert by playing a recording of Eminem's "Lose Yourself," which would then segue into Paul Rodgers's performance of "Reaching

Out." That very song ended up in the hands of Eminem himself, Marshall Mathers, and a live recording of it was sampled on his 2008 single "Beautiful."

Aside from being another example of a Queen song being indelibly linked to hip-hop through the miracle of sampling, it also means that Don Black, who originally wrote the song with Andy Hill, now has credits on an Eminem song to go alongside his work with Brian May and Kerry Ellis and on later Brian May solo material.

But as is so often the way with Queen, the money really rolls in when the tour bus rolls out. After the release of *The Cosmos Rocks*, it was time for the kind of Queen tour that hadn't happened since the 1980s. While Queen + Paul Rodgers had completed a world tour to announce themselves in 2005, the *Rock the Cosmos* tour saw the band filling stadiums and open-air arenas on a much larger scale in the autumn of 2008. Indeed, the tour was full of notable happenings, from Queen's first-ever official appearance in the Middle East at the Dubai Festival City venue to the prime minister of Latvia joining the band on drums for "All Right Now" during their show at the Arena Riga.

Visually, these shows took advantage of the size of their arenas and the optical wizardry now possible. The introduction to "Cosmos Rockin'" opened the show, with huge video screens showing spinning stars, falling rain, and lumbering planets, all before the more traditionally Queen-esque strains of "One Vision" began the show proper. During a fan-shot video from Moscow, it's possible to hear Paul Rodgers's new interpretations of well-known Queen standards, ad-libbing interstitial ideas. It's also possible to hear concertgoers singing along to the version they know best: the Freddie Mercury version. Heard in tandem, it's a jarring but effective representation of the problem faced by Queen + Paul Rodgers, the problem that dogged the whole existence of the project.

"Of Course I'm Not a Bloody Hired Gun"

After Queen + Paul Rodgers's world tour had finished and all the receipts had been counted, on paper, there was nothing to suggest that the collaboration couldn't continue as it had been, delivering the hits of Queen direct to fans with an inspired vocal interpreter. But in May 2009, the band announced that their partnership had come to an end in an amicable fashion. Paul Rodgers confirmed that he would go back on the road with Bad Company that summer, effectively drawing a line under his time with Queen and returning to his natural home. A final DVD release of the band's 2008 concert in Ukraine followed, arriving in stores a month after the announcement.

Although *The Cosmos Rocks* had shifted units among fans, there was a general feeling among the band that more could've been done by EMI to promote what was, after all, the first Queen album in more than a decade. With typical frankness, Roger Taylor complained in a later interview with *Classic Rock* that "we were on tour in Europe, and I went into record stores and we weren't in them. And I remember being furious, thinking, 'Why did we make this fucking record?'" Much later, in 2014, Taylor also told the *Toronto Sun* that the singer who eventually succeeded Paul Rodgers, Adam Lambert, was a superior choice: "Paul has one of the greatest rock voices but it's more blues and soul orientated. . . . I would say, with all due respect to Paul, that Adam is more suited to a lot of our material."

It makes for slightly uneasy reading now, but it seems Rodgers also accepted that there was a musical gulf between him and Queen, one that they perhaps hadn't admitted to noticing before. In a 2014 interview with VH1's *On Tap*, Paul Rodgers was asked about being a "hired gun" in Queen + Paul Rodgers, in other words, a vocalist drafted to occupy a role that could theoretically be filled by anyone with the right range. "Of course I'm not a bloody hired gun," he quietly fumed. "God damn it. I'm my own man." Rodgers then characterized the band as a machine: "They've got this amazing machine, and all it lacks is the frontman. You put the right frontman in and it'll operate."

Rodgers is right in a sense: the band is a machine. But it is not a machine in which replacement parts can keep it humming along. Having operated essentially as a large business brand since the late 1970s, Queen is still now its own entity, one that has such strong gravitational power that it can erase the musical traits of its members. Paul Rodgers may have spent a few years delighting fans and upsetting bystanding critics with his blues-ified versions of the Queen canon, but ultimately, it wasn't comfortable for the express reason that he wasn't Freddie Mercury. It would take a talent wholly different in style and execution to even mount an attempt to harness this machine.

35

A New Muse

Adam Lambert

"I Think You Are Theatrical"

In January 2009, American television audiences see twenty-six-year-old Adam Lambert strolling purposefully into the audition room on season eight of *American Idol*. Despite his apparent confidence in front of the television cameras and the judging panel of Simon Cowell, Kara DioGuardi, Paula Abdul, and Randy Jackson, he grips the cuffs of his jacket. The song he chooses to sing, he informs the panel, is "Bohemian Rhapsody." Jackson enthusiastically reports that this is a good choice because it's Simon Cowell's favorite. Lambert's rendition is brief and whinnying but technically impressive, hinting at a stratospheric upper range. It is, in the context of *American Idol*, an interesting voice, honed onstage and as such, according to Cowell's assessment, "theatrical." There is much discussion among the panel about whether such a voice, undoubtedly impressive as it is, deserves a place in a competition that aims, among other things, to locate a future international pop music icon. Lambert makes it through to the next round in spite of the heated debate about whether his voice is governed too strongly by traits of musical theater and is shown running down the street outside clutching his golden ticket.

Four months later, Lambert is sharing a stage with his one remaining fellow finalist, Kris Allen. They're singing Queen's "We Are the Champions." Allen takes the first couple of lines and smiles as he sings them. Lambert, on the other hand, is not smiling as he sings "And bad mistakes, I've made a few." Crashing in behind the two of them, revealed as the *American Idol* logo rises from the stage to the rafters, are Brian May and Roger Taylor. Allen continues to smile through his lines, and Lambert continues to simper defiantly through his, ad-libbing wildly and refusing to break the character of the song. At one point, he places his hand on Brian May's shoulder as if the two had shared stages across the world.

Lambert didn't win *American Idol* in 2009, but rumors immediately appeared in the press stating that the elastic-voiced singer was in line to become the next long-term fixture in the Queen + era. Although May played down those rumors, he did confirm to *Rolling Stone* just a few weeks after the *American Idol* show that, yes, he and Taylor planned to have a "meaningful conversation" with Lambert. Lambert, on the other hand, chose to prick the interest around his sexuality, which had been a topic of no little media speculation during the show's run, and confirmed that he was both gay and actively exploring his sexuality. In a move that now seems revealing of the media's attitude toward sexuality in recent history, Lambert had refused to comment on it until that point so as to avoid his orientation having a negative impact on his chances of winning the show.

On a more industrial level, Queen's involvement with a fellow juggernaut like *American Idol* has seen them return to the show as mentors and performers, keeping them on American prime-time television and, strangely, reversing a lot of the market indifference the band encountered in the second half of their career with Mercury.

But it wasn't until 2011 that May and Taylor's mooted partnership with Lambert would be revealed to the public. At the MTV Europe Music Awards in November 2011, held in Belfast, Northern Ireland, Lambert made his first official appearance as part of Queen + Adam Lambert, performing a medley of "The Show Must Go On," "We Will Rock You," and "We Are the Champions." Lambert's appearance is striking: a black leather trenchcoat and high-heeled leather boots with his hair whipped into a shuddering peak. Performing with his new colleagues, he carries the hallmarks of a front man, using the physical vocabulary of someone in charge of his own stage. At one point near the end of "We Are the Champions," Lambert strides down the central gangway of the stage with such speed and intent that Brian May literally has to jog to keep up with him while manhandling a tricky solo out of his Red Special.

It's not quite an all-encompassing triumph of a performance, but it is solid, and it looks good on television. More important, it's the beginning of a new dynamic within the band, one that could redress the band's imbalances and reinstall a front man for whom performance is a process of command and delivery. For all the times over the years since Freddie Mercury's death that May or Taylor had said of their latest project, "I think Freddie would have loved it," this was perhaps the closest they'd yet come to making that claim seem believable.

An Exclusively Live Experience

Initially, live appearances after the MTV Europe Music Awards were confined to one-offs and a small tour. No one even mentioned the possibility of recording an album: for the time being, this was to be a live experience over and above anything else. Lambert's first test was to join the band for a special concert in Ukraine, specifically in Kiev's Independence Square as part of a joint show with Elton John. The scale of the show was as ambitious as usual, but the set list was all Queen: no compromises, no experiments, and, tellingly, not a single track from *The Cosmos Rocks*. Deeper cuts from the Queen back catalog immediately resurfaced, including an extended version of "Dragon Attack" replete with an eye-wateringly indulgent bass solo. The Kiev show was in every sense a professional one, with Lambert's nerves under the control of a seasoned performer. Occasionally, it's possible to see him glance to the side of the stage, seeking cues from keyboardist and veteran linchpin Spike Edney. Also part of the band in this incarnation, it's worth noting, is Roger Taylor's son Rufus, handling auxiliary percussion.

The demand for this version of the Queen experience was immediate and obvious. A clutch of European dates was announced, including a headline slot at 2012's Sonisphere festival at Knebworth Park, the scene of some of Queen's most triumphant and well-attended performances. However, the festival was canceled just a few months before it was due to take place, and the band hastily booked three consecutive nights at London's Hammersmith Apollo instead (the Hammersmith Odeon, where Queen played so many times in the mid-1970s, was no longer in existence). For these shows, Lambert would imitate Mercury's vocal tics on "Under Pressure" with Roger Taylor taking the David Bowie role and Brian May playing his part on a double-necked Red Special. Lambert also dueted with a video of Freddie Mercury during "Bohemian Rhapsody," another in a string of examples of self-reference. Writing in the *Telegraph*, critic Neil McCormick was more baffled than impressed by the spectacle of the show: "They deliver the hits with crowd pleasing gusto but it never really feels like a band. It's a Queen show. But it's not Queen." Caroline Sullivan in the *Guardian* was kinder overall but still took issue with Lambert in comparison to Mercury: "The late singer still inhabits every one of Queen's songs, and the best Lambert could do was sing them with verve."

This popular interpretation of Queen + Adam Lambert as a kind of jukebox experience is not completely groundless, but it does negate the agency of Lambert as a solo artist. For these early shows, it is clear to see the debt that Lambert owes not only to the existing Mercury recordings but also to the built-in temptation of a trained singer to simply perform the songs accurately.

The Queen Brand Extends

Gradually, live commitments began to stack up, and Queen + Adam Lambert became fixtures at summer festivals and regulars on television. The brand of Queen suddenly became far more visible and reached increasingly more varied audiences through the sheer force of their aptitude as a traveling spectacle, accompanying the finalists of *The X Factor* in a group rendition of "Somebody

Adam Lambert's first London show with Queen.
Davide Traversi / We Will Rock You Official Italian Queen Fan Club

to Love" for a prime-time TV audience and performing in Westminster under the shadow of Big Ben as 2014 turned into 2015. That New Year's show, broadcast live on BBC 1 and seen by more than 10 million people, is something that could have been achieved only in this branded phase of Queen. This scale of live television performance was something curiously missing from Queen's initial phase (with an obvious and roaring exception of Live Aid). Aside from the fact that live television concerts were not so common in that incarnation of the band, it was almost as if the band's maniacal managerial control over their own interests—the belief in keeping affairs internal—excluded such things. But in the twenty-first century and with a lead singer forged in the fire of reality television and stage musicals, Queen's profile became still more pervasive. That it was based partially on the achievements and contributions of someone who had passed away in 1991 was the subject of much criticism and the source of constant "Freddie would be rolling in his grave" rhetoric in live reviews.

Queen's often tempestuous relationship with the press and their history of less-than-glowing reviews has long earmarked them as a band impervious to the negative thoughts of a critical intelligentsia, seeing far more worthy evidence in a full concert hall of scarf-waving enthusiasts. An emergent immunity to even the harshest criticism has now closed like a suit of armor around the band, deflecting the many slings and arrows as they assume the position of a traveling party band.

A more substantial touring schedule was established for 2016, taking in multiple open-air productions across Europe and Asia. Among these dates was the band's first-ever concert in Israel, specifically in Tel Aviv's Yarkon Park to an audience of 50,000. The schedule wasn't hugely inflated from the busy itinerary maintained by Queen + Paul Rodgers, but the set lists were pure nostalgic indulgence, the very essence of the band's greatest-hits collections given an invigorating new voice and stagecraft to match.

Mass visibility continued to come naturally for the band with Lambert as its new focal point. In an extended sketch for *The Late Late Show with James Corden* from early 2017, Lambert duels with Corden over who would make the better front person for Queen, while May and Taylor gamely run through snippets of hits like "Another One Bites the Dust" and "Somebody to Love" (which sees Corden fare particularly well in the complex timing of the final chorus). May and Taylor are simply called on to play the hits and be humorously glib: the star of the segment is undoubtedly Lambert, by now effortlessly comfortable with *his* role in *his* band.

It's a sign of the times when Queen, one of the longest-serving heritage acts on the planet, is gleefully co-opted into contemporary formats for ever-wider audiences to experience, in this case, the television segment curated for viral online consumption. The front-man battle segment stands proud with more than 15 million YouTube views at the time of this writing, but in context, it's one of Corden's more modest hits (for context, views of similar videos with the likes of Paul McCartney and Adele reach into the tens and even hundreds of millions). This aside, what's clear is that this multi-platform version of the band has successfully set up camp in the Internet age.

Further lucrative live shows were booked for 2017 and 2018 that would take the band around the world again, this time with a longer sojourn in the United States. This culminated in ten nights at the Park MGM theater on the Las Vegas Strip (formerly the Monte Carlo), something Queen had never done before. This leg of the tour was knowingly named "The Crown Jewels" and represented something of a victory lap for the band, their bulletproof commerciality in America now cemented.

Fan-shot footage of these shows tells us so much not only about the performance but also about the temperature and fever of the band's fan base. One YouTuber claims that his self-shot footage of one of the Park MGM shows focuses so heavily on Lambert alone because he is himself "a Glambert" and that there are many alternative videos out there that show May and Taylor more generously. He'd spent a small fortune on tickets and getting to the show: he'd document it how he liked and focus on his favorite member of Queen if he wanted to. It's almost unfair to say it, but this kind of thing, this level of adoration, just didn't happen with Paul Rodgers in the band.

Why Does Adam Lambert Work Well for Queen?

A simple answer to this question would be that Adam Lambert's voice is technically superior to that of both Freddie Mercury and Paul Rodgers. Its range is wider, its athleticism more daring, and its control more rigid. His rigorously established base level of vocal proficiency is impressive, the product not only of formal training but of extensive experience as well. There is the sense that his instrument is so muscular that it could deal with the rigors of any Queen song, from whisper to scream and from giggle to caterwaul.

Visually, too, Lambert is able to harness a certain flamboyance that marks him out from his bandmates. On a purely practical level, it was genuinely hard to see Paul Rodgers from the back of an arena because he just looked like a guy in a T-shirt, almost indistinguishable from any auxiliary musicians onstage. Lambert, on the other hand, peacocks elaborately enough to be seen from a helicopter.

But these are cold and factual reasons: surely, there must be a spiritual connection, something less tangible, that explains the clear relaxation of the whole ensemble in this configuration in comparison to the collaborations that had

Queen and Adam Lambert onstage, Milan, 2018.   *Alice Lorenzini/lunaelive.com*

come before. Even in the comparatively short years in which he's been part of the Queen story, Lambert's demeanor as a performer has evolved from that of a spirited soloist to something approaching a unique artist. It could be that Lambert's slotting into the role seems so effortless because he is, on some levels, similar to Freddie Mercury: a rangy tenor, imperious and impish in his stage work. Another way to sum it up could be to say that the shock of hearing Paul Rodgers singing "I Want to Break Free" is far more jarring than the comparatively pleasant surprise of hearing Adam Lambert singing "We Are the Champions." Regardless of whether he has or not, there is something innately more convincing about Lambert assuring a crowd that he has lived in a belladonic haze.

Lambert's stage credentials could lead one to a conclusion that Queen + Adam Lambert as a whole is simply another approximation of the Queen experience rather than a musical entity with its own agency. Certainly, watching Lambert interact with nostalgia live onstage would support this: watch him in videos of the band's Park Theatre shows as he blends his voice into the chorale that begins "Bohemian Rhapsody" or aping the vocal tics of Freddie Mercury on the fast version of "We Will Rock You," and this is clear enough.

But there is just enough of Lambert's own personality to distance his performances from mere homage. It goes beyond costuming and presentation and sits more squarely with Lambert's gradual journey into artistic comfort. Compare and contrast his first performance at the MTV European Music Awards with a show on the band's 2015 tour, which regularly saw Lambert sliding louchely onto a purple chaise longue and delivering "Killer Queen" while cooling himself with a gold fan. Lambert acknowledges his relationship with Mercury onstage and in his social media (a March 2019 Instagram post on his official account was merely a picture of Mercury in the mid-1970s and a love heart) but has still managed to hollow out the right areas of the Queen catalog so that he might claim them for himself. And whether or not that process is comfortable for the listener is, understandably, the source of much speculation even today.

Mercury Lives Onstage

One of the more poignant results of Queen's continued presence on live stages across the world is that one song in particular, "Love of My Life," still manages to entrance audiences despite its composer long having left the stage. Mercury's ballad for Mary Austin was a concert favorite in his lifetime, but contemporary performances of the song see Brian May assume the role of soloist, playing his own twelve-string arrangement and taking the lead vocal for the main part of the song. Stagecraft and technology is such today that it's unremarkable for duets to happen from beyond the grave, but the final section of "Love of My Life" is surely one of the most poignantly realized examples. The usual format is this: May will perform the song, accompanying himself on the guitar (with a little extra synthesized strings in the background from Spike Edney), but Freddie Mercury will appear on the large video screen behind him to sing the final section and, in effect, "lead" the audience in a sing-along. The footage of Mercury is taken from the band's Wembley Stadium show in 1986, the very peak of their potency as a live band and, as such, one hardwired into the collective nostalgia of Queen fans.

There are many versions of this performance available for viewing online, but one taken from Queen + Adam Lambert's 2014 headlining slot at the Summer Sonic festival in Japan shows perfectly the power of this nostalgia hit. Fans are delirious with emotion at Mercury's sudden on-screen appearance, dabbing at their eyes with replica Queen scarves while a visibly moved May thanks them in Japanese. As we see next, there are countless arguments for and against the ongoing use of Mercury's image in this way, but based on the reaction of hundreds of thousands of adoring Queen fans the world over, that "Love of My Life" can still be sung by its composer is a source of comfort and delight.

Was It Right for Queen to Continue without Freddie Mercury?

This is without doubt the most difficult question to answer in relation to Queen's ongoing and multifarious existence—and far be it from this book to attempt to make a moral judgment with more insight than any other bystanding pontificator. As Queen + Adam Lambert continue to enjoy significant success in live arenas and across endless television and online broadcasts, it's hard to balk at the obvious demand for these songs to be reinterpreted for audiences old and new alike. But aside from this, there are questions about motivation. Why didn't the whole band retire in the 1990s like John Deacon? Is everything they do fixated on commercial gain? How can they ignore public relations storms like the severe backlash from the LGBTQ community over Mercury's depiction in *Bohemian Rhapsody*?

A reputation that has dogged Queen since their inception in the mid-1970s is that they were and still are acutely interested in money above most other things. Old and spurious *NME* articles accusing the band of being manufactured by Trident are more bluster than actual evidence, but incidents like their infamous decision to perform in apartheid South Africa haven't done anything to mute this common accusation leveled at May and Taylor, who are the effective caretakers of the brand along with manager Jim Beach. Each increase of Queen's visibility, each television appearance and its resultant second life online, each sellout tour: all of them perpetuate the band's ongoing legacy and invite both criticism and adoration.

The simplest way to question motives here would be to ask, if money were a motivation for May and Taylor (and, indeed, Adam Lambert, who has an entirely separate and successful solo career), then wouldn't they have just retired for a life of answering occasional music licensing requests? There has to be a base level of creative desire to keep the juggernaut on the road. Surely, no reasonable human with endless financial resources would maintain Queen's touring schedule unless they actually wanted to do the touring. Fans, teary-eyed at the sight of their heroes Brian May and Roger Taylor playing music together decades after many imagined they would quietly retire, must surely be the reason to carry on.

But with that fan base and its level of dedication there comes an entirely new dynamic. It would be naive to suggest that fans of rock bands are as much customers as they are enthusiasts, but Queen's ability to serve their fan base with opportunities to spend money is prodigious. A quick glance at the band's official online merchandise store shows a panoply of related items: you can avail yourself of a Brian May–endorsed *Jazz* sixpence guitar plectrum at £7.99, a *Flash Gordon* mug at £12.99, and a replica 1979 Japanese tour T-shirt at £19.99. The more adventurous might plump for jewelry, specifically a ring made from the Zildjian cymbals favored by Roger Taylor ("you heard it... now wear it!") for a cool £325. And have a look at the official Brian May Guitars website for a surprisingly wide range of products and price ranges, too. Again, merchandising is not new, and, in the digital-first landscape of the twenty-first century, it's essential. Queen's use of it is undeniably mercenary, but it's worth noting that all commercial proceeds for a one-fourteenth-scale replica of the famous Freddie Mercury statue that overlooks Lake Geneva do in fact go to the Mercury Phoenix Trust.

As things stand, Queen operates from a position where nostalgia is commodified through every possible channel. The moral temperature of this position simply depends on your tolerance for that nostalgia and the way in which it is continually served, whether it's through blatant methods like merchandising or through slightly more covert methods like Queen + Adam Lambert's live shows, which at least attempt to veil some of their self-reference with new interpretations of classic songs. Perhaps the question shouldn't be whether it was right to continue Queen without Freddie Mercury but rather whether this was the only way in which to do it.

36

Is This the Real Life?

The Queen Movie

The term "development hell" is one not unfamiliar to anyone with an interest in movies and refers specifically to those big-screen projects that, for whatever reason, end up in a production hinterland, destined either to never see completion or to be released in a version unrecognizable or significantly compromised in comparison to its original concept. In a way that is perhaps fitting (or at least typical) for Queen post-Mercury, there was an almighty production upheaval before *Bohemian Rhapsody* finally made it to cinemas in 2018.

The upheaval began in good spirits, though, and with a seemingly perfect casting choice for the central role of Freddie Mercury. In 2010, British comedian

Joe Mazzello as John Deacon, Ben Hardy as Roger Taylor, Rami Malek as Freddie Mercury, and Gwilym Lee as Brian May. *A Bailey/20th Century Fox/Kobal/Shutterstock*

Sacha Baron Cohen, known for guerilla character creations like Borat and Ali G, was revealed by Brian May in an interview to be tackling the part. Also revealed to be involved at this time was screenwriter Peter Morgan, whose previous credits include *Frost/Nixon* and who later went on to create the multi-award-winning Netflix series *The Crown*. It was every inch a classy project, with a bold central casting choice and involvement from May and Taylor as consultants.

However, disappointed with the narrative direction the movie was taking, Baron Cohen left the project in 2013. A few years later, he claimed in an interview with Howard Stern that in an early incarnation at least, the remaining members of Queen had intended Freddie Mercury's death to occur at the midpoint of the film, leaving the second half open to tell the story of how the band was reborn. Baron Cohen, perhaps predictably given the nature of his oeuvre, had been keen to explore the more lurid side of Mercury's sexual and narcotic activities but maintained that this was not the story the band wanted to tell. Later, in 2016, Brian May fired back with a little more candor, claiming, "Sacha became an arse."

Shortly after Baron Cohen's departure, in late 2013, Ben Whishaw became unofficially attached to the part of Mercury, riding high after playing Q in the James Bond movie *Skyfall*. Around this time, Dexter Fletcher also became involved as a director for the project. Fletcher had previously been a noted actor in films like *Kick-Ass* and *Lock, Stock and Two Smoking Barrels* before directing *Sunshine on Leith*, the acclaimed musical based on the songs of the Proclaimers. However, after reports of creative differences between Fletcher (who was in favor of a harder depiction of the story more line with that of Baron Cohen) and producer Graham King, Fletcher left the project in early 2014. It was Fletcher, though, who would ultimately ensure that the movie made it into theaters—but not before a storm of controversy threatened to topple the production completely.

From Bad to Worse

Before his tenure began on *Bohemian Rhapsody*, director Bryan Singer was famous for critically acclaimed hits like *The Usual Suspects* and blockbuster installments in the X-Men franchise. When he became attached to direct *Bohemian Rhapsody* (as well as produce it alongside Jim Beach and Graham King), it seemed an apt choice—here was a director used to substantial budgets and character-led pieces, an award winner and plaudits winner in equal measure. His directorship was reported in late 2016 along with the casting of Rami Malek (star of *Mr. Robot*) as Freddie Mercury.

Production on the movie crept forward for the following months, and footage of a delightfully accurate re-creation of the band's Live Aid set that showed all the principal cast members emerged in October 2017. All appeared to be relatively encouraging, with online reaction to the footage registering as generally very positive. For the climactic scene, a facsimile of the Wembley Stadium stage was built at Bovingdon Airfield near Hemel Hempstead, Hertfordshire. Gwilym Lee, who played Brian May, later revealed that hand doubles had been employed for the Live Aid scene to make close-ups of instrumental flourishes appear more convincing, but such was the actors' collective commitment to accuracy that the hand doubles were never actually used. Interestingly, this was also the first major block of filming for the movie, leading Lee to comment further on the dynamic of the band of actors: "Day one on set was us running out onto the stage, fear, adrenaline and it was very real. You either sink or swim in that situation, it's a real baptism of fire, but it forged us together as a unit."

However, despite the positive reactions, reports of an unhappy set began to emerge in the press, culminating in 20th Century Fox putting a stop to production due to Singer's unexpected nonappearance after Thanksgiving weekend 2017. The explanation given for his absence was that his mother had fallen ill during this time, but elements of the press drew lines between Singer and then upcoming investigations into historical and current accusations of sexual abuse. *The Hollywood Reporter* also claimed that sources close to the project were worried about the deterioration of the working relationship between Singer and Malek.

The strain on the production became so much that Singer was eventually fired in December 2017. In a series of events that made even the recording of an early Queen album look acrimony free, the long-mooted project was stuck near to the end of principal photography with no director, press reports of an unhappy lead, and a distinctly unsavory attachment to a major criminal investigation. All this, remember, was happening outside of whatever creative decisions were being made—surely, the final product would at best be severely compromised in whatever form it arrived.

Fletcher's Return

Within just two days of Singer's being fired, a replacement was found to bring the movie home. Dexter Fletcher immediately took the helm once more. Speaking in May 2018, he offered this matter-of-fact assessment: "They sort of said, 'Look, this is a film that needs to be finished,' and they trusted me with that responsibility."

In January 2018, a month after Fletcher was rehired, Brian May posted the following on his Instagram account: "The entire BR company has been through storms which would have sunk many a ship, but they're all still on board, full of optimism—and with a team spirit stronger than ever. There's such a great feeling of pride in this movie." Positive messages aside, the fact remained that there was an inescapable issue of tonal balance to overcome, a tussle between

Fletcher's R-rated vision and the PG-13 version favored by Graham King and the remaining band members. By the time *Bohemian Rhapsody* was completed, in accordance with the rules of the Director's Guild of America, the director's credit remained with Bryan Singer due to the proportionately large amount of work he had completed on the project.

After completing *Bohemian Rhapsody*, Fletcher went on to direct a film with remarkable factual and thematic crossovers: the Elton John biopic *Rocketman* (although the role of John Reid is tackled in this film by Richard Madden rather than Aiden Gillen).

What Did the Movie Get Right and Wrong?

Looking at the final product, it's difficult to disagree with at least part of Baron Cohen's initial assessment of May and Taylor's creative input. Although the narrative "snapping point" of Mercury's death in the middle of the movie didn't actually come to fruition, it's certainly true that *Bohemian Rhapsody* depicts only the merest hint of the band's (especially Mercury's) more extreme behavior. Characters and timescales are conflated, songs appear at points when they hadn't yet been written, and critics noted a more troubling reading of the film in which many homosexual characters are seen as wholly corrupting influences purely by dint of their sexuality, that the movie was guilty of what was termed in more than one review a "queer erasure."

This final issue in particular is an uncomfortable result of the creative process. It could be argued that May and Taylor, who were largely separate from Mercury's personal life during the time depicted in the film and as creative consultants on the film, were unqualified to correctly characterize it. It is true to say that, almost without exception, every homosexual character in the movie is a negative or malign influence, tacitly caught up with the AIDS crisis and leading Mercury astray (incidentally, there are plenty of compelling arguments in interviews to suggest that Mercury was perfectly happy to lead himself astray). At one point toward the end of the film, shortly before Malek as Mercury resolves to change his ways and return to Queen for Live Aid, a gaggle of leather-clad men led by Paul Prenter seem to circle and stalk Mercury like a pack of predators. It is a major dramatic pinwheel of the film for Mercury to break away from this apparently insidious and darkly threatening lifestyle, and it takes a conversation with Mary Austin to make it happen.

Aside from the troubled nature of the depiction of Mercury's homosexuality, there is much to savor for fans. In much the same way as latter-day installments of the *Star Wars* saga or movies from the Marvel Comic Universe, *Bohemian Rhapsody* is utterly peppered with obscure references and moments designed to prickle the neck hairs of Queen enthusiasts. We see Smile performing "Doing All

Right," we see Brian May unenthusiastically contemplate "the operatic section" of "Bohemian Rhapsody" itself, and we see Mike Myers play an amalgamated record company boss character (presumably based in part on EMI's Roy Featherstone) who makes a rather on-the-nose reference to the popular appearance of "Bohemian Rhapsody" in Myers's own *Wayne's World*.

And while we're on the subject of industrial representations in the movie, the depiction of Jim "Miami" Beach differs somewhat from the impression given by the likes of Howard Blake earlier in this book and other onlookers elsewhere (Beach himself is credited as a producer on the movie). At no point does Beach appear as the spiky and controlling lawyer; moreover, he's a benevolent, almost reluctant leader for the band during their time of need, growing into a trusted and kindly figure capable of crucial insight. Watch, for example, as he secretly tampers with the Wembley Stadium mixing board as the band takes the stage, ensuring theirs will be the loudest performance of the day.

The commitment of Rami Malek in the lead role is plain to see, and he does absolutely nail Mercury's mannerisms, his quiet conversational ways balanced just so with his bravura onstage persona. The casting of the rest of the band, too, is largely uncanny—especially former *Jurassic Park* child star Joseph Mazzello (now Joe Mazzello) as John Deacon, who somehow manages to mine the comparatively limited Deacy material available and create a surprisingly deep characterization.

Ultimately, *Bohemian Rhapsody* is rather more liberal with factual accuracy than it perhaps needed to be, especially given the material on offer, but the technical accuracy achieved in the climactic Live Aid sequence is truly remarkable (if, again, a little rose tinted). In the film version of this episode, presumably for reasons of narrative tension, Mercury's AIDS diagnosis happens in the weeks before he takes the stage at Wembley in mid-1985 rather than the actual date of 1987. Further than that, the day of Live Aid also, in a pure narrative contrivance, is the same day Mercury introduces Jim Hutton to his parents—*and* the same day his father finally tells him he is proud of his son's achievements.

Speaking to *Attitude* magazine, Malek defended what some critics and viewers saw as a rather light depiction of Mercury's AIDS diagnosis: "The film needed to approach it in a delicate manner. You can't shy away from it. It was an important moment to have in the film, one that ultimately is very sad but also empowering in a way."

Perhaps the best way of summarizing these various narrative conveniences is to say that *Bohemian Rhapsody* contains a litany of "Chubby? Hmm . . ." moments. This phrase, coined by journalist Jon Ronson and popularized by film critic Mark Kermode, refers to the tendency in biographical movies (especially those based on musicians) for protagonists to very obviously do "the thing" for which they are famous. For example, the 1989 TV movie *The Karen Carpenter Story* features a scene in which Karen Carpenter (played by Cynthia Gibb) reads a review of a recent Carpenters gig in which she is referred to as "chubby." The camera dramatically zooms in on her face, and it signifies the very beginning of her tragic journey with anorexia nervosa. In *Bohemian Rhapsody*, almost every opportunity is taken to shoehorn in such moments, including the composition of songs like "We Will Rock You" and "Another One Bites the Dust."

Who Else Appears in *Bohemian Rhapsody*?

Because, as we've established, Queen is a terminally self-referential band fixated on weaving themselves and their legacy throughout any product with their sign-off, there are also some intriguing cameos in *Bohemian Rhapsody*. In the background as Rami Malek strolls through a club prior to joining Queen, none other than Luke Deacon, son of John, is staring directly back at him in quiet wonder. You'll also see May's daughter Emily Ruth standing alongside Lucy Boynton as Mary Austin during an early live performance. Both May and Taylor also appear very briefly, as does Jim Beach, in a scene that was eventually deleted from the movie itself (although some Internet speculators claim it's possible to see May leaning against a television camera reading the *Sun* in the final cut).

But undoubtedly, the strangest cameo comes during one of Queen's early U.S. tours. Malek as Mercury is on the telephone outside a gas station talking to Mary Austin when a mustached trucker catches his eye, an unspoken look shared between them suggesting that Mercury should join him in the bathroom. The trucker is in fact played by Adam Lambert. The bizarreness of this frivolous in-joke barely warrants explanation, but the many-layered notion of the singer who went on to replace Mercury having an off-screen liaison with a fictional version of that very singer seemed to be received as a mere lark. Lambert himself appeared to confirm his cameo in the film in a tweet accompanied by a picture of himself as the trucker, simply saying, "Who is he!?" and advertising the then forthcoming digital download release.

One other appearance worthy of note is a purely sonic one rather than a traditional actorly cameo role. Tim Staffell, former singer and bassist with Smile, lent his vocal talents to a new recording of "Doing All Right." May and Taylor also rerecorded their vocals to suit, making it a kind of remote Smile reunion. The song remains largely unchanged, but there is perhaps a little more timber in Staffell's once feathery delivery.

How Did the Movie Perform?

Unsurprisingly, given the immense production buildup and fan anticipation of the film's eventual release, it was a box office hit. More than that, it quickly became the highest-grossing musical biopic of all time, surpassing the box office total of 2015's *Straight Outta Compton* (which detailed the career of NWA). At the time of this writing, it has grossed more than $900 million against its budget of approximately $50 million, a legitimate commercial powerhouse that, in terms of sheer financial power, is among the most lucrative projects ever commissioned by the band. However, Brian May claimed in a BBC Radio 2 interview in May 2019 that he and Taylor were yet to make a single penny from the movie.

As has been briefly mentioned earlier, the critical reaction to the movie was mixed, with the issues of timescale, factual inconsistencies, and the depiction of homosexuality (Mercury's and others') the common threads picked at. This didn't stop the movie being heavily garlanded throughout the awards season of 2018 and 2019. Most notably, Rami Malek won a BAFTA, a Golden Globe, and an Academy Award for his lead performance as Freddie Mercury, remarking in his acceptance speech at the Academy Awards on the positivity of making a film about "a gay man, an immigrant who lived his life unapologetically himself."

It's fair to say that *Bohemian Rhapsody* and Queen verily dominated the Oscars in 2019. Not only did the movie itself scoop four awards, but Queen + Adam Lambert actually opened the televised show with a performance of "We Will Rock You" and "We Are the Champions." The performance is met with an atmosphere almost of disbelief that a rock band would be permitted access to a black-tie event and, furthermore, that it would be Queen. Emma Stone looks confused and delighted, Jordan Peele nods sagely to the beat, and Mike Myers points excitedly as the screen behind the band shows footage of Freddie Mercury. Adam Lambert is wearing a jacket that cost $10,000.

Despite the visibly adoring reception in the theater itself, Spice Girl and sometime TV talent show judge Melanie Brown (known professionally as Mel B) delivered her critique of the performance directly to Roger Taylor during a televised interview for *Good Morning Britain*, telling him, "I wanted more pizzazz." Taylor's response is a weary "Oh, blimey," the reply of a man for whom Mel B's opinion on the culmination of nearly half a century of music making couldn't matter less.

What Does *Bohemian Rhapsody* Mean for the Queen Brand?

The remarkable performance of *Bohemian Rhapsody* after such a troubled genesis is a sign of several things. First, it's a sign the Rami Malek's lauded performance was convincing enough for him to be decorated with multiple accolades. Second, it's a sign that controversial story decisions and problematic character representations are of little consequence to a ticket-buying public. Third, and perhaps most important, it's a sign that the Queen brand has rarely been more visible.

Queen's brand differs from that of their stadium-filling heritage act peers, the likes of the Rolling Stones or U2, in that it repackages its nostalgia using ever-diversifying methods. Their peers may keep recording new material, but Queen has barely written a note (certainly nothing that would make it into a live set anyway). Instead, they've used their catalog to build a constant and evolving monument for themselves, one that extends into increasing media and formats across countless platforms. Queen's evolving nostalgia can be expressed with equal force in an Adam Lambert ad lib, in a Roger Taylor Instagram post, or in a $50 million Hollywood movie. Plenty of their peers come close, but none can quite match Queen's industrial levels of musical activity in the modern cultural landscape.

37

The Music of Freddie Mercury

Elsewhere in this book, you'll find plenty of discussion and dissection of Freddie Mercury's songs written for Queen, so this chapter aims to cover the highlights of his recording career away from the band, as a solo artist and collaborator. But perhaps it's most important, first of all, to establish what kind of writer Mercury was. We so often think of him as a one-off in the entertainment world, a firebrand possessed of a singular creative voice: this could be argued convincingly. However, to go a level deeper, that inspiration for that creative voice, be it through songwriting, vocal sound, or stage performance, was the result of intense study rather than divine, untraceable inspiration.

Few musicians of the rock 'n' roll age have managed to incorporate such a wide panoply of influences into their compositions, and fewer still wore them so plainly, the default position being to hide one's influences deeply, cleverly, within the music as if their detection would be a game for critics to play. Mercury, unlike Lennon and McCartney, Carole King, or Leonard Cohen, would gleefully let all his listeners know exactly what music he was into just by listening to his songs.

It's also important to note that Mercury did see himself as a solo artist—albeit one sensible enough to know when he had the perfect collaborative vehicle in Queen. He knew his singing voice was distinctive enough to be a product on its own, away from the band, and as such, his career is strewn with projects and oddities that add an alluring richness to his oeuvre.

"Love Kills"

Giorgio Moroder had been a circling figure in the Queen story as they gravitated toward Munich at the turn of the 1980s. The band had recorded at his Musicland studio facility, and some accounts suggest that the disco pioneer mystically masterminded their pairing with his long-term associate Reinhold

Mack as producer. But with Mercury in particular showing clear aptitude and enthusiasm for the kind of dance music Moroder was producing, they eventually teamed up for a single named "Love Kills," intended to be part of the sound track for Moroder's 1984 reedit of Fritz Lang's seminal 1927 science-fiction film *Metropolis* (alongside songs by Canadian stadium rock band Loverboy as well as Bonnie Tyler and Adam Ant).

It would be difficult to consider this first solo release proper from Mercury anything other than a failure regardless of the track's musical merits. Moroder's project was quite universally reviled, and the sound track was one of the main critical bugbears. It was nominated for two infamous Golden Raspberry awards (known in the movie industry as the Razzies), specifically for Worst Musical Score for Moroder and Worst Original Song for "Love Kills."

Desperate to harness Mercury's power as a solo talent outside of the Queen machine, CBS Records had already offered him a substantial two-album deal. By the time *Metropolis* had sent critical ripples, Mercury was almost finished with his first solo album.

Mr. Bad Guy

Mercury released two solo albums during his career, both of them during separate periods of hiatus from his work with Queen. The first, 1985's *Mr. Bad Guy*, is a natural musical partner to Queen's *Hot Space*, written and partially recorded after Queen's infamous disco-inflected "misstep," but also acts as a signifier for the musical enthusiasms Mercury entertained away from the band. Although disco and dance are strong and persistent influences and time spent in the clubs of Munich clearly had its effect, songs like "Made in Heaven," with its Wagnerian music video and dense choral arrangements, show Mercury as a songwriter aiming for operatic grandeur.

Since his youth, classical music represented an ambition, a lofty, romantic complexity to which Mercury would aspire. Songs on his debut solo collection joyously collapse under the weight of his references to the genre, resulting in a remarkably funky bass line of lower strings, brass, and bassoon on the title track as well as a rhapsodic Rachmaninov-inspired outro of pianistic excess, choral backing vocals, and Mercury himself exploring the soprano range of his singing voice.

The writing and production of the album took place in Mountain Studios, Queen's own studio sanctuary, with Reinhold Mack operating the controls with the composer. Mercury painstakingly arranged the instrumental elements with synthesizers, while a hired cast of studio musicians took care of the more traditional guitar, bass, and drum work. It was, in many ways, an album in direct opposition to anything Queen may have produced, exercising Mercury's tendencies for excess without the usual filter of three other composers to shut down any wilder ideas. Because of this, *Mr. Bad Guy* paints a fairly consummate picture of Mercury in the early 1980s, reaching for the divine using only earthly means and suffering their limitations.

Despite the crucible of their composition being immersed in the homosexual underground, several of the songs on *Mr. Bad Guy* are overwhelmingly heteronormative in their worldview. "Foolin' Around" makes reference to the "sexy lady" with whom Mercury is enjoying romantic dalliances, and the elaborately staged video for "I Was Born to Love You" shows him in raptures of devotion for the female object of his desire. As an expression of his sexual status, though, the album inevitably captures only portions of the whole story. Worryingly dark lyrics on "My Love Is Dangerous" ("My love is dangerous, always makes you bleed") jar with the breezy cod reggae and take on a new and uncomfortable meaning in the context of Mercury's later illness. "Your Kind of Lover," however, shows him in more comfortable territory, blithely cruising for a partner: "I wanna boogie down with you, brother, boogie down with bassman, win love on the grandslam, I'll be there waiting when you call."

Mr. Bad Guy wasn't exactly the commercial juggernaut that CBS had been hoping for. "I Was Born to Love You" reached number eleven on the U.K. singles charts and a lowly number seventy-six on the *Billboard* "Hot 100," while the album itself managed to crack the U.K. top ten. It was a grand artistic statement of intent dressed up as a hit generator, weighed down by what was seen as Mercury's pretension and silliness. Scanning the album's liner notes, it seems the silliness ran even as far as the dedication: "This album is dedicated to my cat Jerry—also Tom, Oscar and Tiffany, and all the cat lovers across the universe—screw everybody else!"

Freddie Mercury at a press conference in Australia in May 1985.   *Gill Allen/Shutterstock*

What Happened to the Songs Freddie Mercury Wrote with Michael Jackson?

After watching them play live in Los Angeles several times, the King of Pop was an avowed fan of Queen and was naturally drawn to Mercury's songwriting. Wanting to collaborate further, the two found time between touring schedules to work together on a suite of songs (one of which, in Mercury's estimation, could've ended up on Jackson's *Thriller* album had they finished it in time). Rather than the adversarial atmosphere of collaboration that David Bowie brought to the studio during sessions for "Under Pressure," Jackson's vibe on his home turf at his home in Encino, California, was wholly confusing to Mercury. The sessions were fruitful to begin with, and the pair worked on three songs: "There Must Be More to Life Than This" (which was originally intended for *Hot Space* but didn't make the cut), "State of Shock" (which Jackson took away with him to work on and eventually featured vocals from Mick Jagger), and "Victory" (which remains unreleased). The first song from the sessions did find its way onto *Mr. Bad Guy*, but the duet featuring both vocalists became available only in 2014 in a reconfigured version for the release of the *Queen Forever* compilation.

The sessions themselves were reportedly interrupted by an unwanted visitor to the studio, however. Queen manager Jim Beach took a call from a perturbed Mercury, who wanted the sessions be canceled as soon as possible because Jackson insisted on bringing his pet llama, Louie, into the studio while the pair were working. Or, according to an account from journalist David Wigg, it was Jackson's pet chimpanzee, Bubbles, who caused the sessions to stall, as Jackson would interminably seek the chimp's opinion between takes, even sitting him between the two singers on the piano stool. There is another side to the story, though: the version given to the *Sun* newspaper by an assistant years later claimed that it was in fact Jackson who brought the sessions to a close after finding Mercury snorting cocaine through a banknote.

Mercury as an Interpreter

Mercury's skill at interpreting the work of others made him a surprisingly adaptable musical presence in spite of the unique qualities of his voice. However, those excursions into work composed by others were fairly limited in number (see chapter 5 for discussion of his first recorded cover versions). Before he set about working on his second solo album, Mercury worked with his old friend Dave Clark (of the Dave Clark Five) on the latter's new rock musical: *Time*.

On paper, the medium of the stage musical is a perfect fit for Mercury. His soaring pop voice shows so many traits of classical aspiration (dizzying vibrato, sensitive rubato), occupying the same middle ground between rock roughness and classical refinement as his great idol Liza Minnelli. In practice, Mercury's involvement extended to only two songs. Clark's vision for the musical extended to a concept album of songs from the show, performed by a varied cast of artists, including Mercury, Julian Lennon, and Dionne Warwick. For the stage show itself, the perennially popular British easy-listening denizen Cliff Richard was cast in the lead role (later replaced by David Cassidy), while the venerable Laurence Olivier appeared in a pre-filmed "hologram" role as a disembodied head named Akash. This was just one of the show's technical marvels, which were heralded widely at the time and throughout its eventual two-year run.

The first of Mercury's contributions to the concept album was its title track, a gloopy but effective piece that allows his voice to rocket to the limits of its range. It was released as a single in May 1986 and limped to number thirty-two on the U.K. singles chart despite the success of the musical itself. The second was "In My Defence," which remained relatively unheard until after Mercury's death. It's buried in the middle of the concept album but is one of Mercury's most untamed vocal performances from this period. Almost Michael Bolton–esque in its vertiginous bravura, "In My Defence" revolves around the line "I'm just a singer with a song," itself a pre-echo of the inscription on the statue of Mercury overlooking Lake Geneva (although Brian May eventually penned it "Lover of life, singer of songs"). His trademark vocal rasp is in full effect, but with it, there are cracks—signs of wear and fatigue that we don't see anywhere else in his entire discography. On its eventual single release in 1992, it peaked at number eight on the U.K. singles chart.

During *Time*'s run, specifically on April 14, 1988, Mercury performed "In My Defence" and another song, "It's in Every One of Us," live with Cliff Richard at the Dominion Theatre, where the show was resident. It was to be Mercury's final truly live performance (his later appearances with Montserrat Caballé to perform "Barcelona" were mimed). Bootleg recordings of the performance show Mercury's voice to be bell-like in its clarity, an overpowering foil to Richard's distinctly feathery tone with little trace of rasp. His ad libs are accomplished and slick, bouncing instinctively off Richard, who is relegated to a supporting role as Mercury deftly outclasses him. Although it was far from the last vocal performance Mercury would deliver, it's heartening that the final live recording should be one in which he sounds so effortless.

"I'm Wearing My Heart Like a Crown . . ."

Shortly after his work on Dave Clark's *Time* concept album, Mercury recorded a cover of Buck Ram's "The Great Pretender," as made famous by the Platters. On the surface, it's the perfect song choice: Mercury even confirmed in an interview that the song's title chimed with his feelings on performing for a living. But looking more deeply, it's possible to hear Mercury searching for a musical home.

His performance is convincing, witty, and flamboyant with idiosyncratic delivery intact (clipping lines like "My need is *such*" to an overtly percussive effect, growling through "I played the game"). As a stand-alone recording with no visual element, it is perfectly Mercury yet still in service to the song itself. But as we know from Queen's videography, the tendency is always there for self-reference: it's as if every musical artifact from the second half of the band's career must in some way be viewed in relation to what's gone before, whether it's retooled live footage or getting children to dress up as the band in the video for "The Miracle." As such, the lavish video for "The Great Pretender," directed by David Mallet, is riven with Queen tropes.

Barely a lyric goes past without its being reflected in the video in relation to Mercury's past glories with Queen. "I'm wearing my heart like a crown" is suddenly accompanied by a shot of Mercury onstage in full royal regalia during a Queen encore, and he capers around in various re-creations of previous Queen and solo music videos ("I Want to Break Free," "Radio Ga Ga," and "I Was Born to Love You"). At one point, he is surrounded by an army of cardboard-cutout Freddie Mercurys, a visual comment on the song's themes of personality erosion and the emotional toll of constant performance and adoration. And if these references weren't obvious enough, Mercury drafted Roger Taylor and his close friend and musical collaborator Peter Straker to dress in drag and play his backing singers.

To convincingly use an existing pop song to knowingly comment on one's own career in the same industry is on one hand boldly metatextual but on the other could suggest that Mercury's real desire was to work on his own material rather than a cover version. Buck Ram, well into his eighties by the time the cover was released, was pleased to know the song was experiencing a second life but had no idea who Mercury was. His solo career and the attached albums were undoubtedly successful, but Mercury's achievements paled in comparison to those of Queen in terms of commercial success and general notoriety. Perhaps it was a sore point.

Barcelona: Mercury Meets His Match

The clearest manifestation of Mercury's obsession with classical music and particularly opera was his lengthy collaboration and friendship with the Spanish soprano Montserrat Caballé. To Mercury, she represented vocal perfection, an ideal instrument capable of accessing the deepest levels of emotion without any apparent effort. Seeing her perform as far back as 1983 immediately lodged

Mercury and Caballé on stage in Ibiza, 1987.   *Ilpo Musto/Shutterstock*

her in his mind, and a campaign of messages began to flow from Mercury to Caballé's camp, to no avail.

Mercury would continue to publicly sing the soprano's praises and privately mount his campaign to convince her to sing with him for the next few years. Conjuring a project in his head, Mercury wrote songs and duets that the pair would sing together in an ideal world, when the formidable Caballé finally granted him a meeting. Eventually, it worked, but it wasn't until 1987 that the pair met, initially to discuss the idea of recording duets together. In the lobby of the Ritz in Barcelona, instead of simply explaining his plans for a collaboration to his singing idol, Mercury sat at the hotel's piano and played an embryonic version of "Exercises in Free Love," one of the songs he proposed they would sing together. The soprano was impressed with his clear musicality and agreed that the pair would reconvene at Mercury's house in London.

Caballé had already been earmarked for a performing slot at the opening ceremony for the 1992 Olympic Games, to be held in Barcelona. Knowing full well that this was the case, Mercury presented her with a song named after the city itself when the two met in London. Their creative relationship was instantly a musical infatuation: he was already devoted to her, but in Mercury, Caballé found a sympathetic, considerate, and vocally electrifying sparring partner who involved her in the compositional process in a way she would never encounter in the world of opera. A demo of "Barcelona" was made during the lengthy working sessions at Mercury's house and presented to the Olympic committee.

Work on a full collaborative album began shortly after, albeit remotely, as the two singers struggled to find time to dedicate to the project between their own touring commitments. Mercury spent much of 1987 recording demos with Mike Moran in which Mercury would sing Caballé's intended vocal lines in falsetto so that she knew what recordings she should send back from whichever opera house or concert hall she might currently be in. Working with Mercury and Moran to round out what would become *Barcelona* was the lyricist Tim Rice, who contributed words for two songs on the album. Rice also happened to be living at the time with the West End musicals star Elaine Paige, who was putting together her own album of Queen covers with orchestral backing (Mike Moran also worked on this release).

Classical and orchestral influences are unsurprisingly the most pervasive on *Barcelona*'s eight songs, which range from the kind of pastiche pieces you'd find reference to on Queen albums to fully orchestrated romances with synthesizer augmentation. It's interesting also to hear how Mercury operates as part of a duo: when he sang with David Bowie on "Under Pressure," there was, despite its miraculous feel, much toe stepping as the two duked it out for vocal supremacy, but with Caballé, Mercury appears sensitive, singing soft and low beneath her soprano on "La Japonaise."

For his part, Mercury appears on *Barcelona*, in the staged photographs and music video with Caballé, as happy as he ever did in his working life. The pageantry and formality of classical music appealed to him in an aesthetic sense: the somber, dramatic staging and the stark lighting and comparatively restrained wardrobe drew a clear distinction between this project and his work with Queen, while musically he was able to tackle material that would only be glimpsed at elsewhere in his oeuvre. For Caballé, *Barcelona* was a complete leap of faith, specifically her faith in Mercury's ability to convincingly sell himself as her musical equal. Arguably, Caballé had more to lose in the classical music world than Mercury did in the pop world, which by now was quite accustomed to his capricious career moves.

The album itself spawned a modest hit single in the title track on its original release in 1987 but performed much better on its reissue in 1992 after both the opening ceremony of the Olympic Games and Mercury's death. There is no readily available footage of the pair singing live together, but their mimed performances both in Barcelona and on a huge outdoor stage at the Ku Nightclub in Ibiza display their connection clearly enough: both are respectful of and at ease with each other's talents.

A Social Musician

Mercury's social life revolved around music to such an extent that his major personal relationships would be instigated and then governed by it. During his time bouncing between the gay districts of New York, Berlin, and Munich, the emerging club sound and disco music were the catalysts for his musical ideas both inside and outside of Queen. Everything, from his outfits to his style of dancing, was influenced by his social experiences during this key period.

Later in his life, ensconced in his Garden Lodge mansion in Kensington, Mercury would spend evenings leaping to and from the piano stool in turn with friends like Peter Straker and Mike Moran. A recording exists of one such evening from 1988 in which the three friends, joined at points by Brian May, cycle through dozens of examples of pianistic frippery, from Liszt's "La Campanella" and Mozart's so-called "Queen of the Night" aria to Gershwin's "Summertime" and "Happy Talk" from *South Pacific*. It is clearly a casual evening, but it is also one dominated by music, the only interruptions coming when Mercury makes sure a lightly intoxicated May calls a cab to get home rather than drive.

As with his performative streak and the corresponding social shyness, there was a quieter side to Mercury's music making. Contrasting this image of a supremely gregarious composer and musical bon vivant is that of the private noodler who, legend has it, spent a chunk of the 1970s sleeping with his head under a piano keyboard so that he could reach his hands up in the night to tinker with new ideas. It's a romantic image, one referenced heavily in the *Bohemian Rhapsody* movie, and one we can take with a pinch of salt. But we do know that Mercury composed mostly alone at his preferred instrument, the piano, bemoaning his own skills with the guitar, the default instrument of rock composition.

Ultimately, though, he needed colleagues once the toil of composition was complete. Comparable in some senses to Brian Wilson, who would also require the support of similarly skilled and sensitive musicians to eke out and make real his compositional ideas, Mercury's musicality was naturally geared toward collegiate participation. Sharing his work made it real, and he understood that writing the songs was only half the battle. To win it, he would always require reinforcements, whether it was Reinhold Mack, Mike Moran, Giorgio Moroder, or Montserrat Caballé. Alone and later in life, Mercury was happy to putter around with drum machines and keyboards, making demos for collaborators to pore over, to make flesh.

And although he was a perfectionist and an obsessive when it came to the execution of his own material, Mercury's role in the studio was to cajole and encourage, to conjure from those collaborators the most extraordinary results through sheer force of personality. Outtakes and isolated tracks from Queen recording sessions show him to be fixated on musical results but not at the expense of working environment: easily more Brian Wilson than Phil Spector. Indeed, his bandmates recalled fondly their time spent together during sessions for the then untitled follow-up to *Innuendo* despite the knowledge that his life was likely to end before work on the album was complete. Ultimately, it is this dedication to the craft of composition that defined him as a musician.

38

"Give It to Me One More Time!"

The Greatest Voice in Rock?

Few instruments in rock music have impacted culture so indelibly as Freddie Mercury's elastic, rasping tenor voice. This is all the more remarkable given the elements already jostling for attention in Queen: to compete with Brian May's guitar alone would be a challenge for any singer, but Mercury's voice achieved something close to invincibility even in this most idiosyncratic of lineups.

Naturally, there are technical triumphs that Mercury birthed and grew himself, but the raw instrument itself possessed such innate virtuosity and versatility that it's hard to imagine him working too hard at polishing what he already had. As strong in chest voice as he was in falsetto (and with almost five octaves at his command), Mercury is unique in the rock pantheon—more natural than Robert Plant and Axl Rose, more versatile than Brian Wilson and Michael Jackson, and at least a rival to Aretha Franklin and Beyoncé in sheer power.

What Does He Actually Do Differently?

A 2016 analysis by Professor Christian Herbst points specifically to the quality and range of Mercury's vibrato (the artful undulation of pitch on held notes) as the source of his uniqueness in the rock pantheon, and it is a valid musicological explanation of his base vocal sound. But aside from this, there are little signifiers of vocal character littered throughout Mercury's canon that are solely his. These tics and behaviors may have been inspired by Little Richard or extrapolated from Maria Callas, but they are his alone and together support the defining qualities of that voice.

These are the qualities that, above and beyond his contemporaries, make Mercury's perhaps the greatest voice in rock history:

- **Imitability** Mercury was, first and foremost, a melodist. That Queen fans needed to be able to sing these songs back at the band from the terraces of Wembley Stadium was not lost on him. Each of Mercury's vocal melodies is singable by almost anyone at its most basic level. You might not be able to exactly match him word for word on "Another One Bites the Dust," but the tune itself hits only a handful of perfectly achievable notes. Equally, you might miss every other word of "Good Old Fashioned Lover Boy," but its salon-ditty melody could be adhered to by a school choir.

  While we like to think of Mercury's voice as being beyond imitation, it is its very imitability that makes it an instrument for the masses. It's no coincidence that at the Freddie Mercury Tribute Concert, five months after his death, the roll call of Mercury's contemporaries who interpreted his finest vocal moments spanned gender, genre, and generation—from Liza Minelli to George Michael and Metallica's James Hetfield and Annie Lennox. Chameleonic in the extreme yet always within the realms of imitability, this was the magical middle ground that Mercury's voice occupied.

  To that end, Mercury's vocal work with Queen's audiences proved him to be the master of call-and-response. Besides the obvious bonding benefits of involving one's audience in a mass sing-along, something that singers have done since the invention of amplification, Mercury incorporated a certain wit to his interactions, goading and challenging the crowd to match his vocals. Wordless, two-note cries of "Eeehh-oh!," "Dee-oh!," and "Eeeh-do!" would prompt audiences to respond perfectly in kind as Mercury gradually challenged them further.

- **Flamboyance** We know that Mercury was heavily influenced by opera. Aside from the clear stylistic debts in the middle section of "Bohemian Rhapsody," there are several nods to specific operatic excerpts littered throughout Mercury's back catalog. The introduction to "It's a Hard Life" is almost a direct quotation of the opening vocal attack of "Vesti la giubba" from Leoncavallo's opera *Paglicacci*, one given typical Mercurian color by his decision to flit from chest voice to falsetto in alternate phrases, as if the tenor was desperately clawing to reach the soprano range and finally succeeds.

  What makes that particular example special is the attack. Whereas an operatic aria of the romantic period—the likes of Verdi, Puccini, and Leoncavallo—would contextualize the bombast of the voice with an orchestral introduction or the mood of the surrounding drama, "It's a Hard Life" begins with that belting anacrusis, Mercury in full voice, bursting from nowhere without warning. It is a rock convention applied to a classical format, a trick we often see played with Mercury's voice.

  Similarly, the middle-eight section of "Somebody to Love" shows Mercury at his most playfully virtuosic, almost whooping his way through an improvised-sounding series of swooping melismas, culminating in one of his most famous vocal moments—the final iteration of the song's title, with that tumbling descent and recovery on the word "love" (although musical pedants may argue that he actually doesn't *quite* make that magical final note, an E-flat, on the first attempt). During live performances of the song, Mercury would sometimes cruelly call on the audience to sing that particularly tricky passage, leaving him visibly delighted at their fudged attempts.

- **Sensitivity** Deeper album cuts showcase the quieter characters of Mercury's vocal range. The gentler performances are easier to find at the beginning and the end of his work with Queen, with "Dear Friends" from *Sheer Heart Attack*, "I'm Going Slightly Mad" from *Innuendo*, and "The Great Pretender" sticking out as fine examples. In "Dear Friends," which lasts barely a minute, the vibrato rattles quickly, but the melody itself is completely unadorned, devoid of the ornamentation we associate with Mercury's voice.

"My Melancholy Blues" from *News of the World* sees Mercury ostentatiously pastiching a sequined jazz singer, but the control he displays in keeping a lid on his performance is formidable. Unusually, the voice is quiet, playing very simply atop the accompaniment and achieving impressive evenness of tone at the edges of its range. As storytelling, as mood setting, it shows a voice under control and strategically deployed for purpose.

- **Violence** Mercury was not afraid to punish his voice for musical effect. When he yells, "Give it to me one more time!" at the end of "Hammer to Fall," it's a thrill to hear the voice crack under the vocal pressure. Just prior to this in the same song, he enunciates a rasping "Ha!" twice in duet with Brian May's guitar riff, almost challenging the guitar to come back louder still. It's symptomatic of the power of, well, power: used wisely, Mercury's vocal power is a weapon that took on many guises.

In Queen's earlier material, which bore a stronger hard rock and heavy metal influence (see chapter 9), Mercury's voice doesn't resort to the conventional vocal effects his contemporaries may have employed (growling, screaming, and so on); rather, he operatically forces more and more volume into his performance in full voice. The consequence is a vocal tone that sounds constantly at its limit. The peaks of "White Queen" and "The March of the Black Queen" (both from *Queen II*) display this, recorded as they were at a time when Mercury's recorded voice was noticeably less inclined to rasp and rattle.

Although his vocals toward the end of his career naturally calmed, there were moments in which he was required to summon that rasp once again. A supporting anecdote: when he and May were working on "The Show Must Go On" during sessions for *Innuendo*, Mercury's illness was so severe that he could barely stand. But when May questioned whether Mercury was up to the challenge of singing such an intense song, Mercury reportedly told him, "I'll fucking do it, darling," and immediately laid down the vocal track.

Eleven Key Freddie Mercury Vocal Performances

- **"Hammer to Fall" (live version from Live Aid, 1985)** Although other songs in Queen's Live Aid set have been discussed more frequently, this particular performance of "Hammer to Fall" just so happens to capture Mercury at his most capricious. Beginning with perhaps his most widely seen instance of call-and-response crowd work, it partially devolves into a sweat-slicked series of spoken words and muffed notes—but it is, in a career of true vocal performances, one of the truest.
- **"Killer Queen"** Halfway between loungey chanteur and circus ringleader, Mercury's spackled leather voice on "Killer Queen" was, for many fans, the first time they heard him simply mucking about. The dashed-off nature of those complex lyrics only serves to demonstrate his true virtuosity here.
- **"Under Pressure"** Mercury's nonverbal vocalizations passed into legend with this recording. The whole song is based on doodle-like fragments, so it follows that his vocal contribution (sparring with none other than David Bowie) should be equally spontaneous. Mercury left most of the actual words to Bowie, making his vocals on "Under Pressure" all the more remarkable for the meaning he still manages to convey.
- **"It's a Hard Life"** The introduction is an almost direct quote of Ruggero Leoncavallo's "Vesti la giubba" from his opera *Pagliacci* and, as such, sees Mercury at his opera-aping best. Even when aspiring for that classically trained perfection, he can't resist his own character: as the performance develops, he gradually relaxes its discipline until, at a zenith perfectly attuned to the melodrama of the lyrics, he fades out on a triumphant scream of "Love."
- **"Mustapha"** Beginning with Mercury's voice alone, seemingly in another room altogether, "Mustapha" is one of the very strangest songs in Queen's entire catalog. Sung partially in Arabic (or at least an impression of Arabic), it is simultaneously meditative, devotional, and demented—worth repeated listens for the sheer brass neck of combining these sounds with a chugging metal rhythm section.
- **"Gimme the Prize"** This is another explosive vocal arrival, heralded appropriately with a yell-sung "Here I am! I am the master of your destiny!" Typically for his mid-1980s vocal performances, Mercury's rasp is in full effect, all the comparative smoothness of the 1970s supplanted by this more mature display of power.
- **"White Queen (As It Began)"** One of the most successful examples of Mercury's early 1970s sensitivity, this *Queen II* cut sees the voice very gradually, in measured pace and with demonstrable control, build from narrative whisper to banshee wail and, at its climax, back down to nothing once again.

- **"Staying Power"** (live version, Milton Keynes Bowl, 1982) The wordless vocal pops come thick and fast ("Hey!" "Ha!"), and Mercury's irresistible rasp haunts the tail end of his longer chorus notes in this particularly tight version of a *Hot Space* number, benefiting from a more pronounced role for Roger Taylor's drums. It's notable also for Mercury's flawless vocal mirroring of the guitar lines in the song's middle section (replacing the horn section on the original recording).

- **"Barcelona"** It's telling that, when seeking collaborators for his solo material, Mercury aspired to the technical ideals of opera, dueting with coloratura soprano Montserrat Caballé. His performance of the verses is pure restraint, but the choruses are Mercury turned up to eleven. Interestingly, Caballé matches him in volume but sounds far more comfortable in so doing, altogether more effortless.

- **"Somebody to Love"** One of the most imitated moments of Mercury's entire career: it's worth comparing several live versions of this song for the full range of interpretations (the enunciations during the middle eight from Queen's 1977 Earls Court show are plain bizarre), the breadth of which show this to be one of the most playful and endlessly reinterpreted songs in the canon.

- **"The Show Must Go On"** Just before Brian May's guitar solo, at the extreme upper edge of his chest voice, Mercury sings, "I face it with a grin, I'm never giving in: on with the show." There are myriad contextual reasons that make this an especially poignant line in a powerful song, but in sheer practical terms, it's the haunting sound of a severely ill man, screaming perfectly. Due to the halt in Queen's touring schedule in the years leading up to "The Show Must Go On," Mercury never performed the song live—you wonder, had it come earlier in the band's career, what impact it may have made in person.

39

The Music of Brian May

As perhaps the most restlessly creative composer in Queen, Brian May's work outside the band spans dozens of much smaller, one-off projects in several different areas of popular culture. It is this itinerant streak in May's musical character that makes him the band's most able collaborator, happy not only to rally artistic colleagues but also to work in various ensembles as a contributor rather than a ringleader.

Across his oeuvre, there is one rather obvious guitar-shaped signifier of his presence on any recording, as much a calling card as Mercury's voice. Throughout what we might term his "extracurricular" work as a kind of musical locum doctor and his more autonomous work with Queen, May's considerable compositional voice reveals many tics and traits exclusive to him and a steady evolution toward pop slickness and studio-based confidence as a producer of the work of others.

In March 1991, while Queen was deep in the recording sessions for what would become *Made in Heaven*, May was invited to join legendary self-builder and one of rock guitar's founding fathers, Les Paul, for an onstage improvised jam in New York. Clambering to the front of the stage at Fat Tuesday's in New York, May is outwardly nervous about playing with an established legend, something that never seemed to trouble him in Queen. Paul and May trade licks, but the Red Special is brash and strange in comparison, and May knows the sounds aren't as compatible as they might be were he playing a traditional instrument. It's a rare sight indeed to see May performing in a state of confusion, asking, "How does it go?" when Paul asks him to kick off a jam in C. Of course, there are extenuating circumstances (Mercury's illness placed significant emotional pressure on May, and he'd come to the gig straight from the airport), and he does cover himself well, but it makes for an interesting example of his nature as a musician. Thrust into a lead role unprepared, he is clearly uncomfortable.

Star Fleet Project

Watching television with his young son Jimmy in the early 1980s, Brian May stumbled across something that appealed directly to the child in him as much as it did the adult. *X-Bomber* was a short-lived Japanese television show for children, taking very liberal inspirations from the puppetry and supermarionation techniques of British marionette pioneer Gerry Anderson and the science-fiction behemoth that was *Star Wars*. Repackaged and redubbed for various international territories, *X-Bomber* was known as *Star Fleet* in the United Kingdom and broadcast its heavily trailed first episode on the same weekend that *Star Wars* was due to have its television premiere.

The puppetry on display appears rudimentary to modern eyes and was thoroughly and mercilessly parodied by Matt Stone and Trey Parker's *Team America: World Police*, but when the dubbed version arrived in the United Kingdom, and indeed the home of Brian and Jimmy May, it was exotic and invigorating, a science-fiction creation that traded heavily on its visual effects. May's natural softness for anything technical, scientific, and child-like in its wonderment was such that he decided to create an alternative theme tune for the program. In so doing, May quite inadvertently created an EP that would remain forgotten and largely unheard despite the fact that it brought the guitarist together with one Eddie Van Halen, then perhaps the most famous electric guitarist in the world thanks to his promulgation of the "tapping" technique and his appearance on Michael Jackson's "Beat It" single from 1982.

In April 1983, May managed to convene Van Halen along with Fred Mandel (by then an established Queen sideman, contributing keyboards to *Hot Space* and live shows), Alan Gratzer of REO Speedwagon on drums, and seasoned session bassist Ray Chen in the Record Plant in Los Angeles, just half an hour's drive from Van Halen's 5150 Studios, where his band was working on their soon-to-be-huge *1984* album. The ensemble laid down three lengthy tracks, the first of which being an eight-minute theme for *Star Fleet* with Roger Taylor on backing vocals and featuring a squalling guitar duel between May and Van Halen. The theme already existed as the sound track to the show's closing credits, composed by Paul Bliss, but May's version is substantially and satisfyingly noisier: for his part, Van Halen's guitar work on the song is a typically virtuoso display of histrionics, quite perfectly suited to the laser blasts and explosions that would accompany Captain Shiro and his team's on-screen exploits.

Although May had taken the odd lead vocal on Queen songs, this was the first substantial solo vocal performance under his own name. As an intended theme for a children's television show, the lyrics are necessarily broad ("Always daring and courageous, only they can save us"), but May's vocal is a restrained wonder. In a promotional video cut together from clips from the show itself, May appears as a disembodied head floating through space, charmingly wonderstruck as the Dai-X robot wantonly does battle with the evil forces of Makara, the show's antagonist. Appearing on British TV's *The Saturday Show* to promote the release of the EP while wearing a *Star Fleet* logo T-shirt, May is a clear and unrepentant nerd for the series itself, making the EP's existence all the more heartwarming.

The remaining two tracks on the EP, which was released under the name of Brian May + Friends (and note that the very same + symbol would eventually sit between Queen and their various guest vocalists in decades to follow), take the form of loose blues jams. Both "Let Me Out" and "Blues Breaker" are a musician's pure indulgence, languorous affairs that place instrumental solos above most other elements and have little capacity for self-editing. Pity any plucky young *Star Fleet* fans (or even Queen fans for that matter) expecting three songs along the lines of the TV theme and being greeted by these luxurious curios, the last of which in particular being a nest of borderline-masturbatory blues bar excess.

Stepping into the Light

It would be nine years before another record emerged under the sole marshaling of Brian May. The interim period was, naturally, heavy with Queen activity, culminating in the loss of Freddie Mercury. But May had been squirreling away material for a prospective solo album for most of that time and managing to record the odd piece here and there, songs like "Headlong" and "I Can't Live with You," which would eventually be retooled for Queen's *Innuendo* album with a joint songwriting credit. In an interview with the *Boston Globe* from January 1993, May went as far as saying he already felt "a little distant" from his work with Queen. This is especially interesting given the eventual dominance his work with Queen would have over the rest of his career. Perhaps around the 1992 release of his debut album, *Back to the Light*, May was feeling buoyant enough to believe that his solo material would deliver him ongoing worldwide success.

The album was indeed a success, mostly thanks to "Driven by You," a single released just two weeks before Freddie Mercury's death in November 1991. A suitably driving pop-rock confection, Brian May capitalized on the song's commercial power by reworking it in conjunction with the Ford Motor Company, which used an exclusive version in television advertisements for its range of cars. Rather than "Everything I do is driven by you," the chorus now ran "Everything we do is driven by you," and the opening verse contains the line "We build for the country's needs, wheels turn, power at your feet." Undoubtedly, this would have been a lucrative move for May, who showed the same instinct for a financial boost that Queen had in general throughout their 1980s heyday. In its original form, though, "Driven by You" performed well, peaking at numbers six and nine on the U.K. singles and U.S. mainstream rock charts.

As a whole, *Back to the Light* captures May actively seeking commercial success, a viable furthering of his career as a pop musician. Although he takes on the majority of instrumental and programming duties himself, Cozy Powell of the Jeff Beck Group, Rainbow, Whitesnake, and others handled percussion for the album. Powell also proved a champion of May's work during his period of mourning for Mercury, in which the guitarist uneasily remodeled himself as a front man. May's preferred method of hurling himself into a state of constant activity around this time was, he later admitted, an attempt to deal with the grief of losing Mercury and the end of Queen in its most recognized form.

As a result, there are some bizarre artifacts from around this time, such as the music video for "Resurrection," in which Powell and May appear surrounded by countless small fires and whirling computer-generated rock formations. At one point, a stunt double with an unmistakable mop of brown curly hair precariously scales a rock face, and at another point, an earthquake cracks the floor between May's Adidas sneakers. It is an attempt, May notes in the YouTube description for the video, to cast himself as a "singing guitar hero," a guise he initially struggled to inhabit convincingly.

A Streak of Sentimentality

For his second and final traditional solo album, 1998's *Another World*, May had originally intended to release a record of cover versions of songs originally recorded by his favorite artists. When it came to assembling the songs and guests to play them, however, May found that his own compositions were more diverting and set about turning them into fully fledged, radio-ready rock hits. Again, the role of front man is an engagingly difficult one for May to assume on this album, something that is evidenced by the mammoth list of thank-yous in the liner notes. Aside from thanking the family dogs and cat (Ron, Max, and Brandy), May also thanks "Roger and John, and Freddie, if you're listening."

Three of May's proposed cover versions eventually made the cut, each one proving that the fondness for the blues he'd worn more lightly throughout his time with Queen was now beginning to show its full impact. Jimi Hendrix's "One Rainy Wish" and Larry Williams's "Slow Down" are fairly straight readings of their source material, but May's version of Mott the Hoople's "All the Way from Memphis" features Ian Hunter himself and is a measure of the band's ongoing musical influence on May's life. It is, in all senses, an album of friendly gestures. But in another blow to May's confidence, Cozy Powell, who had provided musical and personal support to May in the years since the death of Freddie Mercury, was to meet his end in a car crash in April 1998 before work on *Another World* had been completed. Powell was replaced in the Brian May Band (as was their touring name) by KISS drummer Eric Singer.

Around the time of release, in one of May's many appearances on a breakfast television interview, he shows a crew from GMTV around his house and home studio. Even though it is a promotional interview and May is called on yet again to speak about the enduring influence of Freddie Mercury on his life, there is a delicate frankness, a bucolic shyness to his demeanor. Asked to name the inspiration for *Another World*, May's simple answer is "Life, really." And while there are moments of what we might call May's more comfortable rock expression on the album, it is one guided ultimately by sentimentality and self-assessment. The album opens with a doodle, a synthesizer drone over which May plaintively sings, "I'm going to make a little space around me, a very special place around me. No-one can come in." On the song that follows it, "The Business," he opines that it is "a hard business to make it on your own." Later in the same song, he sings, "I've got nothing in my life but trouble, but I feel I've got a lot to give," which could be a sentence uttered toward the end of a desperate job interview as much as a song lyric. In short, even though much of the music on the album is strident, May is by his own admission completely lost in this musical territory, an unnatural front man.

This tension of May's discomfort on these recordings is what marks them out from other solo albums from Roger Taylor and Freddie Mercury. With Mercury a natural front man and Taylor an eager facsimile of a rock singer with a golden voice, May is the reluctant intermediary, the gilded musician with star-pulling power to spare but an endearing lack of confidence in his own material. Even on a song like "Cyborg," which on the strength of the title alone should see the guitarist in comfortable sci-fi territory, May clings to genre-aping metal growls and Van Halen–inspired finger tapping rather than choosing to express himself or any inventions of his own. However, it is worth considering that "Cyborg" was actually composed for the video game *Rise 2: Resurrection*, the packaging of which was topped with a sticker proudly proclaiming, "Featuring music specially written and performed by Brian May!"—another example of May's willingness to compose to order and for commercial gain.

May at the Movies

Given his natural predisposition to sound tracking as displayed on *Flash Gordon*, it's surprising that work on movies wasn't a larger part of May's musical grasshopping between projects. Still, he did contribute a song named "What Are We Made Of?" to the 1996 movie *The Adventures of Pinocchio*, the sound track of which also featured songs from Stevie Wonder and orchestral music composed by Rachel Portman. The film, which starred Martin Landau as Geppetto and featured marionette work by Jim Henson's Creature Shop, was a commercial and critical flop, one that May was no doubt attracted to by the involvement of Henson's pioneering effects work.

In lieu of a third solo album, May began work on an original sound track to director Alexandre Aja's French-language horror movie *Furia*, itself adapted from a short story by the noted Argentine author Julio Cortázar, in 1999. After watching a rough edit of the movie, which stars Marion Cotillard in an early French-language role before she took on the Oscar-winning role of Edith Piaf in 2007, May composed the opening theme to *Furia* in just one night. Creatively awakened by the prospect of a full orchestral sound track, May worked closely with Aja to craft soundscapes over which he could drop musical pellets using his Red Special.

Perhaps unexpectedly, there is a pervading influence of John Carpenter's prototypical synthesizer sound tracks, composed by the director for his own movies, such as *Assault on Precinct 13*, *The Fog*, and *Escape from New York*. As well as May's impressive mastery of the synthesized aspects of the score, he also confirms his gift as a melodist. The main melodic motif in the movie is passed around among flute, violin, and wordless voice in a manner reminiscent of Ennio Morricone's music for the movies of Sergio Leone, apparently sharing nothing in common with the rock idiom. But when May uses that same melody in "Dream of Thee," a medievally tinged ballad with arcane language to suit ("know the love that I keep for thee is safe and secret in my heart, lest thou shouldst dream of me"), it becomes once again a May pop composition.

In the liner notes that accompanied the CD release of the sound track, Aja himself described May's work on *Furia* as "an indestructible link between the characters, a simple and limpid music in which a certain idea of love and liberty shines through."

May as Guest Star

Some of the stranger examples of May's extension throughout the music world have been the result of his penchant for appearing as a guest, another manifestation of his powerful collaborative urge (although perhaps it would be more fitting to describe these guest spots as being filled by May's Red Special rather than May himself, as they are almost exclusively nonvocal appearances). Some of the less conventional examples of May lending his talents to the compositions of his contemporaries and colleagues are listed below:

- **Cliff Richard—"Move It"** Cliff Richard occupies a unique place in British music history: a proponent of early rock 'n' roll and a contemporary of the Beatles, Richard's later cultural life has arguably been defined by his strong advocacy of a Christian lifestyle and seemingly inexplicable chart success across a sixty-year career. In short, there would be many arguments to suggest Brian May wouldn't be an ideal duet partner. But with "Move It," Richard channels the energy he displayed on his only major U.S. hit, "Devil Woman," while May's contribution seems to be mostly interstitial guitar licks and a lengthy blues solo.

- **Hank Marvin—"We Are the Champions"** Hank Marvin was originally well known as the guitarist of the Shadows, which also happened to be Cliff Richard's backing band. In the autumn years of his career, bespectacled Marvin continues to release instrumental music led by his inimitably lyrical Stratocaster twang, but in 1992, he managed to convince May to duet with him on a version of Queen's "We Are the Champions" for his album *Into the Light*. It is a uniquely interesting experience to hear Marvin's reduced take on the bombast of Mercury's original, seemingly with much of May's squalling flourishes removed. There is, however, an interesting interplay between the two instruments as the version progresses, though inevitably it suffers in comparison to its source material.

- **Dappy—"Rockstar"** May's status as a legend for hire had been clear for a long time by 2012, when British urban artist and provocateur Dappy (formerly of the tabloid-baiting trio N-Dubz) called on the guitarist to wail a Red Special solo over the closing seconds of "Rockstar." It was, however, May who approached Dappy after being impressed with the young rapper's lyrics. May even went as far as appearing live on BBC Radio 1's *Live Lounge* for a rendition of "We Will Rock You" with Dappy on lead vocals.

- **Soundgarden—"New Damage"** As the alternative rock boom of the early 1990s enjoyed its heyday, Greenpeace oversaw the release of a compilation album that brought together grunge denizens like Sonic Youth and L7 with the likes of U2, James, and the Disposable Heroes of Hiphoprisy, all of them contributing new versions of existing songs recorded in a studio powered by the sun's energy. Soundgarden's contribution was a reworked version of their song "New Damage" from their influential *Badmotorfinger* album, over which Brian May draped a tonally wild guitar solo. It's interesting to hear May abandon traditional licks for this all-out frenzy of notes, ungoverned by the blues scales that fall so easily under his fingers. It has the air of a musician stretched—cajoled into trying something different. In an interview with *Rolling Stone*, Soundgarden's Kim Thayil dismissed it as merely a "very Brian May-ish guitar solo," which seems to be damning it with unnecessarily faint praise.

A Collaboration That Stuck

Musical pairings have taken countless different forms since May first worked on *Back to the Light*, but one of the longest-lasting partnerships has been with the singer Kerry Ellis. Ellis appeared in the original London cast of *We Will*

May and Ellis perform together in Belarus during their *Acoustic by Candlelight* tour.

Rock You after May watched her in the role of Eliza Doolittle in a West End production of *My Fair Lady* and urged her to audition for the musical he was working on with Ben Elton and Roger Taylor. With Ellis, May has released a live acoustic album and a collaborative studio album but taken on a more pastoral role as producer and chief musical partner across a variety of different projects. Ellis's albums and live work often feature Queen songs (thanks in part to her having performed them in the role of Meat in *We Will Rock You*), but May has also composed songs both with and specifically for her.

From Ellis's first solo album, *Anthems*, "Dangerland" is a solo May composition that references the chug of Metallica's "Enter Sandman" and the Arabian-inflected guitar licks of Led Zeppelin, but Ellis's polished vocal performance is pure stage musical, luxurious in its heightened drama. May also collaborated with lyricist Don Black for Ellis's track "I Can't Be Your Friend (This Can't Be Over)," aligning the project with a rich history of musicals (Black was a lyricist for stage productions from Andrew Lloyd Webber and John Barry, among others). *Anthems* works as a kind of joust between the worlds of rock music and the stage musical even to the extent of drafting Foo Fighters drummer Taylor Hawkins to play on Ellis's versions of "Defying Gravity" and "I'm Not That Girl" from *Wicked*.

Besides recording albums together, May and Ellis have shared a consistently active touring presence and found success with shows that teeter between their established stage musical and rock backgrounds but also include reimagined versions of Queen standards, with an understandable lean toward those written by May, such as "Save Me" and "No-One but You (Only the Good Die Young)."

The pair's first studio album on which they share joint billing, 2017's *Golden Days*, sees their musical partnership deepen on a series of perky and frivolous numbers with titles like "The Kissing Me Song" and "It's Gonna Be Alright (The Panic Attack Song)." A glance at the YouTube comments underneath the official video for "Roll with You" is, contrary to almost anything else with any kind of Queen connection, a mix of polite disappointment and outright rage at what appears to be an uncharacteristically formulaic composition.

Exploring New Horizons

On January 1, 2019, Brian May released his first official solo single in twenty years, direct from NASA headquarters. This was to be his first official solo single (not released with another artist or as part of a larger ensemble project) in more than twenty years. "New Horizons (Ultima Thule Mix)" was composed as a commission of sorts from NASA as the organization planned to mark its ongoing mission of a space probe named *New Horizons*, which was due to approach a Kuiper Belt object named (486958) 2014 MU69, otherwise known as Ultima Thule, on January 1. The song was played as the flyby happened.

May's extensive experience as an astrophysicist meant he was an ideal collaborator for NASA's mission regardless of his musical pedigree. The guitarist has a long history of involvement with space exploration, having also founded Asteroid Day in 2014, which occurs every June 30 and has as one of its central aims "heightening awareness of the asteroid hazard and our efforts to prevent impacts." In 2016, May demonstrated yet again his ability to effortlessly marry astrophysics and music by performing alongside movie sound track composer Hans Zimmer at the Starmus International Festival. With an ensemble, the pair performed the main theme from Zimmer's sound track to the movie *Inception* as part of a program on the theme of "Beyond the Horizon: A Tribute to Stephen Hawking."

And so it was that with "New Horizons (Ultima Thule Mix)," May found another way to pay tribute to Professor Stephen Hawking. Before the bouncing triplets and multilayered vocals of the song itself begin, a quote from Hawking is played in the late professor's iconic and instantly recognizable computerized voice. As far as musical collaborations go, this is surely one of May's most cosmic. The song itself sees May fuse a sense of intergalactic wonder with peppy blues licks, with lyrics addressing the mission of the *New Horizons* probe itself. Again, in his solo work, May seems somehow more comfortable working to commission or a set theme rather than endlessly exposing emotional truths about himself.

The Eternal Colleague

Unlike Mercury (or Taylor and Deacon for that matter), May has always required a muse. Mercury needed collaborators to make his musical dreams a reality, and May was only happy to occupy the role of facilitator in that regard, but his naturally collegiate character gives May something approaching a permanent auxiliary role. Even when working ostensibly as a producer or backroom influencer, he is unable to resist picking up the Red Special and contributing musically. This instinct was so strong during his work in 1988 with Anita Dobson (whom the guitarist would later marry) that May would end up standing behind her, shrouded in dry ice, miming his guitar solo for "Talking of Love" on the rather polite BBC chat show *Wogan*. With Dobson, May shed all inhibitions: clearly in love with the woman who wasn't quite yet his wife, he mugs and capers with her during music videos, sings the "and I do and I do" backing vocals on her cover of Phil Spector's "To Know Him Is to Love Him," and even donates to her his rejected Christmas song initially intended for Queen, "I Dream of Christmas."

Brian May onstage in 2018.

Alice Lorenzini/lunaelive.com

Perhaps the musical nadir of May and Dobson's musical creation was the song "Funny Old Life Ain't It," in which Dobson impersonates a moaning schoolchild for a series of spoken verses over a quite insultingly simplistic hip-hop pastiche backing, complete with record scratches and processed horn fills. It also contains the line "school dinners stink and I'd rather have a drink and me dad's bent, brown and bitter," which is as illogical as it is misguided and offensive in its expression: a rare dalliance in extreme bad taste for a project associated with May.

However, it would be wrong to dismiss May as merely a sideman, as it somewhat negates his rich pedigree as a composer of chart-bothering hit singles, but allowing the right interpreters to tackle his work was so often key to its success. Mercury in particular was able to sell convincingly even the loftiest or most pompous Brian May lyric with ease ("He told of death as a bone-white haze, taking the lost and the unloved babe"), in a fashion that May arguably could not.

Suddenly left creatively alone after the demise of Queen, it's no wonder a musician so reliant on collaboration suddenly turned and continues to turn to a vast horde of associates to continue his music making in a fragmentary manner, completely unique to him. And it is this work ethic, this maxim, that fundamentally defines his work: Brian May simply works better with others.

40

The Music of Roger Taylor

Before a career's worth of solo material had been written, Roger Taylor released his first single as a lone artist in 1977, a full four years before his debut album would appear. Rather than punt out one of his hallmark songs about cars or women, Taylor instead opted to release a heavily reinterpreted cover version of Parliament's "I Wanna Testify," originally a steaming funk workout here given a shuddering makeover, complete with layered vocal harmonies, a severe tempo increase, and new lyrics (among them an appropriate manifesto for his creative output thus far: "Women and drinking, loving and thinking"). Appropriately enough given how much it sounds like a jazzed-up T Rex song, Taylor appeared on Marc Bolan's television show *Marc* in September 1977 to mime along to the song.

That the work of Parliament was a part of Taylor's listening diet somewhat negates John Deacon's claim a few years later that he was the only member of Queen to really listen to nonwhite artists and throws further confusion around the precise inspirations of what was to become Queen's *Hot Space*. Regardless, the cover version was a one-off: the real interest in tracing Taylor's compositional history lies in the single's B-side, a Taylor original named "Turn On the TV." It's a pleasingly louche piece that begins with an almighty falsetto screech and a cough, a nugget of in-studio banter that would likely not have made the final cut of a Queen album. Similar to Queen's "Dragon Attack" in its sense of riff and groove, it is lyrically about as Taylor-esque as it gets: "Turn on the TV as it takes a horizontal hold on your energy," he sings in what sounds like an ironic paean to slovenliness. Musically, however, it captures Taylor as his development beyond rock and blues was in its infancy.

In a statement presumably designed to mark out some musical territory for himself, the inner sleeve of the single release proudly stated, "Roger Taylor is one quarter of Queen. He made this record himself."

Early Solo Albums

Taylor has the distinction among Queen members as the first to write, record, and release a solo album. Coming four years after "I Wanna Testify," the timing of 1981's *Fun in Space* suggests Taylor was perhaps the most restless member of the band at this time or at least the most underrepresented in terms of songwriting credits (until this point, his credits generally went as far as one song per Queen album). To that end, he told *Modern Drummer* magazine in 1984, "I felt I was getting more creative, and I wanted a bigger outlet for it than Queen gave me. I wanted, I suppose, to be more than just a member of the band."

Just like Queen's albums, it was released via EMI and Elektra but fared comparatively poorly, especially in the United States. Recorded partially at Mountain Studios in pockets of downtime from Queen activity, Taylor was free to explore his influences in peace, unencumbered by the thought of fighting for his material's inclusion on whatever the next ensemble release might be. Tellingly, the songs on *Fun in Space* take a diversion from the paths explored by Queen until that point, as if Taylor had been waiting for an opportunity to unleash a new musical persona.

Streaks of sentimentality and nostalgia vie with Taylor's natural aptitude for the lurid and the technical, not dissimilar to Brian Ferry with a blues howl on "No Violins." "Future Management" sees him abandon the howl for a more reserved, thinner vocal sound that has an undeniable similarity with David Bowie, while the song itself is ponderous, romantic, and dark: three character traits in which Taylor had previously shown no interest. "Magic Is Loose," on the other hand, sees Taylor aiming for Pink Floyd levels of progressive grandiosity, with vaguely mystical lyrics like "All through the Orient, like a shroud around a sphere."

Also emerging on *Fun in Space* is a sense of political weariness: not the activism of genuine protest songs but, rather, sheer tiredness and apathy, a rejection of the machine and organized society in general. On "My Country I & II," Taylor tells us that he "don't have no truck with no power games" and he "don't have no part of no partisans," both blankly antiauthoritarian statements, the sentiments of which resurface throughout Taylor's later solo works. It's a harder and glibber stance than, for example, Brian May's continual reference to global injustices in his material. Certainly, Taylor's popular perception as a freewheeling rock 'n' roller whizzing around Europe in sports cars between international touring jaunts was at odds with the role he'd cast for himself on his solo material.

This confusion in image didn't quite alleviate itself on Taylor's follow-up, 1984's *Strange Frontier*, although the music was, he admitted, leaner than the experimental approach he'd taken on *Fun in Space*. The album's title track and lead single, interestingly, has the sound of a Bruce Springsteen rabble-rouser but is shot through with cynicism in its lyrics: "Freedom fighters come and go, bloody righteous and mentally slow." Its music video, based partially on *Rebel without a Cause*, sees a clearly uncomfortable Taylor as a huffy romantic lead in a protracted road race, interspersed with archive footage of miscellaneous fascist rallies (specifically accompanying the line "People say it could never happen here, but this is a strange frontier").

Albums after *Strange Frontier* would be more sporadic as Taylor's commitments with Queen demanded more of his time, but he was able to remain surprisingly prolific and continued to explore new musical territory.

The Cross: Roger Taylor as Front Man

After Queen had completed their promotional tour and extensive outdoor concerts for the *A Kind of Magic* album and effectively entered another period of hiatus, Taylor turned his efforts to a new project. Freddie Mercury was taken up with his first solo album, and May was occupied with leisurely collaborations with other musicians, while John Deacon hoovered up smaller projects: but Taylor needed to be in a band again. After corralling longtime Queen live keyboardist Spike Edney, Taylor placed a newspaper advertisement to fill the remaining slots in what would become the Cross, formed to play live versions of an album's worth of songs Taylor had already written and recorded.

The Cross saw Taylor slide into the role of front man for the first time, one that he seemed predisposed to excel in, given his natural charisma onstage and his throaty rock voice. But again, the material Taylor composed sought to expand his musical horizons, to specifically attempt sounds and address issues that would perhaps have been shouted down by his less receptive colleagues in Queen. That first album, graced with the unsubtle title of *Shove It*, was released in April 1988 and failed to make an impression on either the U.K. or the U.S. top forty album charts.

Most notable to Queen enthusiasts among the Cross's recorded output is undoubtedly "Heaven for Everyone," which not only featured Freddie Mercury for a few snatches of lead vocal in the song's introduction and outro (for the single version) but also went on to be reworked as a full-blown Queen production for the *Made in Heaven* album. The single release was augmented by a big-budget music video filmed at an East London industrial gasworks in a typically Queen-esque cinematic style, featuring Taylor strumming a guitar on a fake beach while homeless men warm their hands on a trash fire below him. The version that ended up on *Shove It* featured Mercury on lead vocals across the entire track, making the album's disappointing chart performance all the more surprising.

Taylor's heavily synthesized compositions on *Shove It* incorporate nascent sampling and editing techniques to create something of a *concrète* sound, a tendency that may be symptomatic of his desire to extend his sound. Despite this, the lyrical sensibility he displays on certain songs still sees him in transition, yet to mature beyond a narrow range of subjects. On the album's title track, for example, the knowingly daft chorus runs simply, "Girls! We love it! Cars!

We love it! More girls! We love it!" It is still, however, one of the album's more technically adept songs.

The Cross toured Europe with success, however, filling the kinds of halls Queen hadn't played in more than a decade. It was an enormous novelty to see a bona fide multimillionaire rock star performing in Nottingham Rock City or the University of East Anglia's Student Union building, for example. A 1988 video of the band performing at Montreux's Golden Rose festival shows a packed venue and Taylor sporting his by-now signature sunglasses, the band's convincing swagger paying no small debt to Roxy Music and "Addicted to Love"–era Robert Palmer.

But as Taylor was drawn inexorably back into creative work with Queen, crafting songs for *The Miracle*, he ceded songwriting duties to the other members of the Cross. Both of the albums that followed *Shove It*—1990's *Mad Bad & Dangerous to Know* and 1991's *Blue Rock*—featured a majority of material contributed by the rest of the band and only a couple of Taylor solo compositions. Inevitably, the songs on those albums form more traditional rock sets, while Taylor's minimal songwriting contributions capture him in a state of enervation.

Blue Rock ended up becoming something of a collector's item thanks to the band's having been dropped by EMI prior to its release. Surfacing only in Japan and parts of Europe, its scarcity in physical form has been rendered somewhat moot by the Internet. The material is anthemic and technically accomplished but distinctly vanilla in its identity, indebted to U2 and written with the hope of filling halls larger than they ever would.

A promotional video created to mark the release of *Blue Rock* shows the band engaging in a series of clichéd rock sketches: physically lunging at one another for comic effect, sunglasses indoors, and staged interviews in which band members sit on instrument flight cases and list influences as "diverse" as Jimi Hendrix, Santana, and ZZ Top. When asked about the effect of "sharing" Roger Taylor with Queen, the Cross's drummer, Josh Macrae, tellingly says of the times when Taylor is unavailable, "One has to busy oneself in other ways." Shortly after, Spike Edney simplifies the difference between the two bands: "They're rich, we're poor." It is hard to shake the impression that Taylor's bandmates needed this more than Taylor.

Return to Solo Albums

After the faint reception afforded the last two albums from the Cross, Taylor went back to being billed as a solo artist. However, it wasn't until 1994 that he would release more material: an album called *Happiness?* railed on his familiar bugbears of worldly injustices ("Nazis 1994") and the press ("Dear Mr. Murdoch"). "Dear Mr. Murdoch" is notable for its ribald but arguably unsophisticated attacks on the notorious newspaper magnate and his publications the

News of the World and the *Sun* ("bad news is good business, you're the king of the tits!"). Along with Brian May, Taylor has a long history of personal objections to the tabloid press, something that found its way into Queen songs like "Scandal," but the clear strain of anger in "Dear Mr. Murdoch" is far coarser than anything he may have been able to squeak past the rest of the band.

Both of Taylor's remaining completed solo albums—*Electric Fire* from 1998 and *Fun on Earth* from 2013—contain multiple examples of his ire in these same directions. Before the release of *Fun on Earth*, Taylor asked in a press release, "What happened to the protest song? Music is now so polished, shiny and predictable, we have forgotten to try and say something with it."

What Are Roger Taylor's Most Outspoken Songs?

- **"Nazis 1994"** One of the baldest expressions of Taylor's political songwriting is his 1994 single "Nazis 1994," a song he claimed was a visceral reaction to a then rising tide of far-right political activity and activism across Europe. Due to its confrontational nature, the song was banned from commercial radio stations in the United Kingdom (at the time, the noncommercial BBC stations did not ban records for fear of publicity, sending them further up the singles charts, but consigned them to limited off-peak airplay). It is, though, undeniably justified in its rage, a simplistic statement: the repeated lyrics on the single release include "we got to kick those stinking Nazis" (a remixed version of the single, produced by Danny Saber, retains Taylor's original lyrics: "we got to kick those fucking Nazis"). The controversy around the airplay ban, coupled with a music video that intersperses contemporary and archive footage of Nazi rallies with Roger Taylor beating an oversize bass drum and snare, was enough to see "Nazis 1994" reach number twenty-two on the U.K. singles chart.

- **"A Nation of Haircuts"** While not quite on the same ideological plane as "Nazis 1994," Taylor's ire was raised on his *Electric Fire* album by what he saw as a nationwide lack of practical heartiness. "We don't make ships and we don't make cars, but we look real good hanging out in bars": these sarcastic lines could be seen as wantonly and hypocritically ignoring Taylor's own status as a Kensington fashionista and artless gadabout during Queen's early days, but the more likely truth is that age and wealth, as it so often does with rock stars, has simply made him grumpy and detached.

- **"Gangsters Are Running This World"** There is a nihilistic calm to Taylor's 2019 single, which levels still more everyman accusations at the powers that be. Although less specific in its targets than previous songs of this nature, "Gangsters Are Running This World" is as close to a bona fide protest song as he has come in a career full of admirably bilious attempts. References to civil unrest, rising crime rates, and unscrupulous financial markets are gradually replaced by peace-and-love sentimentality: "I wanna tear down every border and wall, I wanna take part in the human race." That this is all within the confines of a gloopy piano ballad shows once again Taylor's favorite musical duality between sentiment and execution: his angry songs are almost sarcastically pretty.

Who Has Roger Taylor Collaborated With?

After the disbanding of Queen, Taylor found a sympathetic musical cousin in Yoshiki Hayashi, known simply as Yoshiki, the drummer and songwriter with Japanese rock legends X Japan (formerly X). On a surface level, the two artists have much in common: both are drummers and songwriters with internationally renowned bands, both have become synonymous with the excesses of rock in their home territories, and both have active and far-reaching solo careers. When the two collaborated for a single track called "Foreign Sand" on Taylor's 1994 album *Happiness?* the result perhaps inevitably was an orchestral ballad with an excess of hands-across-the-ocean sentimentality. The line "Red, yellow, black and white, every man stand in the light" is particularly cloying, but, paired with a glossy music video containing helicopter shots of billowing flags, children running hand in hand across beaches, and a large amount of Roger Taylor in soft focus, it is an exercise in mawkishness.

Both Brian May and Roger Taylor have collaborated on multiple occasions with Foo Fighters, most commonly with the band's leader Dave Grohl and

Roger Taylor on stage in 2018.   *Alice Lorenzini/lunaelive.com*

drummer Taylor Hawkins. Several examples of collaborations between Queen and Foo Fighters have occurred over the years, spanning live performances and occasional recording projects, including a 2019 reworking of an instrumental track written by Dennis Wilson (late original drummer of the Beach Boys and posthumously feted solo artist) named "Holy Man," which features Taylor Hawkins, Roger Taylor, and Brian May. But Hawkins and Taylor, united by their status as generation-leading rock drummers, share an especially close musical bond. In 2010, Hawkins's band, which goes by Taylor Hawkins & the Coattail Riders, invited Taylor to sing backing vocals on the song "Your Shoes" for their album *Red Light Fever*. In a live video from the same year, Hawkins and his band played that song at the Scala venue in North London not only with Taylor on backing vocals but also with Taylor's son, Rufus, playing drums alongside Hawkins. (Rufus Taylor has himself since become an important part of the ongoing Queen story, performing and recording with his father on several occasions.)

Bouncing into Something Better

Taylor himself explained his work as a solo musician and member of the Cross as a series of "bounces" between Queen and those other projects, with each bounce making the next more interesting. Without completely contradicting a primary source, it could be more accurate from an observer's point of view to characterize Taylor's solo output as being purposefully separated from his work with Queen (with the noted exception of "Heaven for Everyone"). Compositions honed and varnished through in-studio back-and-forth with Deacon, May, and Mercury simply have a brighter pop sheen than, say, the Cross's *Blue Rock*. It mightn't be too strong to say that Taylor actively needed conflict to produce his best work. Left to his own devices on albums like *Strange Frontier*, even up to "Gangsters Are Running This World," that arguably necessary combative atmosphere at the point of composition is removed.

One of rock's greatest drummers was always going to find himself judged a little more harshly than, say, Brian May, who had a proven way with melody and harmony. But with Taylor, we see his growth and evolution up close across Queen's albums but in even more detail across his work as a solo musician. Uniquely among Queen members, Taylor's journey as a songwriter celebrates its failures and its missteps and shows them off as bizarre trinkets and curios collected on the way. Whether or not his songwriting as a solo artist will eventually result in something that defines his work more than simply being the drummer in Queen remains to be seen, but you can be sure the songs will keep coming regardless.

41

The Music of John Deacon

On a surface-level inspection, bassist John Deacon absolutely lives up to his reputation as the "quiet one" in Queen. He barely sang any backing vocals, was a late bloomer in terms of his songwriting, and seemed in most media appearances to be less than comfortable speaking about anything other than the practical business of being in a band. But to leave this book with that impression would be doing a disservice to a musical linchpin. Deacon's studied approach and reticence to indulge in the more tempting excesses of rock lore actually did him a favor: when he worked on music with others, it was with the express intention of improving the quality of his own output, like a magpie scuttling through the pop music undergrowth with the purpose of bringing back only the sturdiest twigs and branches to the Queen nest.

This book has already discussed Deacon's sojourn in New York at the turn of the 1980s, when he listened in on recording sessions with Nile Rodgers and Chic, but it's worth bearing in mind Deacon's analytical, fact-gathering approach when considering the limited extent of his collaborative work outside the confines of Queen.

But his reputation was in part well-founded, and he was a fundamentally reserved social presence. His retirement from Queen activities after the death of Freddie Mercury effectively marked a barrier between his musical career and a life of public silence.

There are signs of that social quietness, of Deacon's skepticism of extracurricular musical projects, from when the band was still together. In a BBC Radio 1 interview from 1989, Deacon is asked what he's been up to while on hiatus from Queen. He mentions his video appearance with Morris Minor and the Majors (specifically in the comedy rap single "Stutter Rap (No Sleep 'til Bedtime)," but aside from this, he appears outwardly wary toward any potential collaborators: "They usually want the money, that's what they're after."

Deacon within Queen

Unlike the previous few chapters, which have delved exclusively into individual band members' compositional activity exclusive of their work within Queen, a few words here about John Deacon's contribution to the band's oeuvre is apposite. Because his compositions, like Roger Taylor's, are few and far between, his journey as a songwriter is more starkly telegraphed and, as such, makes for a striking progression.

- **"In Only Seven Days"** Deacon's fondness for pop music in its purest form is rarely absent from his songs, and this 1978 cut is no exception. Utterly simplistic in its basic construction but elaborate in its whizzing execution, "In Only Seven Days" has the hallmarks of a dreamy Carpenters single, telling its story of a holiday romance in anguished retrospect: it's important to note that the final line is "I'm so sad alone," a key indicator of classic Deacon songwriting being its downbeat lyrical nature. (Sammy never did escape from the Emerald Bar in "Spread Your Wings," did he?)
- **"Execution of Flash"** and **"Arboria"** According to Howard Blake's account of the composition process of Queen's *Flash Gordon* album, so many musical motifs were the product of rushed or confused ideas being whipped into shape for orchestral reimagining. But these two Deacon-penned nuggets are mostly without augmentation: simple melodic ideas, especially on "Execution of Flash," show Deacon's knack for mood setting. We know already that Deacon's musical influences extended to large-scale orchestral works (he saw Deep Purple's legendary "Concerto for Group and Orchestra" show in 1969 with the Royal Philharmonic), and these similarly doomy soundscapes show he had chops beyond crafting pop songs.
- **"Back Chat"** Perhaps the most significant contribution Deacon made to *Hot Space* was this lithe dance number, entirely built around the guitar and bass lines (spaced an octave apart, a common technique for funk songs of the time, including "Another One Bites the Dust"). It also makes an interesting companion piece to "Picking Up Sounds" (see the next section), showing that Deacon's experimentation in this area of funk and even early hip-hop was burgeoning.
- **"One Year of Love"** Deacon was one of Queen's more plainly emotional composers: "You're My Best Friend," for example, was written for his wife, Veronica Tetzlaff, while "Spread Your Wings" is a forlorn tale of ambition stymied by circumstance. On "One Year of Love," Deacon took a central plot device from Russell Mulcahy's movie *Highlander* (for which Queen provided several sound track contributions via their *A Kind of Magic* album) and expanded it into one of Queen's gloopiest songs. Soaked in strings and tenor sax solos, it could easily have been sung by any number of divas of

the time had Mercury not been available. It's interesting to imagine what Sadé, Annie Lennox, Alison Moyet, or even Prince might have done with the song vocally given its vast reservoirs of sentimentality.

Man Friday & Jive Junior

After *Hot Space* effectively severed Queen's creative ties with funk and disco music, Deacon's enthusiasm for the genre (like Mercury's) spilled out into other projects. His first major collaboration outside of his work with Queen was on a project named Man Friday & Jive Junior, a mid-tier supergroup that hoovered up the likes of guitarist Scott Gorham from Thin Lizzie, Martin Chambers of the Pretenders, and both Bad Company's drummer Simon Kirke and guitarist Mick Ralphs. Released in 1983, their lone single, "Picking Up Sounds," was a low-circulation gem of funk and rap simplicity. Heavily indebted to the Sugarhill Gang's "Rapper's Delight" from four years previous, it is controlled almost fully by cocomposer Deacon's bass line, which is quite unlike his work with Queen. Virtuosic, venomous, and borderline-slapped motifs are stacked together in a manner more befitting Bootsy Collins, a series of thick riffs rather than the lithe and melodic accompaniment he would usually deliver in Queen songs.

A Song for Biggles

Although he was decidedly transatlantic in his musical diet, like Brian May, Deacon also had a sympathy for the cultural heritage of his homeland no matter how unfashionable it might be. The *Biggles* series of children's novels was a staple of wartime literature since the character's first appearance in 1932 in an issue of *Popular Flying* magazine and continued to be popular throughout the twentieth century. A 1986 feature-length film adaptation of Biggles's exploits was, like *Flash Gordon* six years before, a peculiarly British affair that suffered from an imbalance of budget and ambition and eventually performed poorly at the box office. Relocating part of the action to the 1980s, the movie's main conceit involves a time-traveling salesman who happens to save young Biggles's life after mistakenly finding his way back to 1917.

For the movie's sound track, a small number of existing rock songs were bolted on to key scenes, among them Deep Purple's "Knocking at Your Door" and Queen's "Another One Bites the Dust," but Deacon's involvement was to become deeper. After meeting Deacon in 1985, the movie's director, John Hough (who had until this point been working mainly on horror films like *The Legend of Hell House* and *The Watcher in the Woods*), asked him to compose a theme song for his new Biggles project, a song shot through with the requisite amount of derring-do but also reflecting the modern-day setting of the movie. Along with guitarist Robert Ahwai (formerly of Hummingbird), Deacon came up with "No Turning Back," a decidedly bass-heavy composition that also featured Lenny Zakatek on vocals (Zakatek had previously featured heavily on albums by the Alan Parsons Project). Together, the ensemble went by the name of the Immortals.

The song is perky in the extreme but, like the movie itself, didn't perhaps make the commercial impact that its makers had hoped for. A music video for the single release is an entertainingly low-budget affair in which the three band members perform wearing World War I pilot costumes, superimposed over footage from the film of swooping biplanes. Deacon doesn't feature heavily but can be seen enthusiastically grooving and miming along to lyrics like "I'm a restless kind of guy, got to live before I die."

Strangely, "No Turning Back" had a brief second life thanks to Minako Honda, who covered the song under the title "Roulette" and included it on her album *Cancel* from 1986: produced by none other than Brian May.

You Deacy Thing?

The only other really notable collaboration on which Deacon embarked was with Hot Chocolate vocalist Errol Brown (who had guaranteed musical immortality after the band's single "You Sexy Thing" from 1976), although even with the archivist mentality of Queen completists, the results of their working together are frustratingly hard to locate. In a 1986 interview, Deacon confirmed not only that Queen would be unlikely to play any more live shows (one of the earliest suggestions that Mercury's health had been a recognized issue for the band) but also that he had been writing songs with Brown. Surprisingly, Deacon also claimed that he intended to "keep myself very busy" and that he would "have a good look around and see what other things I might be able to do."

As it happened, the only notable public appearance Deacon made without Queen after making this claim was in the video for "Stutter Rap," a comedy rap parody of the Beastie Boys' "No Sleep till Brooklyn" by Morris Minor and the Majors.

A Musical Evolution

That Deacon's oeuvre is so small in comparison to Roger Taylor's and Brian May's (and even Freddie Mercury's) only further reinforces his reputation as the "quiet one." But in truth, we can look at his work both within and without Queen as a concentrated progression. Experimentation forms a key part of his work ethic, as does study and collaboration: comparing something like the ditty-ish simplicity of "Misfire" from 1974's *Sheer Heart Attack* to "I Want to Break Free," which assailed the singles charts a decade later, and the breadth of his ability is clear. And that's not to mention the intervening stylistic behemoth that was *Hot Space* and Deacon's work with Man Friday & Junior Jive.

As with Roger Taylor, this development in songwriting ability is what makes Deacon such a compelling musical force: his contributions to the wider musical world may be smaller in number, but their impact remains strongly felt. "Another One Bites the Dust" is discussed in detail elsewhere in this book but, more than any other charting single composed by Deacon, guaranteed Queen a musical legacy that invaded and dominated unexpected areas of popular culture: this is Deacon's work, pure and simple. It may have fallen to Michael Jackson to suggest the band release it as a single, but Deacon was at a key moment of stylistic malleability when the song was written, open to influence and hungry for experimentation. And if there's one lasting impression we should have of John Deacon's music, this is it. His ability to listen to the work of others and repackage it simply outstripped his colleagues.

Afterword

I Still Love You

As this book was reaching the final stages of its first draft, I was constantly being forced to reconsider everything to be included. This was simply because Queen is an active proposition, and every news story, magazine interview, or red carpet Facetime punted out into online consciousness could potentially color our perception of any event from the band's history. But far from being a frustration, this stream of content merely confirmed something that's always been true about this most multifarious and flexible of musical behemoths: everyone has their own version of Queen. Inevitably, in many areas of this book, it's possible to see the author's version much more clearly than others.

To assess the band's status today is, in a sense, very simple. In 2019, it's clear that the release and subsequent awards season ubiquity of *Bohemian Rhapsody* has undoubtedly done the band more cultural favors than any of Roger Taylor and Brian May's other recent projects under the Queen banner. Importantly, that success is ultimately due to nostalgia rather than a bold step into new creative territory. With Adam Lambert, Taylor and May still sell out huge tours and play the same arenas they would conceivably be playing were Freddie Mercury still alive and John Deacon still musically active. But again, this is all based on accumulated cultural importance, and the appetite for it remains undiminished as the band's fiftieth anniversary rapidly approaches. Indeed, at that point, there will no doubt be a majestic celebration of the band's worldwide impact.

But beneath the surface of Queen as a cultural artifact predicated on former glories, there is still the beating heart of what the band had always tried to do: to keep everything they made within walls of their own construction. May and Taylor's hold on the brand (and it is most definitely a brand as well as a band) remains tight. For better or worse and regardless of how cool or uncool it might make them look, every associated album, concert, collaboration, and licensing deal is scrutinized. When you hear "I Want It All" on a TV advertisement for a furniture retailer, you know that this has been allowed to happen by those who have control of the brand.

I contacted a lot of people associated with Queen for this book, both historically and currently, and almost all of them had shared their stories before in some form or another as talking heads on a TV documentary or as part of a magazine oral history. As outlined in the introduction, the sheer volume of material available makes any truly new spin on the story very difficult to come by. I mention this not as an excuse for any shortcomings (I sincerely hope they are minimal) but rather to reinforce the idea that Queen is unwieldy and difficult to understand not because they are especially mysterious but because there's almost too much of them to go around. This is, in my view, both a strength and a weakness.

This final chapter is subtitled "I Still Love You" in a nod to Freddie Mercury's final words to the public in the video for "These Are the Days of Our Lives" and simply because that is how I feel about Queen. But the very nature of loving Queen as a band requires more forgiveness than one might require in the act of loving, say, ABBA or Kate Bush or the Wu-Tang Clan. A simplistic way of looking at it would be to conclude that some of the band's cheesy latter-day missteps are seen as triumphs by die-hard fans, and some of their murky and inaccessible early material is seen as off-putting by those coming to the band afresh. But, as with almost everything related to Queen, the truth is more complex. As this book has suggested, especially in the chapter on *Hot Space*, to be enthusiastic about Queen can seem at times a thankless task. Personally, I advocate an inclusive approach: if you love Queen at their best, you must at least try to understand them at their worst. For every moment of genuine musical togetherness, every miraculously choreographed flash of dry ice that swelled with the slide of a finger up a guitar neck, there is an equal and opposing moment of forehead-scratching despair, a collaboration with a forgotten boy band that smacked of nothing more than commercial gain.

These extremes run in parallel throughout the band's whole career. You can fool yourself into believing that the band had genuine underground and do-it-yourself credentials as they dragged their homemade kit around the country, but the goal of the band has always, *always* been maximum exposure. And by now, they are extremely good at achieving just that.

Brian May and Roger Taylor (and manager Jim Beach) continue to exercise control over the Queen empire with, we're told, silent approval from John Deacon. There are plenty of well-written and well-argued critiques of why the ongoing activity of a band that contains only 50 percent of its original lineup feels queasy to many fans, but, on paper at least, it's no more ghoulish or uncomfortable than the continuing careers of AC/DC or the Grateful Dead or the Who: it's just that none of those bands happened to have Freddie Mercury as their singer. The graffiti on the walls outside Montreux Casino, like the graffiti on the benches in Viretta Park next door to the home where Kurt Cobain took his own life, shows decades later just how big a hole a singer can leave in the legacy of a band.

Many begrudge Queen their second coming, accusing them of opportunism. These accusations have a firm grounding: the financial benefits of their ongoing work are plainly enormous. As this section is being written, in May 2019, Queen

+ Adam Lambert are about to embark on another U.S. tour, with dates scheduled in 2020 for Korea and Japan and New Zealand and Australia. These are, again, massive shows. The audience remains. But again, the story changes at the last minute: in a recent interview with *Mojo* magazine, Brian May suggests that Queen will resist becoming "a museum piece" by possibly writing new material, and discussion of a potential sequel to *Bohemian Rhapsody* is reported in the press with distracting regularity (director of numerous Queen videos Rudi Dolezal believes there is a movie to be made that *begins* with Queen at Live Aid). All of this activity, whether or not any of it comes to pass, simply tells us that the Queen story is not over yet. Soon, the band will have been without Freddie Mercury longer than it had been with him.

The flip side of these rather puffy press nuggets, which tempt and tease readers into excitement for whatever comes next from May and Taylor, is the near-weekly confirmation that John Deacon is a recluse, a grump who simply hoovers up the cash from whatever Queen project May and Taylor might embark on. Taylor called Deacon a sociopath in a documentary in 2019, though it's unclear to what extent the drummer understood the label's true definition. Clickbait-type headlines simply reiterate the circumstances of his retirement and confirm that he suffered more emotional devastation after Mercury's death, accompanied by a grainy photograph of his furtively smoking a cigarette while May and Taylor wear elaborate jackets and fly around the world. "Look at the difference between this weirdo and the life he could've had," the headlines seem to say.

All this is, in the grand scheme of things, moot. That's because Queen will forever be dominated by Mercury: this is perhaps as it should be and happily accepted by all those involved. It is Mercury's voice we hear on the records—it is his voice we *expect* to hear right up until Paul Rodgers or Adam Lambert or the cast of *We Will Rock You* open their mouths to sing. At the very outset of this book and throughout it, I tried to build a picture of Queen as a band of colleagues and differing personalities that, if one component part were removed, would irreparably reconfigure the ensemble left behind. This has proved to be true, but it just so happened that the most visible component was the first to be removed. It is and always will be Mercury's band, and trading on the nostalgia for his role in it will always be part of it as the brand forges new creative and commercial paths.

I'd like to return to the practice room, the one the band used just before Live Aid. In fact, I'd like to return to any of the practice rooms Queen may have frequented over the years and any empty stadiums as they busily sound checked. For me, this is Queen in their essence. The practical and serious consideration given to what is essentially a series of gauche sound and light experiments produced at maximum expense is heartening, comforting even. To plow such effort into an art form that would be roundly ridiculed (and it was ridiculed—it still is) took a special kind of seriousness. For anyone with an even slightly analytical mind, watching how the band worked in these situations is addictive, almost more so than watching the final production in action.

Arguments would break out during these rehearsals, but the quiet professionalism of each of the band's members would eventually return as they directed their work back toward its ultimate consumer: you and me. Whatever went on away from the rehearsal rooms and away from the stage was irrelevant, and none of it could have happened without that charming dedication to furthering the ridiculous, the beautiful, the wrongheaded, and the triumphant. It takes unimaginable balls to commit to such silliness and to argue over exactly how silly it should be and how it could be best presented to a paying audience. Of course, it would be impossible to predict just how much human drama would follow.

In simpler times, a grind of feedback and a plink of piano, some hushed chatter. Then the magic would resume.

Queen, 1982.   *ANL/Shutterstock*

Bibliography

Black, Johnny. "The Freddie Mercury Tribute Concert: Behind the Scenes." *Classic Rock*, November 2013.

Blake, Mark. *Is This the Real Life? The Untold Story of Queen.* Aurum Press, 2011.

Christgau, Robert. Review of *Return of the Champions. Village Voice*, November 15, 2005.

Coon, Caroline. "Freddie Mercury: Queen Bee." *Melody Maker*, December 21, 1974.

Deevoy, Adrian. "Interview with Brian May." *Event*, April 10, 2016.

Fletcher, Gordon. Album Review, *Queen. Rolling Stone*, December 6, 1973.

Freestone, Peter, with David Evans. *Freddie Mercury.* Omnibus Press, 2001.

Fryer, Greg. "The Legendary Deacy Amp." http://queenwillrockyou.weebly.com /deacy-amp.html (originally published on brianmay.com, June 2005), retrieved January 23, 2019.

Hasted, Nick. "Queen Reborn." *Classic Rock*, February 2015.

Henke, James. "Queen Holds Court in South America." *Rolling Stone*, June 11, 1981.

Herbst, Christian T., Stellan Hertegard, Daniel Zangger-Borch, and Per-Åke Lindestad. "Freddie Mercury—Acoustic Analysis of Speaking Fundamental Frequency, Vibrato, and Subharmonics." *Logopedics Phoniatrics Vocology* 42, no. 1 (2017): 29–38.

Hoard, Christian. Review of *The Cosmos Rocks. Rolling Stone*, October 30, 2008.

Hodkinson, Mark. *Queen: The Early Years.* Omnibus Press, 2009.

Hudson, Jeffrey. "The Invisible Man" (interview with John Deacon). *Bassist*, April 1996.

Hutton, Jim, with Tim Wapshott. *Mercury and Me.* Bloomsbury, 1995.

Jones, Lesley Ann. *Bohemian Rhapsody: The Definitive Biography of Freddie Mercury.* Hodder & Stoughton, 2012.

Kara, Scott. "'Freddie Would Have Loved Queen Musical': Roger Taylor." *New Zealand Herald*, May 25, 2017.

Lewis, John. Review of *The Cosmos Rocks. Uncut*, September 8, 2008.

Logan, Brian. Review of *We Will Rock You*. *The Guardian*, May 15, 2002.

May, Brian. *Wire Choir* column, *Guitar World*, January 1999.

McNair, James. Live Review, Queen + Paul Rodgers, Brixton Academy, London. *The Independent*, March 31, 2005.

Mendelsohn, John. Album Review, *Sheer Heart Attack*. *Phonograph Record*, March 1975.

Richards, Matt, and Mark Longthorne. *Somebody to Love: The Life, Death and Legacy of Freddie Mercury*. Bonnier Books, 2017.

Santelli, Robert. "Interview with Roger Taylor." *Modern Drummer*, October 1984.

Scott, Darren. "Rhap Star" (interview with Rami Malek). *Attitude*, October 2018.

Spencer, Charles. "It's a Killer, Queen." *Daily Telegraph*, May 15, 2002.

Stewart, Tony. "Is This Man a Prat?" *NME*, June 18, 1977.

Taylor, Roger. Letter to *Rolling Stone*. June 25, 1981.

No author. "Queen Street" (interview with Roger Taylor). *Sounds*, December 1974.

No author. "Interview with Brian May." *Sounds*, May 1989.

No author. "Interview with Brian May." *Boston Globe*, January 31, 1993.

No author. "Queen before Queen." *Record Collector*, no. 199, March 1996.

White, Rupert. "Queen in Cornwall." *Lulu.com*, 2011.

Wolff, Matt. Review of *We Will Rock You*. *Variety*, May 17, 2002.

Yates, Henry. *Queen: Classic Rock's Living Legends 2015*. *Classic Rock*, https://www.loudersound.com/features/queen-classic-rock-s-living-legends-2015, October 30, 2015, retrieved February 27, 2019.

Index